Astronomy elicits awe and wonder from those who gaze into the vastness of the universe. Religion elicits even greater awe and wonder of the infinite Creator of such vastness. This book beautifully balances both experiences of wonder.

—John Michael Talbot, bestselling musician and author

This book is an engaging and personal tour of the universe from a respected astronomer who also loves the Bible. Come along for the ride!

—Deborah Haarsma, astronomer and president of BioLogos

This book declares the glory of God and invites us to see in the heavens his handiwork. This is a great resource for anyone who wants to help young people see that science and faith can share the same space!

—Dr. Duffy Robbins, professor of youth ministry, Eastern University

A sweeping account of how the heavens and heaven go hand in hand. Even if you don't completely accept the authors' theological worldview, you will encounter many intriguing insights you won't find expressed so clearly elsewhere.

—Owen Gingerich, professor emeritus of astronomy and of the history of science, Harvard University

A close read of this inviting book will open your mind to see the amazing work of God in an amazingly massive universe. You'll be dually awed by the majesty of creation and the action of the Creator.

—Andrew Root, Carrie Olson Baalson Professor of Youth and Family Ministry, Luther Seminary

Too many people see science and faith in conflict. Leading astronomer David Bradstreet explodes that myth in this outstanding, highly readable book that shows how science has enriched his faith and how Christian faith has enriched science.

—David Wilkinson, author and professor of theology and religion, Durham Univ[illegible]

This book combines an engaging and informed romp through the cosmos with a deep conviction that the heavens declare the glory of God. Bradstreet and Rabey make the case that we live on a privileged planet in a remarkably designed universe.

—KARL GIBERSON, scholar-in-residence in science and religion, Stonehill College

We live in a time when cosmologist Sean Carroll claims that "the evidence is pretty incontrovertible" for atheism. This book reminds us that for those who ask why there's any beauty in the universe, the heavens still declare the glory of God.

—DOUGLAS LEBLANC, author, *Tithing: Test Me in This*

This book will capture the imagination of all who hunger to see God's majesty, creativity, power, and love with fresh eyes. Read this book and you'll never see the heavens the same way.

—TERRY LINHART, author and professor of Christian ministries, Bethel College

This book is a celebration of wonder. In plain, accessible language, Bradstreet and Rabey show us how beautiful and mysterious the universe is. This book helps us love the artistry of our great cosmic canvas.

—DEAN NELSON, coauthor, *Quantum Leap: How John Polkinghorne Found God in Science and Religion*

This book is a primer on the current best science on the universe. It illumines our thinking, helps us grasp our Creator's comets, stars, and meteors, and shows us how we may better love God, the scientific enterprise, and the detailed wonders of the heavens and earth that this enterprise reveals.

—ROBERT G. DUFFETT, president, Eastern University

I've always looked forward to the "new earth." This enjoyable book makes me look forward to the "new heavens" more than ever. For this I'm deeply thankful!

—KEVIN FLANNERY, senior pastor, Church of the Saviour

STAR STRUCK

STAR STRUCK

SEEING THE CREATOR IN THE WONDERS OF OUR COSMOS

DR. DAVID BRADSTREET
AND STEVE RABEY

ZONDERVAN

Star Struck

Requests for information should be addressed to:
Zondervan, *3900 Sparks Dr. SE, Grand Rapids, Michigan 49546*

ISBN 978-0-310-34419-3 (ebook)

Library of Congress Cataloging-in-Publication Data

Names: Bradstreet, David (Professor), author.
Title: Star struck : seeing the creator in the wonders of our cosmos / Dr. David Bradstreet and Steve Rabey.
Description: Grand Rapids : Zondervan, 2016. | Includes bibliographical references.
Identifiers: LCCN 2016012910 | ISBN 9780310344063 (softcover)
Subjects: LCSH: Astronomy--Religious aspects--Christianity. | Cosmology--Religious aspects--Christianity. | Physics--Religious aspects--Christianity.
Classification: LCC BL253 .B73 2016 | DDC 261.5/5--dc23 LC record available at https://lccn.loc.gov/2016012910

Cover design: Faceout Studio
Cover photo: NASA, ESA, and the Hubble Heritage Team (STScI/AURA)
Interior design: Denise Froehlich

First printing July 2016 / Printed in the United States of America

CONTENTS

ASTRONOMICAL FOREWORD

As a professor of astronomy and astrophysics for decades, I never know what my former students will be up to next. In the case of David Bradstreet, he's been busy collaborating on a *tour de force* journey through the most interesting people and most important discoveries in the development of astronomy.

Nearly every aspect of astronomy is covered, including the nature of stars, life on Earth, planets (in our solar system and beyond), comets and asteroids, black holes, galaxies, cosmology, dark matter, the Big Bang, and the future of Earth and the universe. The authors also explore the possibility of alien life in the solar system and beyond—a topic I too have studied.

The scope of the book is as broad as the heavens. From the earliest Babylonian and Greek astronomers to today's billion-dollar space race, the authors show how men and women of deep faith in God have explored the farthest reaches of our universe, unraveling some of its biggest mysteries.

I can imagine some of you saying, "But I've never studied astronomy." No worries. Everything is clearly explained and illustrated. *Star Struck* isn't a stuffy read. It's a very engaging and well-written book that requires little or no scientific background. You'll be helped along by enticing chapter titles and subtitles, relevant biblical references, humor, and plentiful pop-culture references to sci-fi books, TV shows, and movies. The photos and illustrations help reveal what words alone can't describe.

Even better, the book takes us along on the personal journey of a contemporary astronomer. Dave was first star-struck as a child, viewing the myriad stars and planets during all seasons, scanning the skies from his Massachusetts home through bug-filled summer nights and long, bone-chilling winter evenings. His fascination with the stars, the Moon, and planets propelled him to become a professional astronomer. Today, he's a professor at Eastern University, where he has taught astronomy and physics for forty years. He's published more than one hundred scholarly papers and articles and has established a planetarium and an astronomical observatory at his school. David is also well-known internationally because of his computer program, Binary Maker, which is used by many astronomers to analyze eclipsing binary star systems.

Like the psalmist David, and like most of us who encounter the majesty of the heavens, Dave was deeply impressed by the awesomeness and wonder of the starry night sky. As we see in this book, he still retains much of that childlike awe and wonder.

Dave says that this book was written "in the hope that you can experience some of the delight and fascination I first knew as a star-struck child examining this magnificent universe that God has created." Mission accomplished! Strap yourself in for a great read.

—Edward F. Guinan, PhD, Villanova University

THEOLOGICAL FOREWORD

In some religious circles there has been a fear of science. That fear is based on the belief that science will lead people away from God and the truths of the Bible. The famous early-twentieth-century debate over the theory of evolution that had William Jennings Bryan, one of America's foremost political figures, facing off against Clarence Darrow, America's foremost lawyer, convinced most fundamentalist Christians that there was an inevitable conflict between science and true religion and that sides had to be taken.

This book challenges that assumption as it traces the intellectual development of professional astronomer David Bradstreet. Bradstreet's lifelong fascination with science, especially astronomy, places him among the many Christians who have studied the heavens, which Scripture tells us "declare the glory of God." He encourages his students at Eastern University, where he has taught for decades, to consider adopting science as a vocation, assuring them that the more they learn about the cosmos, the more they will sense the greatness of the God they worship.

In the middle of the twentieth century, seminary students were struggling with the assault on evangelical Christianity by Rudolf Bultmann, a German existentialist theologian who argued against the way evangelicals viewed the nature and structure of the universe. He claimed that the commonly accepted beliefs about heaven, hell, and God were all formulated against the backdrop of an ancient description of a three-storied universe that was no longer tenable.

Bultmann pointed out that in ancient biblical times, it was generally believed that there was a dome over a flat Earth on which were fixed the stars. Heaven was believed to be above that dome and hell was believed to be below the flat Earth. Angels, given this cosmology, ascended and descended from heaven, which was "up there," and hell, where God sent those deserving of eternal punishment, was "down there," under the flat Earth on which humans and other living creatures spent their mortal lives.

Bultmann asserted that modern scientific cosmology, largely derived from Isaac Newton, had dispelled that three-storied concept of the universe and, with its demise, the New Testament theology implicit in it. From Newton came the belief that the universe is an infinite expansion of empty space and there no longer is a "heaven up there" or a "hell down there." Since Bultmann's writings in the early years of the twentieth century, however, our understanding of the universe has gone beyond this Bultmannian assertion.

It was my pleasure to introduce David Bradstreet to his coauthor, Steve Rabey. Together they have given us an easy-to-understand overview of the most up-to-date discoveries of modern cosmologists. Along the way, Bradstreet and Rabey help us to recognize that while these new discoveries do not prove the existence of God, they do leave plenty of room for those of us who believe in the biblical message. The authors show us how to understand what contemporary astronomers and cosmologists have to say about how the universe began and what is happening to it now.

Star Struck demonstrates a centuries-old harmony between science and religious faith. In tracing the work of major Christian astronomers—including Copernicus, Johannes Kepler, Galileo Galilei, Georges Lemaitre, and NASA scientists and astronauts—Bradstreet and Rabey show how world-changing discoveries don't threaten what we find in Scripture but rather do much to enhance our sense of wonder and awe about the universe. The authors encourage us to marvel at the awesome work of the creator God, who is ultimately revealed in Jesus Christ.

The time has come to put an end to the supposed war between religious faith and empirical science. This book could do much to bring harmony and peace between them, and it could, in the words of Scripture, go a long way to help those who appreciate science to find "a reason for the faith that lies within us."

—Tony Campolo, PhD, Eastern University

A long pursuit. After a ten-year journey of four billion miles, the unmanned *Philae* probe made history in 2014, landing on Comet 67P/Churyumov–Gerasimenko in 2014.

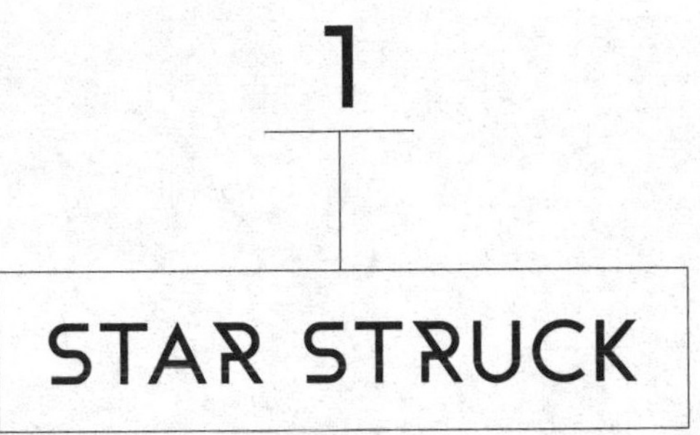

1

STAR STRUCK

THE MYSTERIOUS VISITOR, THE ADVENTURES OF A JUNIOR ASTRONOMER

No one knows when the mysterious traveler began coming around, but Greeks wrote about one visit five centuries before Christ that caused chaos and stirred people's fears.

Chinese chronicles reported on the foreigner in 240 BCE, and Babylonian clay tablets record an eerily similar appearance in 164 BCE. In 837, people in Japan, Germany, and the Middle East claimed they had seen the visitor themselves.

But 1066 was clearly the banner year for this mysterious outsider. Some claimed this visit helped William the Conqueror defeat King Harold of England at the Battle of Hastings. Others said it signaled the end of the age. Artists around the world tried to capture the wonder of this visit. Skilled seamstresses embroidered the vistor's stunning image into France's Bayeux Tapestry, while an unknown artist carved an image of the visitor on the sandstone walls of Chaco Canyon in southwestern America.

Sewing a sighting. For centuries, artists around the world recorded sightings of a mysterious heavenly visitor, including this depiction in the Bayeux Tapestry.

Not until 1705 did we finally realize what was really going on. Astronomer Edmond Halley demonstrated that a single interloper had been responsible for a host of visits recorded over thousands of years. Overnight, Halley's comet became our universe's most famous high-flying ball of gas, dust, and ice.

Halley was a friend of the brilliant scientist Isaac Newton, and he used Newton's new universal law of gravity to study gravity's impact on his comet's 1.7-billion-mile orbit. Laboring over pages and pages of complex mathematical calculations, Halley added everything up and concluded the comet would pay a return visit in another seventy-six years. He wasn't around to see his theory confirmed when the comet returned, as predicted, in 1758.

The comet visited again in 1835, the year Samuel Clemens (a.k.a. Mark Twain) was born. Twain accurately predicted that he would die when the comet returned in 1910. "Now here are these two unaccountable freaks," he wrote. "They came in together, they must go out together."

That 1910 visit brought the comet so close that the Earth actually passed through its long gossamer tail, which stretched through space some 60 million miles. Some people warned that deadly hydrogen cyanide from the tail would poison the entire human race, but the comet failed to deliver the prophesied doom.

A NEW GOLDEN AGE

My only opportunity to view Halley came in 1986. That turned out to be one of the worst years to view the comet, and something tells me I may not be around for its next appearance in mid 2061.

Recently another comet has grabbed people's attention. It has a more complicated name than Halley's: Comet 67P/Churyumov–Gerasimenko. We've learned much about this comet, having landed an unmanned probe on its pockmarked surface.

The European Space Agency's Rosetta mission took a ten-year journey of four billion miles to catch up to Churyumov–Gerasimenko as it sped through space at more than 100,000 mph. The *Philae* probe landed on the surface of the duck-shaped comet's surface in August 2014. (The landing was problematic. See chapter 15.)

Rosetta is just one of the dozens of major missions

currently investigating previously unknown nooks and crannies of our vast cosmos. Right now, a NASA rover the size of a car is slowly rolling across the surface of Mars, analyzing rocks in its on-board chemical lab.

We're living through a new golden age of space exploration. What a great time to be an astronomer!

STAR STRUCK

My love for God's heavens began when I was a boy. Many evenings found me out in the back yard of our Brockton, Massachusetts, home, my eye glued to the eyepiece of a telescope, my mind awed by everything I saw.

My first telescope was a Gilbert Observer, complete with its cheap cardboard tube and rickety aluminum tripod. Some kids played with these telescopes like they were toys, but I knew my trusty Observer had more stargazing power than the telescopes Galileo used.

Unfortunately, the summer skies over Brockton were far from clear, and pesky bugs constantly hindered a young astronomer's concentration. Visibility improved during the winter, so I often took my telescope up to my second-floor bedroom, threw open the window, and saw what I could see.

I couldn't see much. Only a narrow slice of the sky revealed itself to me from my restricted perch. I felt frustrated. I had been studying my older brother's *Golden Book of Astronomy* and wanted to see everything the book described. My family also became frustrated when I kept my window wide open for hours, requiring our furnace to work overtime.

So I devised a brilliant solution. I wrapped myself in layers of warm clothing, grabbed a flimsy, derelict metal chair out of the basement, and headed out to our big back yard, along with my telescope and observation notebook. The dark winter skies were incredibly clear, allowing me to study the heavens to my heart's content as I sat bundled, silent and shivering.

On nights when the frigid winds grew particularly bitter, my numb fingers and bulky gloves made it difficult to write down

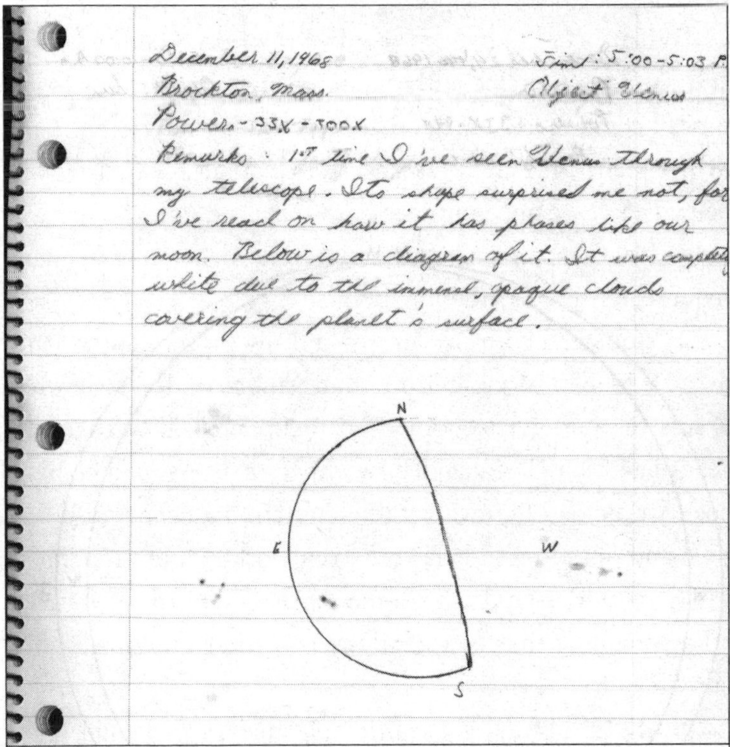
December 11, 1968 Time: 5:00-5:03 P
Brockton, Mass. Object Venus
Power - 33X - 300X
Remarks: 1st time I've seen Venus through my telescope. Its shape surprised me not, fo
I've read on how it has phases like our moon. Below is a diagram of it. It was complet
white due to the immense, opaque clouds covering the planet's surface.

Frigid but focused. My hands were shaking as I recorded my first sighting of Venus on a cold December day in 1968.

my observations in my notebook. But I did so anyway, faithfully recording my sightings of hundreds of planets and stars, including Venus, which I first saw on December 11, 1968.

Alongside my observations I often sketched the alien life forms I was certain inhabited the various planets. Yes, I was a certifiable nerd and a big fan of TV shows like *Star Trek*. I had no doubt that space teemed with all kinds of unusual and bizarre creatures. Like most scientists, I still have an abiding weakness for science fiction.

When I could no longer control my frozen body's shakes and shudders, I reluctantly went inside to warm up. Many times I couldn't feel my hands or feet, but nobody in the family ever called me crazy, at least not to my face. My dad even helped me cart my equipment around. And even though we didn't have much money, my mom never denied my frequent requests for more astronomy books.

Fortunately, both my family and my bigger church family at First Baptist Church lovingly embraced the somewhat obsessive "junior astronomer" in their midst. It wasn't until years later that I realized how different things might have been for me had I grown up in a church that condemned science and discouraged believers from working in astronomy. I still can't understand why some Christians turn their backs on a discipline that powerfully demonstrates the majesty of our Creator.

By the time I was eight years old, I'd made up my mind. I had a clear destiny in life. "This is a great time in history to study the stars, and that is what I want to do for the rest of my life!"

A JOURNEY TO THE HEAVENS

My dream came true. Fifty years later, I'm still happily studying stars.

The equipment I use now is far more sophisticated than my childhood telescope. (I handpicked a Meade Schmidt-Cassegrain sixteen-inch-diameter telescope with computerized movement for Eastern University's Bradstreet Observatory, which is named after me.) But I still experience the same kind of childlike joy and wonder now that I did when I first scanned the heavens.

I'm writing this book in the hope that you can experience some of the delight and fascination I first knew as a star-struck child examining this magnificent universe that God has created.

Will you join me on a journey through the story of astronomy? We will travel through space and time, visiting the people behind the discoveries that have transformed our understanding of our universe and exploring celestial phenomena that baffle even the most brilliant scientists and theologians.

For the first stop on the journey, we will go back—way back—to see how our ancient ancestors tried to make sense of our universe.

Heavenly designs. Ancient peoples around the world used star alignments to design massive ritual structures like England's Stonehenge.

2

EARLY ASTROLOGERS

ASTRO-RELIGIONS, FROM EGYPTIAN SUN GODS AND BABYLONIAN OMENS TO SCIENTOLOGY

An African farmer carefully scans the skies. Should he sow his seed now or later? If he plants at the wrong time, his tribe may suffer hunger or famine.

An Indonesian sailor reads the stars to navigate his outrigger canoe safely home after a voyage to seek out new fish supplies. If he misinterprets his location, he could die on the open sea.

Prehistoric people knew their lives were intimately connected with the heavens, but ancient stargazing involved much more than practical tips for farming and fishing.

Centuries before Christ, pagan holy men interpreted heavenly signs to determine the best times for sacred feasts, rituals, and sacrifices. The movements of celestial bodies influenced when our ancestors slept, ate, had sex, and worshiped their gods.

God knew when he created the cosmos that the movements of the heavens would impact our lives. "Let there be lights in the vault of the sky to separate the day from the night, and let them serve as signs to mark sacred times, and days and years" (Gen. 1:14).

Our ancient ancestors often went overboard, believing that the stars controlled their fates. Today, many of us face the opposite problem, believing that we have little or nothing to do with the heavens.

The truth is we're more interconnected with the cosmos than ever before, thanks to hundreds of orbiting satellites that provide weather reports, transmit TV shows, handle credit card transactions, spy on our enemies, and connect our cell phones.

How many of us thank God for his magnificent heavenly handiwork? Instead, it seems the closer we get to our cosmos, the less we care. As late blues legend B.B. King sang, the thrill is gone.

Can we recapture our ancestors' sense of connection to the cosmos without embracing their idolatry?

I think we can.

This chapter of our journey begins at a time long before telescopes and astronomy, a time when our ancestors used astrology and divination in an attempt to understand the message of the stars.

We could visit five-thousand-year-old sites like England's Stonehenge or Ireland's Newgrange, where ancient communities used huge stones (or megaliths) to build gigantic structures that precisely captured the Sun's rays during the winter solstice. Or we could see Mayan sites like Mexico's Xochicalco, or Pueblo peoples' sites like New Mexico's Chaco Canyon.

Designed for deities. The heavens played a powerful role in Egyptian religion and social life.

But the best place to begin our journey is by visiting two ancient empires that were crazy about the cosmos: Egypt and Babylon.

EGYPT'S EMPIRE OF THE SUN

The flooding of the Nile River brought life and death, growth and destruction. The pharaohs commanded court astrologers to do a better job of predicting these annual floods. After carefully studying the Sun, the astrologers came up with the brilliant invention of the 365-day year. This simple but revolutionary idea made calendars much more accurate and helped Egyptians live harmoniously with the Nile.

Astronomy historian Michael Hoskin says there was more to Egyptian stargazing than flood control. "The sky played a profound role in Egyptian religion," writes Hoskin, "for deities were present there in the form of constellations and immense labor was expended on earth to ensure that the reigning Pharaoh would one day join them."

Astrologers played many important roles in Egyptian society. They determined when the empire would celebrate Ra, the Sun god. They advised pharaohs on when to go to war. They worked with engineers to design massive pyramid tombs, making sure the giant structures accurately aligned with the heavens. They also gave us a phrase that many of us know but few understand.

Millennia before the Westminster Dog Show, Egyptians were mad about dogs. Some Egyptian gods even sported canine heads. Astrologers gave the name Canis Major (bigger dog) to the heavenly constellation home to Sirius, the Dog Star, the brightest star in the night sky. Every year around the fourth of July, the Dog Star rose at the same time as the Sun, so astrologers concluded that Sirius added its own heat to that of the Sun, causing the throat-parching "dog days" of summer.

BABYLON'S OMENS

Astrologers enjoyed status and security in Egypt, but in Babylon they risked death. When King Nebuchadnezzar felt troubled by dreams that kept him awake at night, he summoned "magicians, enchanters, sorcerers and astrologers" and demanded answers:

"If you do not tell me what my dream was and interpret it, I will have you cut into pieces and your houses turned into piles of rubble. But if you tell me the dream and explain it, you will receive from me gifts and rewards and great honor. So tell me the dream and interpret it for me" (Dan. 2:2, 5–6).

Ancient Babylon (which was located where Iraq is today) was a culture captivated by omens. Holy men studied blemishes on the livers of sacrificed animals to ascertain the will of the gods, while astrologers scanned the skies for signs of divine blessings or curses. Omens influenced whether Babylon should raise taxes, go to war, or cease work to seek the will of the gods.

After Nebuchadnezzar conquered Jerusalem, beginning the period of Babylonian captivity or exile, Jews were expected to worship state-sanctioned gods and images. When some refused, Babylon's angry astrologers demanded discipline:

"There are some Jews whom you have set over the affairs of the province of Babylon—Shadrach, Meshach and Abednego—who pay no attention to you, Your Majesty. They neither serve your gods nor worship the image of gold you have set up" (Dan. 3:12).

You may remember from Sunday school that the king sentenced Shadrach, Meshach, and Abednego to death in a blazing furnace. God honored their faithfulness and brought them through the flames unscathed. Unfortunately, most Jewish captives lacked such devotion. Even Judah's King Manasseh was disobedient, bowing down and worshiping strange gods:

"He rebuilt the high places his father Hezekiah had destroyed; he also erected altars to Baal and made an Asherah pole, as Ahab king of Israel had done. He bowed down to all the starry hosts and worshiped them" (2 Kings 21:3).

God had commanded his people to worship him, not his Creation: "And when you look up to the sky and see the sun, the moon and the stars—all the heavenly array—do not be enticed into bowing down to them and worshiping things the LORD your God has apportioned to all the nations under heaven" (Deut. 4:19).

But his people disobeyed these commands, with predictable results. God sent prophets to warn of coming judgment:

> Let your astrologers come forward,
> those stargazers who make predictions month by month,
> let them save you from what is coming upon you.
>
> —Isaiah 47:13

If I could go back and rewrite Jewish history, my revised version would show how God's people remained faithful, even during captivity. They would help the Babylonians realize only one true Creator God existed. They might even develop a uniquely Jewish tradition of astronomy.

But that's not how things turned out.

Baal's Temple. Babylonians dedicated the Temple of Bel (or Baal) in Palmyra, Syria, around the time of Christ's crucifixion. Islamic State militants destroyed this ancient temple in 2015.

Other than helping priests schedule the many religious festivals in the Hebrew calendar, or working with architects to make sure the tabernacle and other sacred buildings aligned toward the sunrise in the east (Exod. 27:13), Jews made few significant contributions to astronomy until the Islamic golden age (approximately 800–1250 CE).

BABYLON REBORN: TODAY'S CELESTIAL CULTS

People still scan the skies for religious revelations, sometimes with tragic results. In March 1997, thirty-nine members of a group called Heaven's Gate dressed themselves in identical black outfits, calmly laid down on identical metal beds in an attractive 9,000-square-foot mansion in the ritzy Rancho Santa Fe area north of San Diego, and methodically killed themselves.

The unusual group's mysterious leader, Marshall Applewhite (who went by the nickname "Bo," as in Bo Peep from the children's nursery rhyme), promised members of his cult they would reach a "level above human" if only they would shed their "containers" (bodies) and rendezvous with a spaceship said to be hiding behind the Hale-Bopp comet.

"Planet Earth is about to be recycled," said Applewhite in a videotaped message he delivered in his clipped, robotic voice. "Your only chance to survive—leave with us."

The most famous celestial cult is Scientology. Founder L. Ron Hubbard, a prolific science fiction writer, unveiled his new faith in the May 1950 issue of *Astounding Science Fiction* magazine.

Celestial prophets? Marshall Applewhite of Heaven's Gate and L. Ron Hubbard of Scientology founded two of the most notorious modern astronomical creeds.

Hubbard proclaimed Scientology was a "scientific" creed, but when hackers from the group Anonymous released the group's wacky theological materials on the internet in 2008, Hubbard's silly cosmology was plainly revealed for all to see. (Hubbard claimed that Earth—which he called Teegeeack—was part of a "Galactic Confederacy" of stars and planets. Astronomers haven't yet located Hubbard's confederacy anywhere in space.)

Heaven's Gate and Scientology are just two of the "extraterrestrial religions" Hope College professor James Herrick has examined:

- Swedish scientist and mystic Emanuel Swedenborg claimed direct contact with disembodied spirits, including spirits from other planets.
- Members of the Urantia Brotherhood study *The Urantia Book*, allegedly dictated by superhuman (possibly alien) beings.
- The Aetherius society says its doctrines were revealed by extraterrestrials called the Cosmic Masters.
- Jane Roberts spent years "channeling" insights from an extraterrestrial being she called Seth.
- Baha'u'llah, the prophet of the Baha'i faith, wrote that "every planet [has] its own creatures."

- Seventh-day Adventist founder Ellen G. White claims to have visited Jupiter and Saturn while in trance states.
- French journalist Claude Vorilhon says he founded the Raëlian movement after meeting a four-foot-tall, greenish alien who offered commentaries on the Bible and other religious revelations.
- Horror fiction writer Whitley Strieber says aliens abducted him, probed his body, and declared him their "chosen one" in his creepy, allegedly *non*fiction bestseller, *Communion*.

As for astrology? Today this ancient pseudoscience has more daily devotees than it did when Nebuchadnezzar ruled Babylon.

AN ONGOING JOURNEY

From the beginning of time, we have sought to understand how the heavens above influence life here below. Our ancient ancestors saw only bits and pieces of this cosmic puzzle. At times, even God's people got confused, worshiping the stars rather than the God who made them.

To understand the whole picture better, we needed God to reveal the true nature of our cosmic connections. That revelation is the focus of the next chapter of our journey.

Evening and morning. Michelangelo portrayed God's creation of the cosmos on ceiling panels in Rome's Sistine Chapel. This panel is titled *Separation of Light from Darkness*.

3

OUR COSMIC CREATOR

ASTRONOMERS EXAMINE THE ARTIST'S BRUSHSTROKES ON THE CANVAS OF CREATION

As soon as I could talk, I sang hymns with my parents at our Baptist church. I did my best to make sense of big theological words like *sanctified*, but I never could quite figure out what the hymn "Come, Thou Fount of Every Blessing" meant when we all sang the words, "Here I raise my Ebenezer."

One other hymn needed no explanation:

> O Lord my God, when I in awesome wonder
> Consider all the worlds thy hands have made,
> I see the stars, I hear the rolling thunder,
> Thy power throughout the universe displayed.

I've probably sung "How Great Thou Art" hundreds of times. When our church sings this classic hymn on a Sunday, I often hear it playing back in my mind the following week as I look through the telescope at Eastern's observatory.

"How Great Thou Art" makes a perfect soundtrack for

today's Christian astronomers who believe God has called us to explore previously unknown mysteries of his universe.

Christian astronomers aren't necessarily supergodly or more devout than the average person, but we're totally out-of-this-world curious to learn all we can about the delightful details of Creation. As sixteenth-century Protestant astronomer Tycho Brahe put it, "Those who study the stars have God for a teacher."

Take my specialty: binary stars. Remember the dual suns Luke Skywalker saw from his home planet of Tatooine? *Star Wars* got it right. Multiple-star systems like the binaries that warmed Luke's skin make up 60 percent of all the stars in our cosmos. Our Sun is among the solo minority. (See chapter 18.)

When I study the light curves coming from distant binaries, I can tell if the gravitational bond between them is strong enough to pull them closer together. When the bond is extremely strong, the two move close enough to exchange energy and mass.

Seeing this process play out is like having a front-row seat for the most amazing show ever. I'm witnessing a vast cosmic dance involving celestial bodies whose power and energy stretch over billions of miles.

In this dance of binary stars I see God.

Not literally. God is invisible. And not philosophically. I'm not a pantheist. (That's the technical term for people who say the universe *is* God.) When I study the heavens, I see God's character expressed in the order, beauty, complexity, and harmony of the many marvelous worlds he has made.

Sometimes I think astronomers are like art experts. If I had spent decades examining paintings by Rembrandt and Warhol, my eyes would be able to detect the unique brushstrokes of each

Designing deities. Mayan gods tried a variety of raw materials before making people out of maize.

artist. We astronomers study the work of the Original Artist, and as Annie Dillard said in *Pilgrim at Tinker Creek*, "The extravagant gesture is the very stuff of creation."

IN THE BEGINNING

The Cherokee say the Earth began as a huge, floating island. A water beetle seeking a solid place to rest dived down into the primordial sea. When he came back up, he brought along some soft mud that expanded to become our Earth.

The Maya believed gods employed a variety of raw materials in their efforts to create the first people. After unsuccessfully using mud and wood, the gods achieved success when they formed people out of maize, a major food staple believed to be sacred.

The many creation stories people have told to explain where everything came from differ tremendously, but most of these origin stories share two big assumptions.

- Assumption 1: Everything has existed forever.
- Assumption 2: The gods in these stories are part of the physical world, not independent of it. If everything that exists were to suddenly disappear, these deities would disappear right along with everything else.

Genesis 1 reveals a truly radical alternative: "In the beginning God created the heavens and the earth." What a simple but profound statement! God created everything out of nothing. (The Latin is *ex nihilo*, meaning "out of nothing," or "out of the void.") The original creation event wasn't the making of something within time and space; that event *created* time and space and everything else from nothingness.

"Almost all ancient civilizations believed that the universe had existed forever," writes historian Martin Gorst. "Throughout the ancient world there was just one civilization that didn't subscribe to this cyclic vision of eternity. Jewish scripture, with the story of the Creation, stated clearly that the world had a beginning."

God revealed his creation story to the Jews. Later, Christians and Muslims inherited this beautiful gift. Today, followers of the three major monotheistic faiths don't always see eye to eye, but they wholeheartedly agree on this much: "All the gods of the nations are idols, but the LORD made the heavens" (Ps. 96:5).

ANYBODY HOME?

I'm a *theistic creationist*, so I see the work of a divine Creator when I study the heavens. Not all scientists share my perspective.

Some astronomers are *atheistic materialists.* They insist that everything arose from impersonal processes of time plus matter plus chance.

Carl Sagan was to the twentieth century what Neil deGrasse Tyson is to the twenty-first: an astronomy rock star. Sagan, a brilliant scientist, made science interesting enough that some 300 million people watched his 1980 *Cosmos* TV series.

But not everything that proceeds from the mouths of great scientists is great science. Sagan famously made many wildly nonscientific claims, such as this bold theological whopper: "The Cosmos is all that is or ever was or ever will be."

Sagan was not the first atheistic materialist to promote a godless theory of origins. A century before Christ, philosophers vigorously debated how everything got here. Some argued that the gods had created it all, but Roman poet Lucretius had no patience for such mystical mumbo jumbo. In his classic book, *On the Nature of Things*, Lucretius expressed the Epicurean view that everything originated through impersonal processes:

"[O]ur world has been made by nature through the spontaneous and casual collision, and the multifarious, accidental random and purposeless congregation and coalescence of atoms."

Will science ever settle these debates about God and

It's all material. Both the ancient Roman poet Lucretius and the twentieth-century astronomer Carl Sagan said the cosmos arose from impersonal natural processes.

creation? I doubt it. Neither theists nor atheists can scientifically prove their positions.

For me and many other scientists, the "God hypothesis" remains the best explanation for why everything exists, and why it exists in the way it does. We think belief in a Creator God makes more sense than believing that everything happened through impersonal processes of time and chance.

One other important reason I believe in a personal Creator God is deeply *personal*. It concerns my identity.

I'm a person with a unique personality. I deeply love another person named Colleen. Through our love, the two of us have brought into existence other wonderful persons named Andrew and Jonathan. Colleen and I are both devoted to people at our church and the students we encounter at Eastern University, where we both work.

Our lives would be empty without the personal relationships that bring so much love and joy. So how do atheistic materialists explain the origin of personhood and personality? They point to the same impersonal processes of time plus matter plus chance.

In the long run, I'm convinced the theistic creationist view offers the best explanation for you and me and everything else. Even better, the personal God who created us in his image (Gen. 1:26) loves us.

THE ORIGINAL ARTIST

Every time humans sing a song, make a flower arrangement, write a blog post, or enjoy a movie, we exercise our God-given creativity. But when God creates, it's on a whole different level.

For one thing, God creates on an incredibly vast scale. No one knows exactly how big the cosmos is (and everything just expanded a bit more during the time it took you to read this sentence).

One way to grasp the mindboggling bigness of Creation is to follow the progress of *Voyager 1*. The probe lifted off from Florida in 1977. It finally exited our solar system in 2012 after a journey of thirty-five years, and will spend the next few billion years passing through our own Milky Way galaxy, only one of the many billions of galaxies floating around out there.

God created a pretty amazing place. That's why the story of the cosmos is the biggest story ever.

Size matters, but it's more than size alone that distinguishes God's work from our creativity. When you and I create something, we do so by assembling raw materials that already exist. Artists use canvas, paint, and brushes to create their masterpieces. Writers use words, rules of grammar, and concepts that existed before they were born. During my years as a model-airplane builder, I used existing materials (first balsawood, then plastic) to build my models. Even creative guru Steve Jobs used existing technologies to make Apple's world-famous, user-friendly devices. Einstein used existing numbers, theories, and formulas.

God's approach is different. He used no preexisting raw materials when he created the cosmos. He started with zero. Nada. Zilch. However you phrase it, when God creates, he truly starts "from scratch."

J. R. R. Tolkien spent more than a decade writing the nearly half-million words in his Lord of the Rings trilogy, but he grew uncomfortable when people praised him for "creating" Middle Earth. In his wonderful essay "On Fairy-Stories," Tolkien described humans as subcreators:

> Man, Sub-creator, the refracted Light
> through whom is splintered from a single White
> to many hues, and endlessly combined
> in living shapes that move from mind to mind.

Each one of us is creative in our own way, but none of us has ever created something from nothing. We improvise something new from something old.

That creative gift is pretty amazing in itself, but God is the one and only Original Artist and Author, "the Father Almighty, Maker of heaven and earth."

THE HEAVENS DECLARE, BUT WHO'S LISTENING?

Why study the heavens? Chet Raymo describes some of the potential benefits in his book, *The Soul of the Night: An Astronomical Pilgrimage*: "fleeting revelations, intimations of grace, and brief encounters with something greater than ourselves, a force, a beauty, and a grandeur that draw us into rapturous contemplation of the most distant celestial objects."

Raymo's religious language conceals the fact that he—like Sagan—is an atheistic materialist. Raised a Catholic, Raymo wrestled with faith and doubt. Doubt prevailed, but the old theological language survived.

I can understand why many atheists speak of "creation,"

even though the word suggests a Creator they don't believe in. What alternative do they have? Their naturalistic language fails them as they struggle to describe the glory they see in the heavens. A universe that came about through time plus matter plus chance doesn't provide a foundation for the beauty and meaning humans experience when we encounter the heavens.

"Science is great as science, but it makes a lousy religion," says Vatican astronomer Guy Consolmagno.

What I don't understand is why so many of my fellow believers seem to feel so little passion or curiosity about the cosmos. Atheistic materialists look to the skies and experience "rapturous contemplation." Christians? Not so much.

Something isn't right here. We've identified a problem I call the "wonder gap." People who don't believe in God sing the wonders of the cosmos while believers are mute.

We may quote Paul's apologetics-friendly words in Romans 1:20: "For since the creation of the world God's invisible qualities—his eternal power and divine nature—have been clearly seen, being understood from what has been made, so that people are without excuse."

We may even meditate on David's beautiful psalm: "The heavens declare the glory of God; the skies proclaim the work of his hands" (Ps. 19:1).

But how often do we take a moment to look up and savor our Creator's awesome display of cosmic handiwork? When do we praise him for the beauty of Creation?

The heavens declare.

Who's listening?

Divine designer. William Blake's vision shows the Ancient of Days at work as Creator and Sustainer.

4

CREATION, CONTINUED

NO "ONE AND DONE" CREATOR BUT A SUSTAINER THROUGH POWERFUL PROCESSES

Members of America's longest-running prime-time TV family are gathered around the dining room table, ready to dive in. But first, grace must be said. Without thinking, Dad asks his bratty son to do the honors.

The boy lowers his head, closes his eyes, and offers up this scorcher: "Dear God, we paid for all this stuff ourselves, so thanks for nothing!"

Viewers wrote letters to the Fox network complaining about Bart Simpson's anti-Christian hostility, but I think Bart's ironic blasphemy performed a valuable public service. It exposed the truth that many of us are closet deists. We *say* we depend on God for our daily bread, but we know deep down that *we* buy bread all by ourselves.

The problem is a whole lot bigger than bread or Bart.

Deism is a commonly held belief among young people who attend churches and Christian youth groups, according to

Notre Dame sociologist Christian Smith's disturbing book, *Soul Searching: The Religious and Spiritual Lives of American Teenagers*.

Smith analyzed data from the massive, multiyear National Study of Youth and Religion, describing the faith of the typical contemporary Christian teen as Moralistic Therapeutic Deism. The MTD creed says God wants us to be good (Moralistic) and happy (Therapeutic), but this God is not really personally involved in the cosmos or our lives (Deism).

Where do these kids get these crazy ideas? Probably from you and me, the very hypocrites Bart was making fun of in his prayer.

Classical deism promotes an impersonal "watchmaker" god who wound up the universe like a big clock and walked away, letting everything run on its own, independent of any divine influence. It's sad, but when I talk to my astronomy students about the heavens, some of them seem to believe in an impersonal, clockwork universe with no ongoing connection to its Creator.

We need to purge our souls of closet deism or it will blind us to God's continuing presence in the world he has made.

CREATOR *AND* SUSTAINER

Scripture paints a balanced portrait of God as Creator and Sustainer. David praised God for demonstrating his ongoing love for all of Creation:

> He makes grass grow for the cattle,
> and plants for people to cultivate—
> bringing forth food from the earth.
> —Psalm 104:14

For David, this love for Creation was personal. He could see God's sustaining presence in our world. Today, I'm not sure we see Creation with the same eyes David did.

"The created world has lost its sacredness," writes Christian author Philip Yancey in *Fearfully and Wonderfully Made*, his bestselling book written with Dr. Paul Brand.

Most of us accept God as Creator, but frankly some of us aren't so sure about the whole Sustainer thing. Our insufficient theology may stem from a Sunday school understanding of the two Genesis creation accounts.

GOD'S LONG NAP?

The God of Genesis 1 is active and hardworking, creating everything in six busy days. The God of Genesis 2 seems more laid back, catching up on some rest after a hectic week: "By the seventh day God had finished the work he had been doing; so on the seventh day he rested from all his work" (Gen. 2:2).

Deists think God is still napping somewhere. After creating the cosmos, God called the project done and went into early retirement.

Jesus paints a completely different picture. When some Jews challenged Jesus for working on the Sabbath, he identified himself with God the worker: "My Father is always at his work to this very day, and I too am working" (John 5:17).

Paul perfectly balanced God's roles as Creator and Sustainer in his sermon to the seekers, philosophers, and spiritual dabblers of cosmopolitan Athens: "The God who made the world and everything in it is the Lord of heaven and earth and does not live in temples built by human hands. And he is not served by human hands, as if he needed anything. Rather, he himself gives everyone life and breath and everything else" (Acts 17:24–25).

Christians believe that God *created* the world, but this past tense verb needs to be present tense too. God *creates* the world.

God's creative action did not end after the sixth day. It's not his nature to create things, walk away, and take a long nap. He creates and continually re-creates all that is. Or as historian Michael Hoskin puts it, "He had entered into a servicing contract with the universe, to demonstrate his continuing care for his Creation."

A PREFERENCE FOR PROCESSES

As a Christian astronomer, I experience God's sustaining power as a concrete daily reality, not just some abstract theological concept. When I study the heavens, I feel as if I'm being permitted to "look underneath the hood" and examine the details of how God creates and sustains.

When I'm watching binary stars dance together, exchanging mass and energy, I can't draw a line between sustaining and creating. The two acts blend into one. That's because when God creates, he exhibits a decided *preference for process*. The act of creation is not a "one-and-done." It's a "now-and-then."

Evidence for process is plentiful here on our own planet. Centuries of scientific study and experimentation have repeatedly shown that our cosmic home is dynamic and ever changing, not some dead hunk of rock.

Ongoing presence. God uses atmospheric processes (weather) and geological processes (the San Andreas fault reveals the Earth's moving plates) to sustain our planet.

God created the Earth and he sustains it through dynamic and ongoing processes (biological, geological, climatic, atmospheric, and more) that keep our beautiful blue planet spinning 'round. These processes also preserve Earth's immense diversity of life.

Some of these processes are violent and brutal. Tragically, we can see the results of these powerful processes in the news. Earthquakes and lava flows can harm or kill people who live nearby, but these violent geological processes are also essential to our planet's ability to sustain life.

We don't live in a wind-up, watchmaker universe. Our Creator/Sustainer is on the job, keeping everything humming through billions of brilliant processes. Our challenge is to *see* what he's doing. Perhaps Frederick Buechner can help us correct our vision:

"If you think you're seeing the same show all over again seven times a week, you're crazy. Every morning you wake up to something that in all eternity never was before and never will be again. And the you that wakes up was never the same before and will never be the same again either."

PERSISTENT PERSONAL PROCESSES

It shouldn't surprise us that God sustains Creation through process because process has been his preferred method of working with us pesky humans from the very beginning.

God revealed himself to his chosen people and worked with them across the centuries to win their love and obedience. That very same God revealed himself to me through his Son, and his Spirit works within me still to continue the lifelong process of sanctification.

Process is how you and I love. When I married Colleen, I didn't just say, "I do!" and walk away. I committed myself to living alongside her and sustaining her for the long haul. Together, we had two sons. We still sustain our boys today, though they don't require as much attention now as they did as infants.

We also can see the importance of process in the way God created you and me. He didn't make us droids or program our brains with every fact we needed. He created us in his image, giving us the gift of creativity that allows us to make new languages, build cultures, and explore the heavens with the tools of scientific inquiry.

SCIENCE REVEALS GOD'S SUSTAINING PRESENCE

Only four or five centuries ago did we begin methodically exploring the heavens using the tools and techniques of modern astronomy. Since then we've learned much about many of the processes God uses in creating and sustaining the cosmos.

Take gravity, for example. Sir Isaac Newton first described universal gravitation in 1687. Before that, we didn't realize that some invisible force holds everything in place and keeps us from floating up into space.

Much about gravity remains mysterious. We don't know where it comes from, or why. We're still in the infant stages of humanity's continuing journey of scientific discovery. So much remains to be learned.

When I say grace at dinner, or when I thank God for keeping everything humming, I'm not saying empty words or repeating Bart's deistic prayer. I mean it. I'm totally sincere. I literally thank God for holding it all together!

St. Augustine said it much more eloquently: "All created things would perish if his working were withdrawn."

A planetary selfie. In the 1960s, humans finally traveled far enough away from Earth to photograph our beautiful home planet. This *Blue Marble* photo was taken by the crew of Apollo 17.

5

OUR GOLDILOCKS WORLD

LIKE THE KID SAID, EVERYTHING LOOKS "JUST RIGHT"

Remember Goldilocks, the persnickety young girl in the popular "Story of the Three Bears" who carefully tested the bears' beds and tasted their preferred meals? She rejected extreme candidates (porridge that was too cold or too hot, beds that were too small or too big) and chose the ones she deemed "just right."

If Goldilocks were an astronomer, she would absolutely *love* planet Earth. When astronomers and astrobiologists (scientists who look for signs of life in the cosmos) refer to ours as a "Goldilocks planet," they're talking about the unbelievable combination of "just right" conditions that have made our world the only known place inhabited by living creatures. One popular Christian DVD calls ours a "privileged planet," citing nineteen essential factors that make our home unique.

In some cases, only miniscule differences distinguish our life-filled planet from all the other lifeless celestial bodies. For example, if Earth were just a little bit closer to or just a little bit farther away from the Sun, we would be much, much hotter or much, much colder. Goldilocks rejected the bears' porridge when it was too cold or too hot, but the temperature on Earth is, again, just right. Otherwise, you and I wouldn't even be here.

Writer Bill Bryson describes our uniqueness in his *Short History of Nearly Everything*, marveling at how "the atoms that so liberally and congenially flock together to form living things on earth are exactly the same atoms that decline to do it elsewhere."

Let's take a brief look at four significant factors that make the difference between life and death here on Earth.

FOUR CONDITIONS FOR LIFE ON EARTH

1. Our Temperate Tilt

Aesthetically, the arrangement looks like a huge mistake. Our planet is out of whack. Everything might look more elegant if our planet rotated with its North Pole pointing straight up and its South Pole pointing straight down, but Goldilocks loves it crooked.

The alignment of the Earth's poles is askew by 23.5 degrees, creating an axial tilt. That minor tweak vastly increases the size of the Earth's temperate zone, the area of our planet's surface most hospitable to life.

A most pleasing angle. Our Earth's tilt vastly increases the planet's temperate zone, where plants and creatures thrive.

If our planet aligned straight up and down, the equator would be toast. Tropical regions would be pummeled by non-stop hurricanes. Canada and Russia would be frozen solid. We would have no seasons. But our tilt creates a vast temperate zone that provides for just-right climate conditions across six of our planet's seven continental landmasses.

2. A Breath of Fresh Air

We inhabit the only known celestial body to be snuggled in its very own protective atmosphere, but things weren't always so congenial and comfy here.

The consensus among today's scientists is that our Earth was created billions of years ago. (We'll talk more about the age of the cosmos in coming chapters, particularly chapter 11.)

So far as we can tell, version 1.0 of Earth's atmosphere was

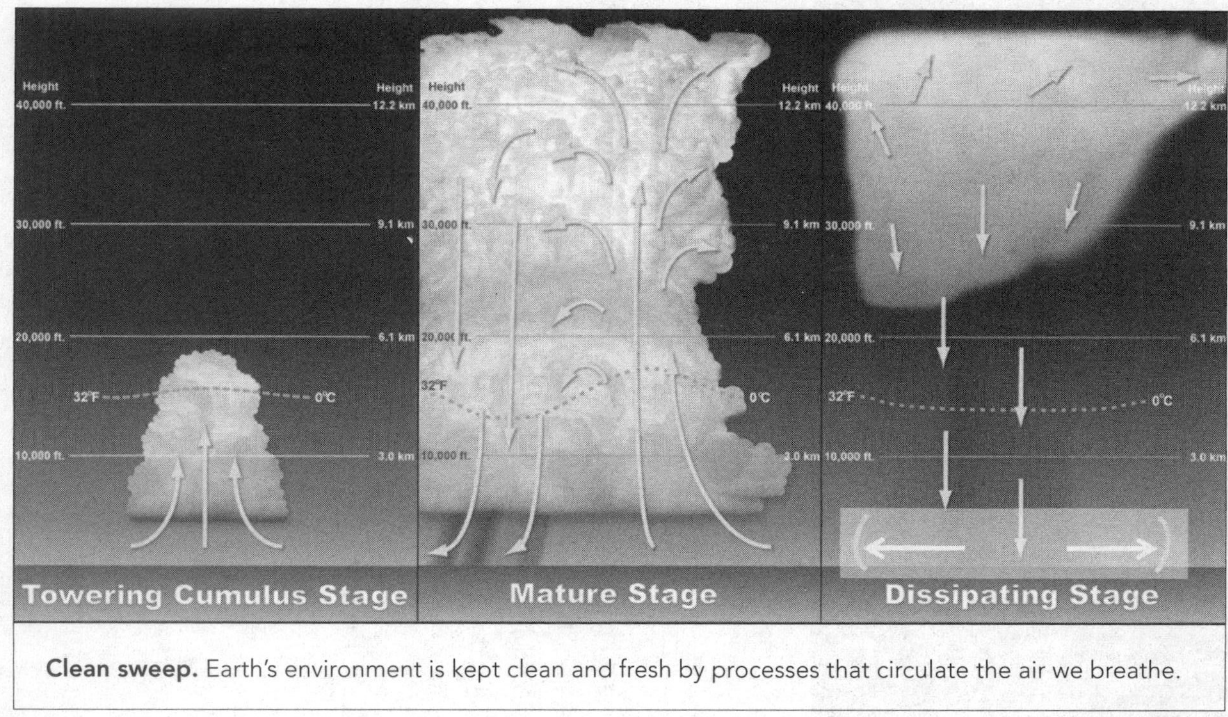

Clean sweep. Earth's environment is kept clean and fresh by processes that circulate the air we breathe.

similar to many young planets: vast clouds of gases (hydrogen, helium, methane, ammonia) with a bit of water vapor.

Next came atmosphere 2.0: a noxious mixture of methane, carbon dioxide, sulfur dioxide, ammonia, and nitric oxide spewed out by the planet's many active volcanoes. That atmosphere was both deadly and stinky!

When the planet's birth pangs finally settled down, Earth's surface temperatures cooled, water vapor condensed, and oceans formed. In time, God gave birth to plants in the oceans and on the land. As these living things took in carbon dioxide and exhaled oxygen, they enriched our planet's life-supporting atmosphere. Our Creator topped things off with an ozone layer that protects us from the Sun's destructive ultraviolet radiation.

One of the powerful processes our Creator uses to sustain life on Earth is convection, which constantly circulates the air we breathe. Every day, as the Sun's rays heat the Earth's surface, hot air rises and cool air falls. This ongoing process keeps things on our planet fresh and generates most of our wind.

Earth's atmosphere exhibits its share of variety and even violence. One village in the Bay of Bengal gets 87 feet of rain per year, while Death Valley receives only a couple of inches. And some 1.5 billion lightning strikes kill nearly twenty-five thousand people every year.

Overall, however, our atmosphere is just right, wrapping us in a self-refreshing, oxygen-rich blanket.

3. A World of Water

When the summer Sun is beating down, do you ever wish you could store some of that heat in a jar until wintertime?

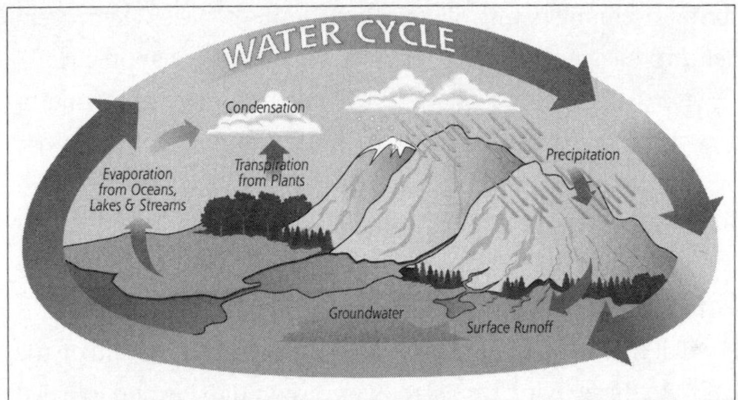

Wonderful water. Water falls to Earth in rain and snow, flows to oceans, and evaporates into the atmosphere to make more rain and snow.

Perhaps that's one of the reasons God created the oceans, which cover three-fourths of the surface of our planet at an average depth of more than two miles. The oceans help regulate our planet's temperatures, turning dramatic highs and lows into averages that are just right for us.

Like oxygen, liquid water is essential to life. And while almost every other planet we've studied lacks flowing liquid water, our world is awash in the stuff, some 352,670,000,000,000,000,000 gallons, according to the National Ocean Service.

And like convection—the process God uses to circulate our air and keep it fresh—our planet's water cycle constantly circulates our water, which evaporates from the ocean, rains down on the land, and then flows back to the ocean to do it all over again.

I could write an entire book about the wonders of water,

a topic explored more fully in the brief NASA film *Water Falls*. For now, I'll just ready myself for the next big Pennsylvania rainstorm and thank God for the precious fluid that cleanses us, cools us, hydrates us, and sustains us.

4. The Ubiquity and Audaciousness of Life

God is evidently very pro-life. Our planet is home to some 10 to 14 million species of living things.

Consider the lowly dandelion. Found on all the Earth's continents, these tenacious plants seem to flourish anywhere and everywhere (particularly where fussy gardeners wish they wouldn't). Dandelion flower heads are perfectly designed for maximum seed creation and dispersal. Each yellow, flowering head can disperse 50 to 175 seeds to the winds. One single dandelion plant can create more than two thousand seeds.

Few of us ever stop to think about the power of plants, but a recent column in the *New York Times* hailed them for being "as close to biological miracles as a scientist could dare admit." As Douglas Tallamy writes, "After all, they allow us to eat sunlight . . . and plants also produce oxygen, build topsoil and hold it in place, prevent floods, sequester carbon dioxide, buffer extreme weather and clean our water."

Life thrives even in the deepest and darkest regions of the ocean floor, where no sunshine ever permeates the gloom. Strange plants grow 20,000 feet below the surface, surviving on chemical nutrients emerging from vents in the ocean floor.

It's this kind of mind-blowing biological diversity that I think about when I'm singing "For the Beauty of the Earth," one of my favorite hymns.

POWERFUL PROCESSES UNDER OUR FEET

The psalmists frequently praise God for the glories of the heavens, but what about the glories buried deep underground? This book is about astronomy, not geology, but I can't resist briefly mentioning some of the powerful geologic processes God uses to sustain our wonderful world day after day, largely without notice.

In school you probably learned about our planet's fundamental structure. At the center of everything lies an inner core, surrounded by a thick mantle that makes up some 80 percent of our planet. All of this material is wrapped in a relatively thin (25 miles deep) outer crust, where we live.

Textbook diagrams may make the Earth's internal structure look static and solid, but under our feet hides an unseen

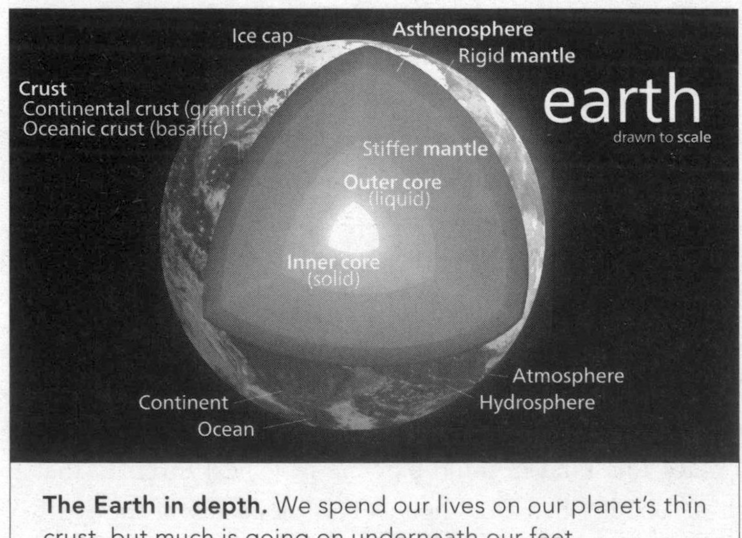

The Earth in depth. We spend our lives on our planet's thin crust, but much is going on underneath our feet.

world of moving, swirling, and sometimes exploding matter and energy.

Over a century ago, scientist Alfred Wegener proposed a shocking new theory called continental drift that said continents don't just sit there. They move.

Today, the science of plate tectonics has shown that the Earth's crust consists of a series of rocky plates that continually migrate to transform our planet's surface. Originally, the Earth didn't have the seven continents we see today. Instead, most of the Earth's landmass was huddled together in one big supercontinent called Pangaea. Over time, plate tectonics subdivided this supercontinent into seven individual continents that hitched rides on the moving tectonic plates as they migrated around the globe.

Like most bold new theories, Wegener's concept of continental drift was dismissed and ridiculed. But as the evidence in its favor accumulated, his theory became the new scientific consensus.

One powerful piece of evidence is found in the shape of today's continents. You can see how the continents could be reassembled like puzzle pieces, especially South America and Africa, which fit snugly together. Further evidence is found in the presence of similar geological and fossil deposits in continents that are now separated by thousands of miles of ocean.

The powerful drama of migrating plates is still at work today for all to see. Earthquakes often result from plates bumping up against one another. After a big quake shook Nepal in the spring of 2015, Chinese surveyors found that Mount Everest had suddenly moved 1.18 inches to the southeast. (Normally, it takes Everest a year to migrate about 1.5 inches.)

We often take our planet's powerful subterranean forces for granted, but musician Bruce Hornsby highlighted these processes in his beautiful geological love song, "Continents Drift":

Continents drift
Across a moonlit ocean
Continents divide
In a glacial measured motion

Such subterranean shifts provide one more example of God's grand plan for sustaining our Goldilocks planet.

OUR FIRST SELFIES

"Oh my goodness! Look at that picture over there!"

You've probably heard budding photographers make similarly enthusiastic comments, but this scene was unique.

The Apollo missions took astronauts to the Moon and back, but they also gave us an unexpected gift: gorgeous photos of our home from the perspective of space.

As NASA's Apollo 8 orbited the Moon on Christmas Eve, 1968, the mission's three astronauts appeared in a live TV broadcast, taking turns reading the first ten verses of the Genesis creation account. Afterward, astronaut William Anders saw something no human had ever seen before. "There's the Earth coming up," he said. "Wow, is that pretty."

The photo Anders snapped was called *Earthrise*, which soon became one of the most iconic and influential photos of all time.

Three years later, the crew of Apollo 17—NASA's last manned Moon mission—took an even nicer selfie. The *Blue Marble* photo revealed Earth in all its spherical beauty, complete with Antarctica's ice cap, a cyclone spinning in the Indian Ocean, and daylight creeping across the African continent.

For the first time ever humans could now see our planet in all its splendor and fragility. As many young people concluded at the time, these images really were "Far out, man!"

ARE WE TRASHING OUR PLANET?

The Earth's first selfies helped inspire 1970's inaugural Earth Day and encouraged decades of environmental awareness and activism that resulted in laws designed to reduce pollution and protect our health.

Some Christians dismissed early environmentalists as "tree-hugging hippies," but today many believers accept stewardship of the Earth as part of our service to a Creator whose promised judgments include "destroying those who destroy the earth" (Rev. 11:18).

No Christian leader has spoken so clearly and forcefully about the environment as Pope Francis, whose namesake, St. Francis of Assisi, is the patron saint of the environmental movement.

The pope's 2015 encyclical *Laudato si'* claimed human activity is the primary cause of climate change and called on all people to turn away from our "throwaway culture" and care for our planet.

"St. Francis of Assisi reminds us that our common home is like a sister with whom we share our life and a beautiful mother who opens her arms to embrace us," wrote the pope. "This sister now cries out to us because of the harm we have inflicted on her by our irresponsible use and abuse of the goods with which God has endowed her."

The Earth's temperatures and ocean levels are rising (the last few years are among the warmest on record), but some people still question the science of climate change and challenge the claim that humans are to blame. I myself wonder whether humans have played a bigger role than our Sun. Many people assume the Sun is a *regular* and *consistent* source of light and radiant energy, but it's not. Our Sun is an inconsistent star that seems to go through moody phases. Sometimes it shoots off huge flares or exhibits huge, dark sunspots. Sometimes it doesn't.

(This inconsistency proved particularly vexing for Galileo. Shortly after this God-fearing, pioneering astronomer became the first person to identify sunspots, they inexplicably disappeared for the next sixty years!)

In 2015, NASA's Magnetospheric Multiscale Mission set out to track down even more data about the invisible forces impacting our planet. Four identical MMM spacecraft will explore physics, magnetic forces, energy particle acceleration, and more in our own magnetosphere (that's the area surrounding Earth where the planet controls the behavior of charged particles).

Meanwhile, the science is already crystal clear about fracking, a technology that shoots pressurized water, chemicals, and sand deep underground to release precious oil and natural gas. Fracking waste products are injected deep into the Earth's surface—and the consequences are Earth-shaking. Literally.

Since Oklahoma began allowing fracking two decades ago, the state has experienced an unbelievable upsurge in earthquakes: from only a few during a typical year to nearly six hundred in 2014. That makes sense. Earthquakes result from tectonic plates and rocks sliding against each other. Injecting fracking wastewater deep underground lubricates these rocks, allowing them to slide more easily and create more earthquakes. The Oklahoma legislature has adopted new guidelines on fracking, and other states are sure to follow.

HOME SWEET HOME

Goldilocks was right. We've got a just-right planet here. The pope is right too. We need to care for our cosmic home: "We are called to be instruments of God our Father, so that our planet might be what he desired when he created it and correspond with his plan for peace, beauty and fullness."

As an astronomer and follower of Jesus, I'm regularly amazed at our Creator's role in our wonderful planet. The more I learn about Earth, the more I want to praise God for creating our unique haven, and the more I want to be a good steward of this amazing gift until Christ returns.

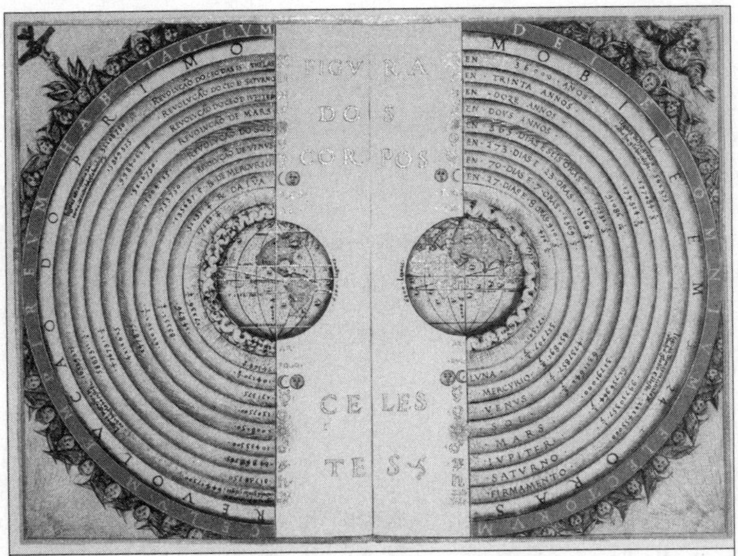

At home in the center. Before the 1500s, most people believed the Earth was the center of the universe.

6

COSMOLOGICAL CONFUSION

GEOCENTRIC, EGOCENTRIC, OR "COSMIC MEDIOCRITY"?

Planet Earth is pretty amazing, but how is our planet connected to everything else in the solar system? People wrestled with this question for millennia, none more fruitfully than a godly man named Niclas Kopernik.

Born into a devout Polish Catholic family two decades before Columbus sailed the ocean blue, he was a devoted lay worker in his parish, but studying the stars was his true passion.

Niclas was a talented artist and painter, as we can see by his self-portrait. His artistic training also may have helped him discern patterns in the heavens that others couldn't see. But mathematics was his strong suit, and he could spend weeks performing elaborate calculations to describe the movements of heavenly bodies.

By observing the skies, seeking out planetary patterns, and doing the calculations, Niclas felt he was able to perceive something that had eluded astronomers for centuries: "the structure of the universe and the true symmetry of its parts."

The problem was that Kopernik—now known by the Latinized name Copernicus—disagreed with just about everyone when he concluded the Earth moved around a stationary Sun. For centuries it had been *obvious* to nearly everyone that the Earth stood still. Copernicus did what scientists typically do: question the obvious.

Fearful that his astronomical work would attract scorn or danger, he steadfastly refused to publish his theories until shortly before his death in 1543. Instead, he kept quiet, carried out his parish duties, and carved out as much time as he could to explore the world's "wonderful commensurability." (Goldilocks would have called it "just rightness.")

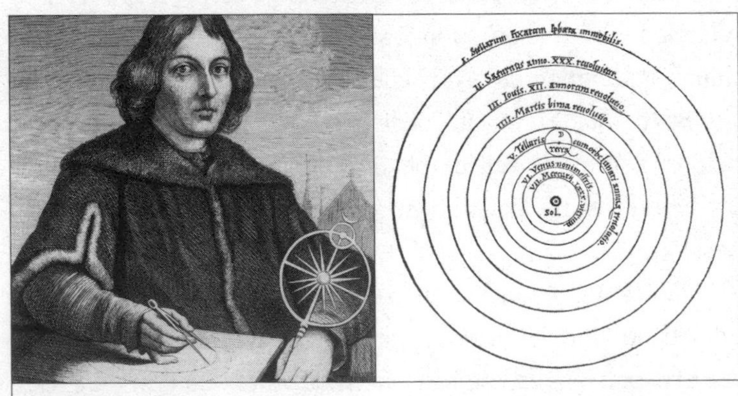

Questioning the obvious. Just about everybody said the Earth was the center of the universe. Copernicus showed that everything orbits the Sun.

When his theories finally were published, they were immediately condemned and ridiculed by both Catholic leaders and Protestant reformers, including Luther, who dismissed Copernicus's efforts to "turn the whole of astronomy upside down."

These theological critiques did little to stop the Copernican revolution that forever transformed our understanding of our world. But debates about cosmology—the structure of the universe—began long before Copernicus's time.

THE SEARCH FOR A "BIBLICAL" COSMOLOGY

Why does the Bible refer to heaven as "up there" and Sheol as "down there"?

What does Scripture mean when it refers to the "ends," "depths," or "four corners" of the Earth?

Is there really a "firmament" (or dome) in the heavens that separates the waters above from the waters below?

And what are those "fountains of the deep" that provided the water for Noah's flood?

Bible scholar Kyle Greenwood explores these and many other questions in his fascinating book, *Scripture and Cosmology*. Earlier we showed how many ancient Israelites embraced the idolatry and divination practiced by their Babylonian captors. Greenwood, associate professor of Old Testament and Hebrew Language at Colorado Christian University, shows that ancient biblical writers went farther than that, largely embracing

Middle Eastern understandings of the universe that were the *pre*scientific consensus of the day.

"The biblical authors wrote according to the best scientific evidence of their time," writes Greenwood. As a result, "biblical cosmology is ancient Near Eastern cosmology." Both Israelites and Babylonians understood the universe to be "small, flat and round."

Greenwood says understanding ancient cosmology helps explain why biblical writers described the world as they did. Most ancients believed in a three-part universe made up of Earth, heavens, and seas:

- Part one was a flat Earth held in place by pillars that supported its foundation.
- Part two was the heavens, the dwelling place of the Sun, Moon, stars, and planets, which passed over and under the flat Earth.
- Part three was the heavenly canopy, or upper heavens. These served as the floodgates for the upper seas, which had been separated from the oceans below. When this canopy opened, rain fell to Earth through windows in the sky.

We can see bits and pieces of this ancient cosmology in various biblical passages. In Genesis, we read that Noah's flood began when "the floodgates of the heavens were opened" (Gen. 7:11) and ended when "the floodgates of the heavens had been closed" (Gen. 8:2).

Job describes Creation according to these ancient concepts:

Where were you when I laid the earth's
foundation?
Tell me, if you understand. . . .
On what were its footings set,
or who laid its cornerstone?
—Job 38:4, 6

Centuries of scientific discovery have given us a much more detailed understanding of how everything works, but these discoveries do not invalidate biblical accounts, says Greenwood.

"Passages like the Job account are poetic in nature," he writes, "using metaphors, anthropomorphic language and other literary devices to convey concepts that would otherwise be foreign to human understanding."

Bottom line: The Bible is true in teaching us about our cosmic Creator. But the ancient pagan cosmological concepts that biblical writers largely embraced have long since been supplanted by more scientifically accurate explanations.

GREEKS ARGUING COSMOLOGY

"All the Athenians and the foreigners who lived there spent their time doing nothing but talking about and listening to the latest ideas," wrote Luke in Acts 17:21.

Cosmology was one of the Greeks' favorite debate topics, says historian Nicholas Nicastro: "The Greek intellectual world . . . was almost fanatically preoccupied with competing models of the ultimate configuration and substance of the cosmos."

Nicastro's book *Circumference* summarizes some of the colorful cosmological concepts that philosophers debated in the centuries before Christ. Thales said the Earth was a flat disk floating on a vast ocean. Anaximenes said our flat Earth was suspended in air. Anaximander said our Earth disk was surrounded by a wheel of fire. Other potential models included a cylinder, a drum, a funnel, and a Frisbee-like disk with an upturned rim.

Aristarchus of Samos (310–230 BCE) was one of the first to anticipate Copernicus's heliocentric theories by arguing that the Earth revolved around the Sun. Philosophers scoffed. It was *obvious* the Earth didn't move.

As the debates continued, Eratosthenes of Alexandria (276–194 BCE) proposed a radical new theory. He said the Earth's surface was curved—and set about to prove his theory by determining our planet's circumference through a brilliant experiment that college students often duplicate today, uploading videos of their projects on YouTube.

Using the principle of triangulation, Eratosthenes and a coworker in a distant city measured the angle of the Sun at the same time from their respective locations. Then Eratosthenes did the math, concluding that the Earth was 24,662 miles around. His results were shockingly accurate: within 1 percent of our current estimate of 24,859 miles.

Aristotle became a card-carrying round-Earther after witnessing the curved shadow of our planet darken the Moon's surface during lunar eclipses. But nobody actually *proved* that the Earth was round until Magellan's expedition circumnavigated the planet between 1509 and 1512.

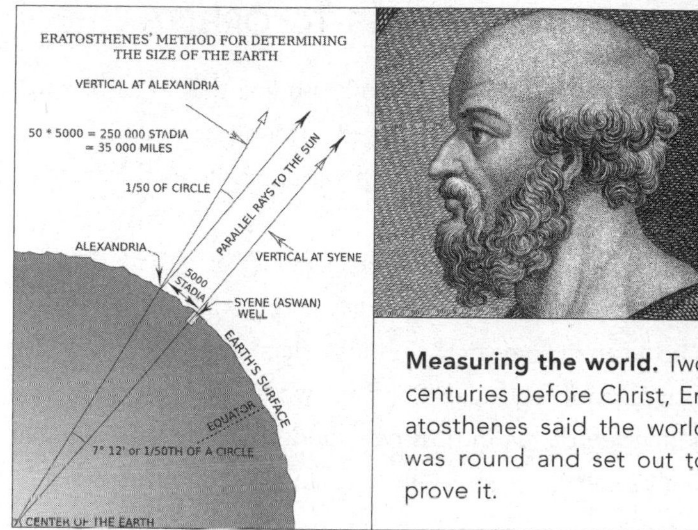

Measuring the world. Two centuries before Christ, Eratosthenes said the world was round and set out to prove it.

That proof failed to persuade everyone. Even today, some folks refuse to give up the notion of a flat Earth. In the 1800s, Bible students and astronomers in Britain founded various flat-Earth groups. America's very own Flat Earth Society counted thousands of members, many of whom kept the faith, even after NASA missions repeatedly photographed our very round planet. The society trumpeted its science-denying attitude in a startling 1977 newsletter headline: "Whole World Deceived . . . Except the Very Elect."

The Flat Earth Society largely disappeared after a 1995 fire in its leader's house destroyed most of its records, but vestiges of the group were resurrected online in 2004. You can join the Flat Earth Society for free, but you will have to pay to be an official Friend of the organization, which gets you a membership card and medallion.

FROM SPHERES TO ORBITS

Long before astronomers carefully studied the orbits of planets, philosophers claimed that the Moon, stars, and planets were affixed to or embedded in various spheres that rotated around the Earth.

Ptolemy (90–168) proposed a model of nested spheres, one inside another, with Earth at the center. Ptolemy's theory was better than some of the philosophers' silly ideas, but it still had significant logistical problems, which Copernicus sought to address with his radical new model. Copernicus replaced Ptolemy's spheres with a "threefold movement of the Earth."

1. The Earth rotates daily on its axis.
2. The Earth orbits the Sun once a year.
3. Earth's seasonal shifts are caused by its tilted axis.

These three principles helped explain why we have night and day, why planets appear to wander back and forth through the sky, and why days vary in length depending on the season.

Scientists were intrigued, but theologians were offended. Luther dismissed the Copernican theories as a vain novelty during a 1539 *Table Talk*: "So it goes now. Whoever wants to be clever must agree with nothing that others esteem. He must do something of his own. This is what that fellow does who wishes to turn the whole of astronomy upside down."

Some scholars suggest that Calvin was equally dismissive, though others argue he never offered the following condemnation: "We will see some who are so deranged, not only in religion but who in all things reveal their monstrous nature, that they will say that the sun does not move, and that it is the earth which shifts and turns."

Luther's associate Philipp Melanchthon even suggested state-sponsored censorship could help rein in unruly scientists: "Wise governments ought to repress impudence of mind," he said.

Today, a few Christians still cling to the belief that the Earth is the center of the cosmos. Supporters of the christianastronomy.org website say their mission is "upholding the Earth-centered cosmos according to God's word."

AT HOME IN A VAST COSMIC OCEAN

"It's not about you" is the opening sentence of the bestselling nonfiction book in US history, megachurch pastor Rick Warren's *Purpose Driven Life*. These four words also provide a pretty good summary of the history of astronomy in the centuries since Copernicus.

For the longest time, we Earthlings reigned at the center of the universe. Or at least we thought we did. And frankly, we loved believing that everything revolved around us. The earlier *geocentric* model was also a pleasantly *egocentric* model.

I can understand why theologians and religious leaders of the past embraced the geocentric model. It seemed to make sense that the God who created us would place us—the beloved crown of his Creation—at the center of everything. Some psalms seem to support the geocentric model: "He set the earth on its foundations; it can never be moved" (Ps. 104:5).

But after centuries of astronomical discoveries made with better and more powerful telescopes, we've been able to see farther and deeper into space. It's now clear that God created billions of galaxies as big as or bigger than our own beloved Milky Way.

Our cosmic address no longer has us located at the crossroads of Creation. The universe is bigger. We are smaller. (See color photo section p. 4.)

Carl Sagan poignantly described our remoteness and apparent insignificance in the grand scheme of things: "We are tucked away in some forgotten corner of the cosmos, our tiny, fragile, blue white world, lost in a cosmic ocean vast beyond our most courageous imaginings."

World-famous cosmologist Stephen Hawking described our lessened status in more dramatic language: "The human race is just a chemical scum on a moderate-sized planet, orbiting around a very average star in the outer suburb of one among a hundred billion galaxies."

Writer Chet Raymo describes our scenario in more desperate terms: "We can no longer look upon ourselves as the favored children of gods. The universe, we now understand, is vast beyond our reckoning, and we are ordinary, perhaps even typical, fragments of that universe. What is required, then, is the courage to accept our cosmic mediocrity . . . the courage to walk a tightrope between arrogance and despair."

I understand what Raymo is saying, but I see things from a different perspective. From the time I was a young junior astronomer studying the stars in my freezing back yard, I never had any problems accepting the fact that I was a very small creature in a very big cosmos. I knew that God and the universe were both incredibly huge.

True, the bigger the universe seemed, the smaller I felt. But that was fine with me. I already knew I was a small creature. After all, I was a kid! My life was limited. I had no money. I couldn't drive a car or do the other cool things all the big people did. Feeling small was a regular part of growing up.

Astronomy was different. Studying the heavens made me feel small in a big way. It still does. The fact that God created our vast cosmos and enables little people like me to look into its farthest reaches makes me feel truly blessed and mysteriously noble.

I'm far from the first person to feel that way. David got there way ahead of me:

> When I consider your heavens,
> the work of your fingers,
> the moon and the stars,
> which you have set in place,
> what is mankind that you are mindful of them,
> human beings that you care for them?
> —Psalm 8:3–4

LOCATING OUR TRUE VALUE

"Location, location, location!" may be the mantra in real estate, but is our "mediocre" cosmic address the truest measure of our worth and significance?

I don't think so. Our location in the universe doesn't determine our value. Only God can determine that, and he values us greatly.

This little blue planet God created is the only place where we know life exists, making us (at least as far as we know) the only creatures created in God's image.

Our Creator values and loves us so much that he sacrificed his Son for our sake. The infinite price he paid for our redemption shows us how much we are valued, even though we Earthlings are comparatively small in cosmic terms.

God thinks small is beautiful when it comes to humans, as we see in his love for the Israelites: "The LORD did not set his affection on you and choose you because you were more numerous than other peoples, for you were the fewest of all peoples" (Deut. 7:7).

Our smallness may even be designed to prepare us for heaven, which is open to the humble but not the proud.

Watching *Antiques Roadshow* on PBS is a great way to gain perspective on this concept of value. It's surprising to see which old objects are considered treasures and which are deemed trash. One painting bought at a garage sale for five dollars is actually a rare masterpiece worth $50,000. Other beautiful objects created centuries ago are worth very little.

Value is a fluid concept, as we can see by the changing calculus concerning the world's most plentiful fluid: water. Once upon a time, water was considered so abundant and readily available that it had relatively little value. Today, as our planet's population grows and more nations and regions face serious drought, water is becoming increasingly valuable.

Value is in the eye of the beholder, and our ultimate beholder is God, who brought us into being on this uniquely privileged planet. That's why I don't lose any sleep over the unimaginable vastness of the cosmos.

The Creator of everything knows me and he loves me. What's mediocre about that?

Celestial trinity. The Earth rises over the surface of the Moon as both are bathed by the light of the Sun, illustrating our intimate interconnection with these bodies.

7

BROTHER SUN AND SISTER MOON

THE INNER WORKINGS AND INTIMATE CONNECTIONS OF OUR CELESTIAL TRINITY

One is huge, hot, and bursting with energy. The other is small, cold, and dead.

One warms our skin, gives us the vitamin D and radiant energy we need, and powers cars, factories, and homes. The other moves our oceans and watches over us as we sleep.

These two heavenly bodies couldn't be more different, but they collaborate seamlessly. If they didn't, we couldn't survive. That's how our Creator set things up in the beginning: "God made two great lights—the greater light to govern the day and the lesser light to govern the night. He also made the stars. God set them in the vault of the sky to give light on the earth, to govern the day and the night, and to separate light from darkness. And God saw that it was good" (Gen. 1:16–18).

Good? It's awesome. I can see why St. Francis—the man

whose image adorns bird feeders worldwide because he preached to birds—praised God for our two heavenly companions in his "Canticle of Brother Sun":

> Be praised, my Lord, through all Your creatures,
> especially through my lord Brother Sun,
> who brings the day; and You give light
> through him.
> And he is beautiful and radiant in all his
> splendor!
> Of You, Most High, he bears the likeness.
> Be praised, my Lord, through Sister Moon and
> the stars;
> in the heavens You have made them bright,
> precious and beautiful.

Let's take a closer look at our brother and sister so we can see how they partner with our planet to create one pretty amazing interconnected celestial trinity.

WE'RE SOLAR POWERED

America's Mojave Desert spreads across parts of California, Arizona, Utah, and Nevada. With more than three hundred days of sunshine per year and temperatures that can soar above 120°F, this Sun-baked hot spot isn't congenial to human life, but it's the perfect place for the Desert Sunlight Solar Farm, where some eight million photovoltaic panels capture enough solar energy to power nearly two hundred thousand homes.

Right now solar power is rapidly being transformed from

a nice idea to a booming global industry. Morocco recently switched on a solar plant than can power a million homes. But the fact is, we humans have been solar powered from day one. Brother Sun bathes our blue-green planet with the light, heat, and radiant energy we living things couldn't live without. If you've ever eaten an apple or used up a gallon of gasoline, you have consumed stored sunlight.

Every second, nuclear fusion deep beneath the Sun's surface converts four million tons of material into energy that's equivalent to 10 billion nuclear bombs. Some of that energy becomes sunlight that travels vast distances to reach us—about 91 million miles in January when we're closest, and about 95 million miles in July.

(One might suspect that Earth would actually be warmer when we're closest in January, but because of the Earth's tilt, things are actually warmer in summer when the Sun is higher in the sky, warming us with concentrated sunshine. In winter, when the Sun is lower, each ray of sunlight covers a wider area, spreading the radiation over a larger area and thus reducing surface temperatures.)

The Sun is so powerful that we sometimes must shield ourselves from its heat, even after that heat has taken an eight-minute journey to Earth, losing a third to half of its radiant energy to the protective atmosphere of our clouds. "Nothing is deprived of its warmth," says the psalmist (Ps. 19:6).

But giving off all that energy takes a toll, and scientists estimate that in a few billion years or so, our brother will finally burn out.

BIG, BUBBLY, AND GASEOUS

Stars are some of our Creator's most amazing inventions. Even though he has already made trillions of them, he continues making more today, personally keeping track of each one. "He determines the number of the stars and calls them each by name" (Ps. 147:4; see also Isa. 40:26).

God is intimately connected with his Creation, knows its innermost workings, and exhibits a deep and lasting commitment to its well-being. Each star is a unique creation, and Paul tells us that "star differs from star in splendor" (1 Cor. 15:41).

These glowing factories of heat and light are not solid and rocky like our planet. Each star is a big ball of gas, mostly hydrogen and helium, powered by an explosive core of nuclear fusion, all of it bound together by the force of gravity.

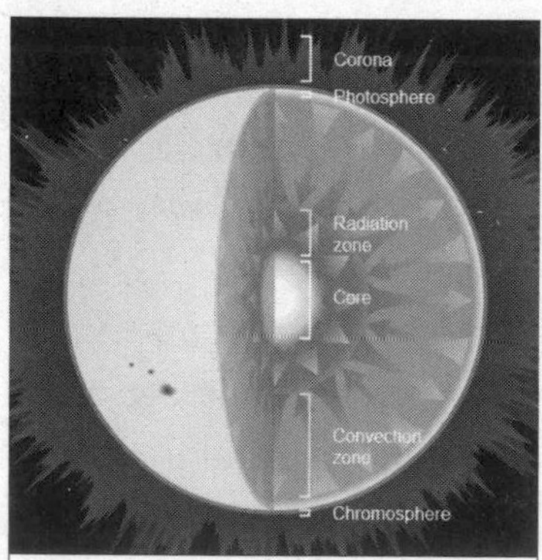

Fiery disposition. Our Sun is a glowing factory of heat powered by an explosive core of nuclear fusion.

Even if you had big, super-thick asbestos shoes, you wouldn't be able to walk across the Sun's turbulent outer layer. Every few minutes, a huge globule of the Sun as massive as one of our Earth's continents boils up to the surface before settling back down. Several million of these globules (astronomers call them granules) come together to constitute the Sun's surface at any one time. We can even see that as the Sun rotates on its axis every 29.5 days, these granules spin *differentially*. That means the granules at the Sun's equator move faster than those at its poles. (For more on stars, see chapters 17 and 18.)

As our solar brother goes through his occasional bouts of wildly erratic behavior, we suffer (or enjoy) the consequences. His storms and flares regularly disrupt our planet's telecommunications, but charged particles from his fast-moving solar winds give us the gorgeous displays of the northern and southern lights, or aurorae.

Not only can changes in the Sun's mood unleash severe storms here on Earth, but inexplicable variations in his energy output can make our planet fatally hot (severe droughts lasting centuries) or fatally cold (brutal ice ages lasting millennia).

Most of the time, though, our brother treats us "just right." For one thing, he's just the right size, compared to other stars that are too small to do much good or so big they gobble up everything in sight.

Our distance from the Sun is also just right. If we were much closer, our atmosphere would vaporize (picture Venus). If we were much farther away, our oceans would freeze (picture Mars).

Our lives—our very existence—depend on our radiant brother.

"Life on earth is nested in the life of the Sun," writes Judy Cannato in *Radical Amazement*, a book that connects the dots between Christian spirituality and astronomical discovery. "She is expending all that she has, expanding all that she is, in order for life to exist. As a result, earth and all her inhabitants flourish in her radiance."

We still don't understand a lot about Brother Sun, but we're working on it. In 2015, NASA dispatched four Magnetospheric Multiscale spacecraft to an area about halfway between Earth and Sun so we can better understand the powerful, invisible forces that connect us across the miles.

OUR SISTER'S GENTLE EMBRACE

The citizens of Assisi, Italy, had grown accustomed to having their slumber interrupted by the drunken carousing of a local troublemaker named Francesco di Petro di Bernardone. This time was different.

After nearly dying in war, Francesco had experienced a spiritual rebirth and received a powerful call from God. Now, on this moonlit night, the man who would later become known as St. Francis, patron saint of ecologists, was loudly praising God.

Overcome by the sheer beauty of the nighttime sky, Francis felt an overpowering mystical connection to the Moon and its Creator. Wanting his neighbors to share his joy with him, he scampered up to the church's bell tower and began furiously ringing the bells.

"Lift up your eyes, my friends," Francis cried out from his perch above the town. "Lift up your eyes. Look at the moon!"

Sister Moon is only one-fourth the diameter of Earth, while the Sun is more than a hundred times larger. But the Moon's closer proximity (less than a quarter of a million miles away) makes our relationship with her all the more intimate.

Astronomers and stargazers witness this intimacy as it plays out in the cosmic dance the Moon and Earth perform together. Our sister is bound to us in a synchronous orbit. Every 27.3 days she completes one complete orbit around the Earth while simultaneously rotating one complete turn on her axis.

Moon and Earth constantly tug and pull on each other. Over time, Earth's more powerful gravity has actually changed the shape of the Moon, making it slightly more oval than round. Likewise, the Moon exerts a weak but steady gravitational pull on us, and while that tug is too weak to alter Earth's shape, it is powerful enough to keep our oceans on the move.

Many scientists think Moon gravity also helps keep the Earth tilted on its axis at a beneficial angle of 23.5 degrees. That slight tweak vastly expands the temperate zone of the Earth, where creatures can be fruitful and multiply.

LIVING AND PRAYING ON LUNAR TIME

Our relationship with our sister goes even deeper. For thousands of years, our companion satellite has played an important role in our daily lives and religious practices.

Jews, Christians, and Muslims observe religious holidays that follow the lunar calendar's 29.5-day months. (Our word *month* comes from the earlier *moonth.*) Each month of the Jewish calendar begins with the new Moon, and these lunar rhythms help determine the dates for Christians' Easter celebrations.

The lunar year is shorter than the 365-day solar year the

Egyptians gave us. That explains why lunar holidays like the Jews' Rosh Hashanah and the Muslims' Ramadan continually move backward through the now-standard solar calendars we rely on.

Sister Moon has played an important role in our religious lives, but does she also possess the power to turn people into lunatics?

In medieval Europe, folks believed the "Transylvania effect" of a full Moon could arouse vampires, werewolves, and other creatures of the dark. Such fears only slowly subsided. As recently as a century ago, Britain's "Lunacy Acts" led to the arrest of people believed to be "moonstruck." Among the unfortunate souls mistakenly thrown into "loony bins" were people suffering from epilepsy, bipolar disorder, or trauma.

Even America's dysfunctional Congress pulled itself together long enough in 2012 to pass bipartisan legislation removing the word *lunatic* from federal laws.

CLOSER THAN WE THOUGHT!

Thanks to dozens of manned and unmanned lunar missions, we now know more about our cold, dusty satellite than any other heavenly body.

For half a century, scientists have been studying lunar rocks retrieved by these missions so we can find out what the Moon is made of. We've also left behind sensors on the lunar surface to transmit data about what's happening on *and in* the Moon. This new information may help us finally settle the "Moon origins" debate that has divided astronomers for centuries.

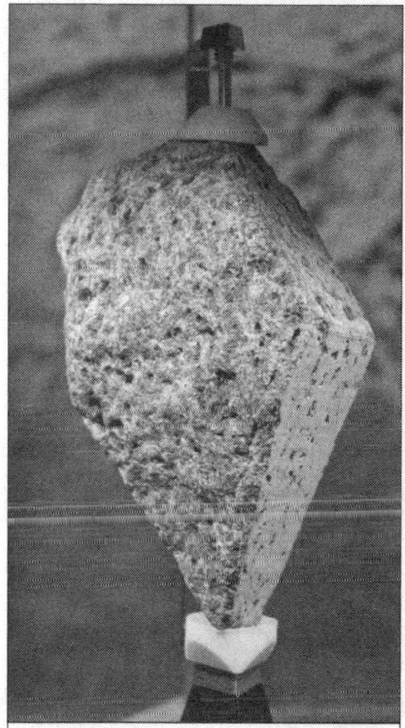

Rock of ages. We've been to the Moon many times, and the moon rocks we've brought back have helped us unravel lunar mysteries.

After the careful consideration and ultimate rejection of a half dozen competing theories, the current scientific consensus is that a Mars-sized flying object hit Earth with a glancing blow long, long ago (moon rocks brought back to Earth by astronauts for analysis suggest about 4.5 billion years ago). The impact of this collision pushed a chunk of Earth stuff out into space, where it gradually coalesced into its own spherical body.

Even after this violent separation, the two bodies have maintained a powerful mutual attraction, although each developed in radically different ways.

Over time, the Moon remained barren and lifeless, while our Earth grew greener, bluer, and more hospitable to every imaginable form of life. We're nestled in a protective atmosphere that insulates us from too much solar radiation. But the Moon travels through space pretty much naked. Its heavily cratered surface boils when warmed by solar radiation, freezes when shrouded in deepest darkness, and bears testimony to many massive direct strikes from incoming cosmic visitors.

RIDDLES OF BIBLIOASTRONOMY

I share Bible readings with my students in class each day. They often ask me—a card-carrying astronomer—questions about Bible verses they've heard in sermons or Sunday school lessons over the years. Here are two of their top questions.

1. What's the deal with the Sun standing still? Some students ask me about the famous passage from the book of Joshua. Joshua was the successor to Moses and as such battled the pagan nations of Canaan so that Israel could possess the land. During one particularly heated battle, Joshua commanded the Sun to stand still:

> So the sun stood still,
>   and the moon stopped,
>   till the nation avenged itself on its enemies,
> as it is written in the Book of Jashar.
> The sun stopped in the middle of the sky and
>   delayed going down about a full day.
> —Joshua 10:13

This is a complicated question. We now know the Earth revolves around the Sun, while most ancients (apparently including the author Joshua) believed otherwise. I trust that God performed some kind of miracle on the battlefield that day, but because of the way this passage is written, I can't scientifically explain what that miracle was or describe how it played out in the heavens.

Pretty much all life on our entire planet would die instantaneously if somebody suddenly stopped the Earth's rotation. Right now, people like me who live in Pennsylvania (at 40 degrees latitude) are traveling around and around at 800 miles per hour. If God were suddenly to apply the brakes and halt the Earth's rotation, I would experience the equivalent of being run over by a bulldozer powered by a supersonic jet engine.

I can't explain what happened with Joshua on the battlefield that day, but neither can I explain the miracles I've experienced in my own life. There's a good reason we can't explain these things. They're miracles. They're mysterious.

2. *What's the deal with the blood moon?* Someone recently showed me a news headline: "Christian Pastors Warn 'Blood Moon' Is an Omen of Armageddon and Second Coming of Christ."

When the Earth passes in between its Brother and Sister, astronomers call this a lunar eclipse, while others call the phenomenon a "blood moon." The Bible briefly mentions a blood-colored Moon in Joel 2:31; Acts 2:20; and Revelation 6:12. In Acts we read:

Blood-red tint. Sunlight filtered through Earth's atmosphere illumines the Moon with an eerie glow.

The sun will be turned to darkness
and the moon to blood
before the coming of the great and glorious
day of the Lord.

On the night of Sunday, September 27, 2015, I joined a bunch of my neighbors and stood outside in the street watching a beautiful blood moon. The Moon grew dim as the Earth blocked the Sun's light from reaching the lunar surface. But the Moon never went completely dark. Remnants of sunlight scattered through the Earth's atmosphere, where they took on a beautiful, deep red tint, just like the clouds in a colorful sunset. It was this reddish light that finally reached the Moon, providing the dim illumination. What a wonderful thing to see!

There have been thousands of blood moons since the time of Christ, but for some reason the 2015 version inspired some preachers to produce sermons, books, and DVDs declaring that this particular blood moon would play some role in fulfilling biblical prophecy.

I remind my students that interpreting prophecy and interpreting astronomical events are two distinct gifts. I also advise them not to get too worked up about biblioastronomical prophecies of doom and gloom that exploit regularly occurring astronomical phenomena and sow misunderstanding or fear. Yes, Acts says a blood moon is a sign of the day of the Lord, but that's only half of the scriptural picture. The Sun must go dark as well. Astronomers consider that impossible, so if this ever happens, end times preachers will have plenty to talk about!

CELESTIAL FAMILY VALUES

When it comes to Sister Moon, God doesn't want us to fear her or worship her. (The ancient Israelites had a big problem with the latter.)

As for Brother Sun, we can appreciate him without becoming card-carrying Umbraphiles. According to *Fortune* magazine, some fifty thousand Umbraphiles regularly travel to locations where they can observe solar eclipses. They will be out en masse on August 21, 2017, when the next total solar eclipse should be visible throughout North America.

God would appreciate it if we would thank him for giving us such a great Brother and awesome Sister. Even if we don't thank him, the Sun and Moon will do so for us:

> Praise him, sun and moon;
> praise him, all you shining stars.
> Praise him, you highest heavens
> and you waters above the skies.
> Let them praise the name of the LORD,
> for at his command they were created.
> —PSALM 148:3–5

Heavenly high priest. Johannes Kepler believed his astronomical work was his way of serving God and humanity. "I have composed this hymn for God the creator."

8

THE CALLING OF A CHRISTIAN SCIENTIST

KEPLER, GOD'S TWO BOOKS, AND THE ELEGANT ELLIPSE

When young people talk to me about what they're going to do with their lives and careers, they often say they are finding their calling. But I'm not sure calling is something we find. In fact, calling was something that found *me* as I pursued my faith in Christ and my passion for astronomy.

Our family spent Sunday mornings and evenings at First Baptist Church in Brockton, Massachusetts. That's where I learned that Jesus loves me and the Bible is God's book.

When I wasn't in church or school, I was out in the back yard, scanning the skies. By the time I was eight years old, I knew astronomy was what I wanted to do for the rest of my life. But could science be my way to serve God?

I knew God called people to serve him in various ways, but in the Bible it seemed he mostly called people to be preachers or evangelists. Could God be calling me to be a scientist?

I wrestled with this question as I watched a Billy Graham evangelistic crusade on TV one evening. After his powerful sermon to the crowd, Graham looked straight into the camera and challenged viewers at home to get right with God. I felt like he was speaking directly to me. I knelt before the TV and recommitted my life to Christ, promising once again to serve God no matter what, even if he wanted me to go halfway around the globe and die as a missionary somewhere. But in my heart of hearts I hoped and prayed I could be an astronomer instead.

When it was time to choose a college, I faced a crucial decision. Should I attend a major secular school with a solid astronomy program? Or should I go to a Christian college where the Bible teaching might be stronger than the science program?

After much prayer, I chose the combo platter! I registered as a full-time student at Eastern University while also taking higher-level astronomy classes at Villanova University. I wanted to grow in my grasp of both faith and science.

I later discovered a spiritual companion in Francis Bacon, the English statesman and author whose "Baconian method" of inquiry helped fuel the scientific revolution of the sixteenth and seventeenth centuries. Bacon saw deep connections between faith and science: "God has, in fact, written two books, not just one. Of course, we are all familiar with the first book he wrote, namely Scripture. But he has written a second book called creation."

I believe God called me to study these two books and teach others how to do the same. I've studied the book of Scripture to become a better disciple of Jesus day by day, and I've learned everything I can about the book of nature, earning both a master's and a doctorate in astronomy and astrophysics at the University of Pennsylvania.

Along the way I've discovered I'm not alone. Right now, hundreds of committed Christian astronomers are busy studying the Creator's handiwork. We work on top government projects, teach at esteemed universities, conduct cutting-edge research, travel to space, and praise God for giving us the awesome privilege of understanding previously undisclosed mysteries of the cosmos.

For many of us, our role model is a devout Christian scientist who centuries ago combined theology, mathematics, and musical theory to explain some of the workings of the Creator.

HIGH PRIEST OF THE HEAVENS

"I wanted to become a theologian. For a long time I was restless. Now, however, behold how through my effort God is being celebrated in astronomy."

It was 1596 and Johannes Kepler was expressing his love for God's "two books" in a book of his own: *Mysterium Cosmographicum* (or *The Cosmographic Mystery*). The book's forty-six-word subtitle explains its focus: "Forerunner of the Cosmological Essays, Which Contains the Secret of the Universe; on the Marvelous Proportion of the Celestial Spheres, and on the True and Particular Causes of the Number, Magnitude, and Periodic Motions of the Heavens; Established by Means of the Five Regular Geometric Solids."

Kepler was a German Protestant who studied theology so he could be a minister, but it was while studying science that he found his true calling. A friend of *observational astronomers* such as Galileo (they look through telescopes), Kepler was a *theoretical astronomer* (they use numbers and formulas, not telescopes).

His constant prayer was that his work would "always be ready to offer delight not unworthy of a Christian, and give relief from sorrow either in the astronomical practices or in the contemplation of the heavenly works of the harmonies of the universe."

Kepler's astronomical theories flowed from his deep faith in God, the cosmic architect and builder. He believed astronomy was one way to better understand the Creator's mind and methods, allowing us to praise him more accurately and rapturously. "Those laws [of nature] are within the grasp of the human mind; God wanted us to recognize them by creating us in his own image so that we could share in his own thoughts."

Faith also gave Kepler the courage he needed to express unpopular ideas at a time when religious conflicts divided families, congregations, communities, and nations. He was well aware that religious institutions used force to suppress heresy. His own elderly mother had been arrested, charged with witchcraft, and threatened with torture and death. And his own Lutheran church denied him Communion because he was too friendly with Calvinists, Catholics, and controversial astronomers like Galileo.

Threatened with exile for supporting Copernicus's new heliocentric theory, Kepler kept his cool and refused to be silenced or censored. "Now nothing can keep me back," he wrote in his 1619 book, *Cosmic Harmonies*. "If you pardon me, I shall rejoice; if you reproach me, I shall endure."

KEPLER'S GIFTS

Kepler earned a hallowed spot in astronomy's hall of fame by applying his mathematical skills to the detailed astronomical observations of others. The result was his groundbreaking laws of planetary motion, which helped solve riddles that had perplexed astronomers for centuries.

His greatest gift to astronomy was the ellipse. Kepler's first law said planets travel in elliptical orbits, not in perfectly circular orbits, as ancient philosophers like Aristotle had taught two thousand years earlier. This simple, elegant solution solved mysteries that had confused astronomers for centuries. The theory also gave further credibility to Copernicus's heliocentric cosmology, causing religious leaders to condemn Kepler's work.

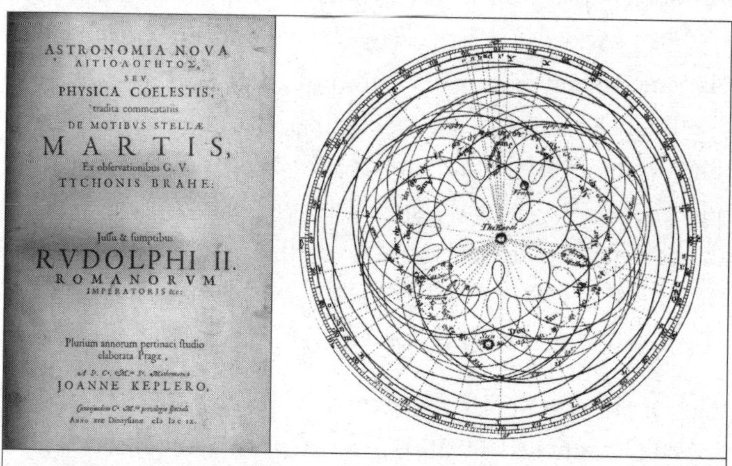
ASTRONOMIA NOVA
ΑΙΤΙΟΛΟΓΗΤΟΣ,
SEV
PHYSICA COELESTIS,
tradita commentariis
DE MOTIBVS STELLÆ
MARTIS,
Ex observationibus G. V.
TYCHONIS BRAHE:

Jussu & sumptibus
RVDOLPHI II.
ROMANORVM
IMPERATORIS &c:

Plurium annorum pertinaci studio
elaborata Pragæ,

JOANNE KEPLERO,

Mathematics and motion. Kepler applied his mathematical skills to the astronomical observations of others to determine laws of planetary motion in his influential book *Astronomia Nova*.

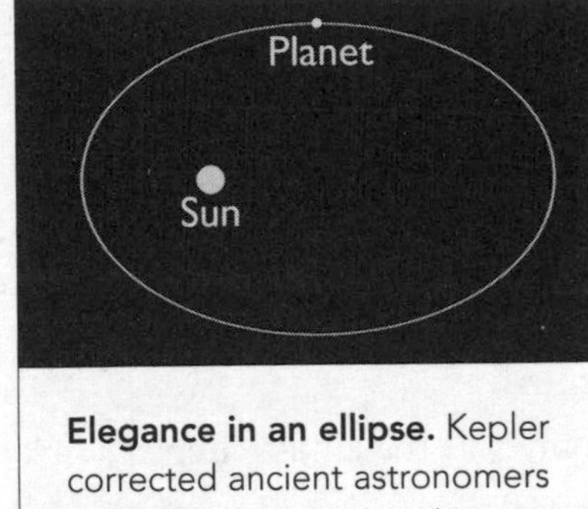

Elegance in an ellipse. Kepler corrected ancient astronomers and philosophers by showing that planets travel in elliptical orbits.

Another Kepler law said planets' orbital speeds vary at different times of the year. They move fastest when closest to the Sun and slower when farther away. Kepler's new theories pointed out irregularities in the heavens, and this further eroded confidence in ancient notions about heavenly perfection.

Kepler also took important steps toward helping us understand the invisible forces that hold the cosmos together. He said the Moon impacts Earth's ocean tides through a "magnetic force." Within a few decades, Isaac Newton would identify that force in his game-changing theory of universal gravitation.

Today Kepler's laws seem obvious, but in his day superstition was more powerful than science. People spent more time on *astrology* (What are the stars saying to *me* about *my* love life and career?) than *astronomy* (How do the heavens work?).

A NAMESAKE MISSION

We can honor Kepler's legacy by following NASA's *Kepler* mission. Launched in 2009, the *Kepler* space observatory's purpose is to seek out Earth-like planets that orbit other stars in our region of the Milky Way. Scientists think these Earth-like planets are the best place to look for signs of life (see chapter 16), and so far the mission has identified more than three thousand potential candidates.

I believe Kepler would have been thrilled to see his namesake mission. He felt certain God had populated other worlds, and he even wrote a book titled *Somnium (The Dream)* that imagines what Moon-dwelling creatures might think about Creation. Carl Sagan claimed *Somnium* was the world's first work of science fiction.

In the long run, the young man who wanted to be a minister became a father of the scientific revolution, praising God along the way.

"I have been made priest of God, the creator of the book of nature," Kepler wrote. "I have composed this hymn for God the creator."

SEEKING CONTEMPORARY KEPLERS

You've probably heard of U2, the acclaimed Irish rock band that performed psalms and other spiritual songs to millions of fans around the world. But you probably never would have heard of U2 if Bono, the Edge, and Larry Mullen had submitted to their spiritual elders in Shalom, the Dublin charismatic Christian community they attended. Shalom's leaders felt certain God would never call followers of Jesus to minister through secular music. After a difficult period of discernment, the three musicians were forced to leave Shalom to pursue their calling.

Today, similar challenges face Christian young people who inherit anti-science attitudes from their parents, churches, or schools. I believe God calls young people to study astronomy, but how can they hear or respond to that call if well-meaning Christians try to scare them away from science?

I thank God that didn't happen to me. My parents and the people at my church supported me as I pursued my calling.

Is God calling you to be a scientist? That's not for me to say. Just make sure you don't let anyone tell you that all scientists are "godless scientists." Believing scientists are everywhere, as a recent survey by the American Association for the Advancement of Science shows.

AAAS found that more than a third of scientists have no doubts about God's existence, 18 percent of scientists attended weekly religious services (compared with 20 percent of the rest of us), and 15 percent of scientists consider themselves very religious (compared with 19 percent of the general population).

BALANCING SCIENCE AND FAITH

If you would like to know a more contemporary example of the working Christian scientist, check out Francis S. Collins, a committed believer who serves as director of the National Institutes of Health, one of the most prestigious science positions in the United States.

Collins explained his dual calling in a 2015 *National Geographic* article, "Why I'm a Man of Science—and Faith": "I am privileged to be somebody who tries to understand nature using the tools of science. But it is also clear that there are some really important questions that science cannot really answer, such as: Why is there something instead of nothing? Why are we here? In those domains I have found that faith provides a better path to answers."

Over the centuries, Christian scientists like Kepler and Collins have helped us see more deeply into God's two books: the Bible and the book of nature. We will need even more such people of faith and science in the future.

A contemporary Kepler? Francis S. Collins is a leading scientist and a committed man of faith.

Martin Luther King Jr. explained why: "Science keeps religion from sinking into the valley of crippling irrationalism and paralyzing obscurantism. Religion prevents science from falling into the marsh of obsolete materialism and moral nihilism."

Studying both books promotes balance, says psychiatrist/author Timothy Jennings: "If we study science without Scripture, we risk falling into the ditch of atheistic evolutionism; on the other hand, the study of Scripture separated from God's laws in nature risks ideologies that misinterpret God and distort his character."

We need more men and women who can help us study both of God's books. May God send more of these scientists our way, and may we bless them and prayerfully support them as they pursue this sacred calling.

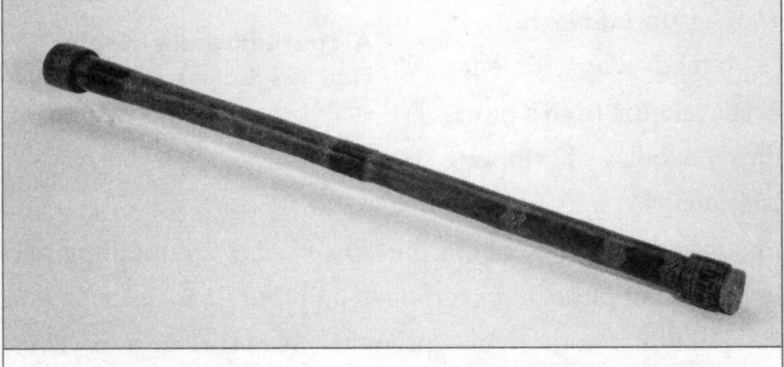

"Observer of marvels." A better telescope helped Galileo see more of God's heavens than anyone had ever seen before.

9

THROUGH THE TELESCOPE WITH GALILEO

GLASS HELPS US SEE UNSEEN WORKS OF THE CREATOR

Hans Lipperhey (or Lippershey) made eyeglasses in a tiny shop in the Netherlands. He never planned on jump-starting a revolution. But one day in 1608, children playing in his shop grabbed two glass lenses, placing one in front of the other. When they looked through the two lenses, the weather vane on a nearby church suddenly appeared three times larger.

The eyeglass maker quickly pounced on the surprising discovery. He secured a patent for this new device, called the "looker," describing it as "a certain instrument for seeing far."

Back then, people didn't have binoculars or telescopes. Astronomers studied the skies with their naked eyes. Navigators used sextants to determine angles and distances of heavenly bodies, but these devices lacked magnifying powers.

Word quickly spread and the new looker became the talk of Europe. Lipperhey made them as fast as he could, selling some to royalty and others to military leaders, who liked calling the devices "spyglasses." Soon an Italian scientist named Galileo Galilei would make his own looker, and that would change everything forever.

"THE FIRST OBSERVER OF MARVELS KEPT HIDDEN"

Galileo was a complicated man. Born in Pisa, he was a devout, if imperfect, Catholic who might have become a monk had his father not prevented him.

But no one could squelch his curiosity. He conducted experiments by dropping objects from his town's famous leaning tower as part of his lifelong quest to better understand "this grand book of the universe, which stands continually open to our gaze."

Working as a mathematics instructor at various universities, Galileo struck some associates as arrogant and offensive. One university held back part of his salary for his repeated refusals to wear proper academic regalia.

When Galileo heard that someone had created a spyglass that could help people see farther than ever before, he decided to grind and polish his own glass lenses so he could create an even more powerful sky-scanning device.

Finally, in November 1609, Galileo turned his new

telescope toward the heavens. He wouldn't get a full night's sleep for the next two months. Peering deeper into space than anyone had ever seen before, he felt repeatedly star struck by the wonder of it all.

Complex Christian. Devout and arrogant. Brilliant and argumentative. Galileo was a complex scientist who changed our understanding of the world.

Strange, marvelous, unknown sights came to life before his eyes.

Turning his gaze on the Moon, he saw alarming irregularities: mountains, big craters, and curious surface patterns.

He also studied the Sun, becoming the first human to methodically study sunspots.

Turning his telescope toward Jupiter, he thought he saw four small stars. After further study, he concluded Jupiter had four orbiting moons of its own. (Today we know them as the four Galilean moons: Io, Europa, Ganymede, and Callisto.)

Galileo was the first person to realize that the Earth's relationship with Sister Moon was not unique in the universe. God had created another planet with its own unique sisters. Overnight everything seemed different.

He also observed Venus changing phases. As he watched the planet going through changes similar to those witnessed on the Moon, he concluded that Venus orbited the Sun, not the Earth.

Much of what he saw baffled him, so he conducted repeated observations of the same heavenly bodies, dozens and dozens of times, night after night, to test and verify what he was seeing, writing down detailed observations and illustrating his notes with simple, elegant drawings.

The more he studied, the clearer it became that these celestial bodies were actually a whole lot messier than the perfect, unblemished spheres Aristotle and just about everybody else had imagined. Concepts that had been obvious for millennia now seemed dead wrong.

Galileo's discoveries also threatened the foundations of Ptolemy's reigning geocentric model, which said *everything* orbited the Earth. His work put him at odds with much of the scientific consensus of his day and would ultimately lead to his battles with the institution that enforced that consensus: his very own Roman Catholic Church.

But his biggest discovery was yet to come. Aristotle had conceived of the Milky Way as a cloud of vapors from Earth, but when Galileo trained his powerful telescope on these heavenly clouds, he saw "innumerable quantities" of previously unknown twinkling stars. Suddenly our universe was vastly bigger and more crowded than anyone had ever imagined.

"I render infinite thanks to God for being so kind as to make me alone the first observer of marvels kept hidden in obscurity for all previous centuries," wrote the sincerely grateful, if not entirely humble, astronomer.

"FATHER OF MODERN SCIENCE"

The telescope clearly gave Galileo an advantage over earlier stargazers. "Until the invention of the telescope, each generation of astronomers had looked at much the same sky as their predecessors," wrote astronomy historian Michael Hoskin. "All this now changed. . . . Galileo saw with his telescope wonders vouchsafed to no one before him: stars that had remained hidden from sight since the Creation."

But Galileo was far more than a lucky guy who stumbled upon a powerful new tool that gave him a temporary edge. He was a scientific pioneer who transformed astronomy from a philosophical exercise into a detail-oriented, observational process of empirical inquiry.

Galileo's revolutionary findings would reveal fatal flaws with the old geocentric cosmology, ushering in a major paradigm shift. Unfortunately, the Catholic Church was behind the old cosmology. Galileo was on a collision course with God's earthly representatives.

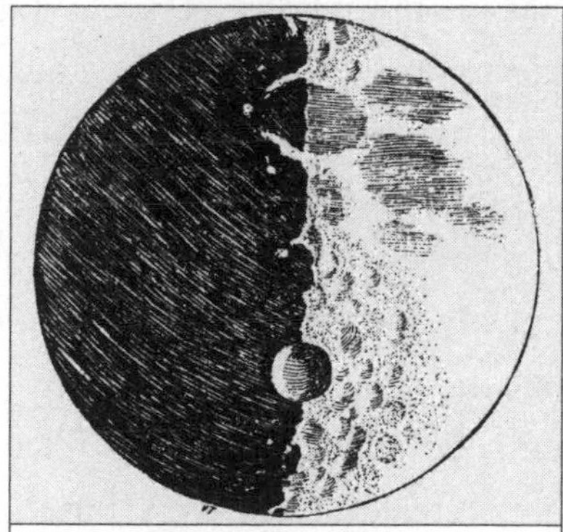

Astronomical artist. Galileo's detailed drawings of our Moon show surface irregularities no one had ever seen before.

The Catholic Church was reeling from the fallout

of the Protestant Reformation. The institution was committed to reining in all forms of dissent, and used various powers of persuasion, including violence, torture, and execution. Plus, people were fed up with instability and change. This was not the ideal time to be Galileo.

TECHNOLOGY'S UNINTENDED CONSEQUENCES

Back in 1969, US Defense Department engineers didn't intend to kick-start a revolution any more than Hans Lipperhey did. But when these engineers linked computers at four American university campuses, they set in motion a process that led to the worldwide web.

In 1995, about 1 percent of the world's residents accessed the internet. Today, billions of us go online every day to communicate, shop, study, travel, work, and invest. In twenty short years, this technology has disrupted industries and changed lives.

That's what technology does. We create newfangled tools to address one challenge, but then our tools generate unintended consequences and new sets of problems. Automobiles quickly and comfortably transport us from point A to point B, but they also bring traffic jams, pollution, and more than a million highway deaths worldwide every year. Solar wind turbines create clean energy, but they also kill birds.

Few technologies have been more disruptive than the telescopic tools Galileo gave the world four centuries ago. But nobody would have heard of Galileo if it weren't for an even *earlier* disruptive technology: Gutenberg's printing press.

THE POWER OF GLASS

Prior to 1450, few people could read. When the mechanical printing press made books accessible to more people, many new readers suddenly discovered flaws in their eyesight. That's how printing paved the way for astronomy. The growing market for books sparked a growing demand for glass lenses.

Glass has been around for a long, long time. Most scientists agree that some 20 to 30 million years ago, a big meteor crashed into or exploded above the Libyan desert in northern Africa, instantly melting acres of sand and creating miles and miles of a glasslike substance that ancient people used for primitive weapons and cutting tools. Egypt's royal craftsmen even incorporated a piece of this Libyan desert glass into a gaudy pendant they buried with King Tutankhamen. People were making glass beads by 3500 BCE, and Roman glassmakers turned out clear wine bottles and glasses in the centuries before Christ.

In time, people recognized the optical properties of glass. Medieval monks who hand-copied precious manuscripts in dim monastic scriptoria slid circular pieces of glass over their pages to enlarge tiny details. When someone connected two of these glass pieces in a simple frame that could be worn on the head—voila!—spectacles were born.

Bestselling science writer Steven Johnson calls glass "one of the most versatile and transformative materials in all of human culture." He writes, "Within 100 years of Gutenberg's invention, thousands of spectacle makers around Europe were thriving, and glasses became the first piece of advanced technology—since the invention of clothing in Neolithic times—that ordinary people would regularly wear on their bodies."

Today, three-quarters of Americans use either glasses or contact lenses to correct their vision.

Glass technology helped people do more than read books. It enabled astronomers to detect previously unseen worlds in the heavens through their telescopes, while allowing other scientists to examine previously unseen worlds inside the human body with their microscopes. Glass helped scientists see everything more clearly.

WHAT WILL ASTRONOMERS SEE NEXT?

Galileo changed our understanding of the cosmos using a simple telescope with two pieces of glass. Four centuries later, astronomers are engaged in "the greatest, most expensive and ambitious spree of telescope-making in the history of astronomy," says *New York Times* science reporter Dennis Overbye.

Today's astronomers have augmented Galileo's primitive technology with two kinds of powerful new telescopes: radio and infrared. These telescopes don't have an eyepiece for an observer like Galileo. Instead they collect invisible data and feed it into giant computers for analysis. These data streams are combined and then analyzed by computers using specialized software as part of a complex process called *interferometry* that converts invisible radio waves into stunning visual images scientists can view and study (see chapter 17).

ALMA (the Atacama Large Millimeter/submillimeter Array)

is the world's most complex and expensive network of radio telescopes. A partnership between the US, Europe, Canada, and other countries, ALMA is perched atop 16,500-foot-high mountains in Chile.

Meanwhile, the Hubble Space Telescope is truly out of this world. Launched in 1990, Hubble circles the Earth in an orbit outside of our atmosphere, enabling its near-ultraviolet, visible, and near-infrared spectrum cameras to take beautiful, distortion-free photos of deep space.

As we will see, these powerful new technologies are helping us unravel even more mysteries of Creation.

Spying on the heavens. The ALMA network of radio telescopes is extending human eyesight even farther and deeper into space.

Burning passion. Philosophers and others whose ideas challenged the establishment could suffer the same deadly consequences as Dominican friar Giordano Bruno.

10

GALILEO: HERO OR HERETIC?

TIMES OF INSTABILITY AND UNCERTAINTY CAN FUEL FEAR AND STIFLE SCIENCE

You could say it was the best of times and the worst of times to be Galileo. While fortunate to be part of a growing movement trying to decipher the hidden workings of the natural world, he was unfortunate to live at a time when bitter religious conflict put people on edge, paralyzing much of Europe's scientific and intellectual progress.

The age of exploration had taken men like Christopher Columbus to new worlds. Galileo now applied that spirit of exploration to the heavens. He knew this was risky work.

Nine years before Galileo first studied the skies with his powerful new telescope, the Roman Catholic Church burned Dominican friar Giordano Bruno at the stake for his many controversial views. (Among his thought crimes was the belief in *cosmic pluralism*—the idea that the heavens provided a home for an infinity of worlds, some of them populated by living creatures.)

Galileo was a committed Christian who saw no conflict between his faith and his calling as a scientist. "Holy Scripture and Nature are both emanations from the divine word," he wrote. But his telescope was providing growing evidence for Copernicus's heliocentric theory, and that put him in conflict with his church, which supported geocentric cosmology.

Galileo didn't worry about the risks he faced. After all, he was a scientific superstar, on par with today's Neil deGrasse Tyson or Stephen Hawking. His Italian patrons and supporters were proud of his work. He was a personal friend of the pope. What could possibly go wrong?

He found out at church one Sunday when a priest twisted Acts 1:11 ("Men of Galilee . . . why do you stand here looking into the sky?") to launch a homily condemning astronomers for practicing "diabolical arts."

The priest was later forced to apologize, but the first shot had been fired in what became an unfortunate decades-long battle that transformed Galileo from an esteemed man of science to a heretic who was condemned by his own church, forced to recant his views, and kept under house arrest for the last eight years of his life.

CULTURES IN COLLISION

Popular culture sees the Galileo affair as a major battle in the ongoing war between religion (often a *conservative* force that looks to the past) and science (often a *progressive* force, because it constantly reveals new things). But the story is much more complicated.

The early 1600s were turbulent times. People felt too overwhelmed by anxiety and fear to welcome any more revolutionary ideas. Wars and rumors of war unsettled many. The Thirty Years' War ground on, causing death, destruction, and famine. And more than a century after the Black Death had wiped out a quarter of Europe's population, localized outbreaks of the plague raised fears in Italy's cities.

Luther's Protestant Reformation further contributed to the instability of the age by questioning the authority of the Catholic Church. Now the Catholic Counter-Reformation sought to regain lost ground. Paranoia ruled within the Vatican, which was divided by political squabbles and threatened by spies and murderers. The Inquisition enforced theological orthodoxy by harassing, torturing, and executing heretics.

Let's journey to Italy in 1615 to understand how Galileo and his church collided in this needless conflict, and see how followers of Jesus can avoid similar showdowns today, a time of even more powerful technological tools and unprecedented scientific discovery.

TRIALS AND TRIBULATIONS

After Galileo's eight weeks of nonstop nighttime stargazing through his new telescope, he caught up on his sleep and came to a conclusion. Copernicus was right. We orbit the Sun. Those who said the Earth is the center (Ptolemy, Aristotle, the Catholic Church, and just about everybody else) were wrong.

Copernicus had published his controversial heliocentric theory back in 1543. Since then, the church tolerated debates about cosmological theory.

Galileo wasn't debating. He claimed his detailed telescopic observations of moons orbiting other planets *proved* the Copernican theory. He was right, but he was mistaken in believing he could convince everyone else to see things in a new way.

Galileo was challenging the Catholic Church, and he hoped he could work out a deal with his old friend, now Pope Urban VIII. But Urban felt he had no choice and assigned his friend's case to the Inquisition. Leading the prosecution would be Cardinal Robert Bellarmine, the so-called Hammer of Heretics, who had presided over the trial that led to the execution of Giordano Bruno.

Galileo was given the freedom to keep working so long as he kept quiet about his findings. But Urban had also made things more difficult by reaffirming the Catholic Church's geocentric position and declaring Copernicus's heliocentric theory a heresy.

Galileo kept quiet much longer than anyone expected, but by 1632 he was ready to come out of the closet, finally publishing his long-simmering masterpiece, *Dialogue Concerning the Two Chief World Systems*. The book would put him in the crosshairs of the Inquisition.

"Until the telescope, the defenders of Christian orthodoxy felt no need to ban Copernican ideas," wrote Daniel J. Boorstin in *The Discoverers: A History of Man's Search to Know His World and Himself*. "But this new device, which spoke directly to the senses, short-circuited the priests' appellate jurisdiction over the heavens."

Galileo wrote his *Dialogue* in a fictional style, but you don't need to be a literature scholar to distinguish the good guys (the witty and winsome astronomer) from the bad guys (the ignorant character representing the Catholic Church hierarchy).

"May God forgive Galileo for having intruded into these matters concerning new doctrines and Holy Scripture, where the best is to go along with common opinion," said the pope.

Called before the Inquisition, Galileo boldly defended himself. While he deeply respected the church's spiritual authority, he had no respect for the ways theologians twisted Scripture to defend erroneous scientific notions. His lack of social skills and excessive confidence in his own persuasive ability didn't help him any.

God's enforcers. Pope Urban VIII couldn't protect his friend Galileo from trouble, and assigned the controversial case to Cardinal Robert Bellarmine, the ruthless "Hammer of Heretics."

In his defense, Galileo claimed the heliocentric theory fit numerous passages of the Bible. "Though Scripture cannot err, its expanders and interpreters are liable to err in many ways," he had written in the *Dialogue*.

Unfortunately, Galileo's use of biblical passages only made things worse. Leaders of the Protestant Reformation had proclaimed the priesthood of all believers, declaring that everyone should read and interpret Scripture. The Catholic Counter-Reformation responded at the Council of Trent, forbidding all but the church hierarchy from interpreting Scripture. Galileo had violated this prohibition by citing and interpreting Scripture in his defense.

With the Inquisition now ready to pronounce the ailing sixty-nine-year-old astronomer guilty of heresy, Galileo knelt and recanted rather than face torture and death. He spent the last eight years of his life under house arrest.

The whole affair saddened Caesar Baronius, a high-ranking church official and librarian of the Vatican. "The Bible teaches us how to go to heaven, not how the heavens go," he said.

In 1992, Pope John Paul II agreed, formally forgiving Galileo and apologizing for the "tragic mutual incomprehension" that led the church to persecute one of its most loyal and famous members. The *New York Times* captured the moment in its headline: "After 350 Years, Vatican Says Galileo Was Right: It Moves."

Galileo had apparently forgiven his church long ago. In a letter he wrote to his daughter Maria Celeste, a cloistered nun who encouraged him throughout his trials, he expressed his trust in divine mercy. "Whatever the course of our lives, we should receive them as the highest gift from the hand of God," he wrote.

MAKING PEACE IN THE "WAR ON SCIENCE"

Things typically don't work out too well when Christian leaders embrace one particular scientific understanding of the world and use their power to censor competing views. As a Christian and a scientist, I have four simple suggestions for believers wanting to find a more redemptive way to deal with science and scientists in the future.

1. Own your interpretation. The Church's persecution of Galileo shows the tragic consequences that can result when people or institutions embrace an idea and twist Scripture to support it. We tread on dangerous territory when we become so enamored with our own beliefs that we become convinced God also endorses those beliefs. All who utter the words "Thus sayeth the Lord" must take care to speak with humility and caution. We need to do our best to interpret Scripture accurately, but we should always remember that our interpretation could be wrong.

(People should show the same humility when interpreting science. Silly claims often accompany new discoveries, and even brilliant scientists like Carl Sagan have made nonsensical comments.)

2. Embrace science as God's gift, not Satan's subversion. I know some believers who consider science an enemy of the church, but I don't see how they can say that. "The heavens declare the glory of God," says Psalm 19:1. More Christians should try to stay abreast of science's exciting new discoveries, and more of us should celebrate these discoveries, praising God for allowing us to comprehend his handiwork in greater detail.

3. *Love a scientist.* If I ruled the world, people of faith would stop demonizing people of science for the new truths of nature they discover. Kepler and Galileo believed science allows us to read God's book of nature. I would love to see more Christians serve God as scientists, and I want the rest of us to do what we can to support believing Galileos in our midst.

4. *Don't "opt out" of science.* Over the centuries Christians have exercised the "opt out" clause, refusing to engage in behaviors they believed would violate their faith. Christian pacifists have refused to kill fellow humans in war. Other believers refuse to celebrate popular civic events or holidays.

At times this opt-out approach has been valuable, preserving religious freedoms while helping fuel the growth of a vast and vibrant Christian subculture of private schools, colleges, charitable institutions, publishers, and musical groups. That's fine, but there's no reason for Christians to opt out of mainstream science, especially if their only option is to embrace alternate kinds of religious pseudoscience.

CELEBRATING NEW WAYS TO SEE

The Galileo affair shows that believers don't need to fear scientists or their bold new discoveries. God is not diminished when scientists discover "new" insights into the operations of the universe. In fact, these insights often give us a better understanding of our Creator's magnificence and incomparable majesty.

I believe knowledge about the workings of Creation should be a crucial component of every thinking Christian's intellectual portfolio. If this were the reality, fewer scientists would think of Christians as ignorant, closed-minded, and academically challenged.

When God created us in his image, he gave us intelligence and a passion to understand our world. What a tremendous blessing and privilege it is to use these gifts in his service, pursuing ever more insights into our Creator's wondrous works!

Time machine. After a lifetime of research, Archbishop James Ussher concluded the universe was created some six thousand years ago.

11

SHOWING OUR AGE

WHY THE ARCHBISHOP SAID GOD CREATED THE WORLD IN SIX DAYS, BEGINNING AT 6:00 P.M. SATURDAY, OCTOBER 22, 4004 BCE

It's the Great Age Divide and I see it open up before me in my classroom each semester as I start new astronomy classes at Eastern University. It's not a divide between young students and old students. It's a division over the age of the world.

Typically about half of my students are "young Earthers." They've been taught that the Bible says everything in our universe was created in six twenty-four-hour days and that the universe is less than ten thousand years old. Some of these students see science as an enemy of the Christian faith and some mistrust so-called secular scientists like me, who accept mainstream scientific approaches.

The other half is made up of students who've never heard much about the young-Earth theory and who consider it silly when I explain it to them. Many of these students took advanced science classes in high school, and most want to learn even more about our cosmos.

When I'm teaching these students together in the same classroom, I sometimes feel as if I'm talking to creatures from different planets. One of the first things I do is tell everyone to take a deep breath and relax.

"No astronomical finding we discuss this semester will diminish your belief in God's role as Creator and Sustainer of our universe," I promise in our first class before launching into a version of the following speech:

> I'm not going to attack your deepest beliefs and values and I will never punish you with a bad grade because of your beliefs. But you are university students taking a university-level science class. I expect you to learn new things this semester. You will earn a bad grade if you aren't willing to do that.
>
> Science involves analyzing and comparing different theories to find the best one, so I will expect you to learn about the "other side" of various topics. This also will help you know what you're talking about when you try to share or defend your beliefs.

By the end of the semester, students may still differ on the age of the universe, but I hope we all will agree on at least one thing. "Our Creator God is really awesome," students tell me after spending a few months getting a better understanding of our cosmic home.

WHEN THE CREATOR CREATED

The Bible clearly teaches that God created everything "in the beginning." But does Scripture also tell us *when* that beginning began?

This question became an obsession for James Ussher, a seventeenth-century Anglican bishop in Ireland who spent decades of study and research in his quest to come up with the best answer. His dogged pursuit of the truth sapped his strength, emptied his bank account, and almost blinded him. But he persevered, concluding that the beginning had begun at 6:00 p.m. on Saturday, October 22, 4004 BCE.

Christian thinkers had debated the age of the Earth long before Ussher, but they could never settle on a date. Theophilus of Antioch, the second-century church father, dated the "foundation of the world" to 5529 BCE. Martin Luther favored 4000 BCE. More than a hundred other dates were proposed and debated. "The lack of agreement was spectacular," writes Martin Gorst in *Measuring Eternity: The Search for the Beginning of Time*.

Ussher was only forty-four years old when he became Archbishop of Armagh, the most prestigious and powerful post in the Church of Ireland. This appointment allowed him to spend the next two decades pursuing his life's true passion: linking all the Bible's historical references to determine the precise age of the Earth.

This quest took Ussher to rare book dealers throughout Europe, where he uncovered dusty tomes of ancient history he could add to his ten-thousand-volume library. He also learned

Samaritan and Chaldean languages so he could connect secular historical dates to various passages in the Bible.

Ussher was in his sixties when he finally finished his research. That's when tragedy struck. All his notes were blown away by a powerful Irish wind. The loss shocked the bishop, who ascribed the incident to God's mysterious will: "He has thought fit to take from me at once, all that I have been gathering together, above these twenty years, and which I intend to publish for the advancement of learning, and the good of the Church."

Helpful townspeople quickly gathered up most of the bishop's windblown papers, allowing him to finally publish his magnum opus, *The Annals of the World*, in 1650.

Ussher's chronology drew mixed reviews. While most praised his scholarship, others scoffed. In 1922, H. G. Wells, a skeptic and author of some of the most enduring works of science fiction (*The War of the Worlds*, *The Time Machine*), dismissed Ussher's dating scheme as a "fantastically precise misconception" based on "arbitrary theological assumptions."

Ussher died six years after publishing his *Annals*, but his dating scheme achieved immortality when an enterprising Bible printer began including his chronology in new Bibles. The Church of England incorporated Ussher's dates in its official version of the Bible in 1701.

(Some Catholics also embraced Ussher's dating scheme, but Jesuit missionaries encountered problems in China when they tried to preach a young-Earth Creator to people who traced their civilization back thousands of years.)

Anno Mundi	I	Anno Periodi Julianæ	Anno ante æram Christianam

ANNALES
VETERIS TESTAMENTI,
à primâ Mundi origine deducti.

1 a. IN PRINCIPIO creavit DEUS Cœlum & Terram. [*Geneſ.* I. 1] quod temporis principium (juxta noſtram Chronologiam) incidit in noctis illius initium, quæ XXIII. diem Octobris præceſſit, in anno Periodi Julianæ 710. 710 4004

Primo igitur ſeculi die (*Octob.* 23. *feriâ* 1.) cum ſupremo Cœlo creavit Deus Angelos: deinde ſummo operis faſtigio primùm perfecto, ad ima Mundanæ hujus fabricæ fundamenta progreſſus mirandus artifex, infimum hunc globum ex Abyſſo & Terrâ conflatum conſtituit; concinentibus & collaudantibus eum ſimul omnibus ipſius Angelis. [*Job* XXXVIII. 7] Cúmque Terra eſſet inanis & vacua, & tenebræ eſſent in ſuperficie Abyſſi: in ipſo primi diei medio creata eſt Lux; quam à Tenebris diſtinguens Deus, illam appellavit Diem, has Noctem.

Secundo die, (*Octob.* 24. *fer.* 2.) creato expanſo (quod Cœlum eſt appellatum) diſtinctio eſt facta inter aquas ſuperiores, & inferiores Terræ circumfuſas.

Tertio die, (*Octob.* 25. *fer.* 3.) Aquis inferioribus in locum unum confluentibus, emerſit Terra arida. Aquas in Mare congregavit Creator: emiſſis interim fluviis, qui in Mare refluerent. [*Eccleſiaſt.* I. 7] Terram omne genus Herbas & Plantas, cum ſeminibus & fructibus, germinare fecit. Præ aliis autem locis, Paradiſum in Edene plantis ornavit: in quibus, Arbor vitæ & Arbor ſcientiæ boni ac mali. [*Gen.* II. 8, 9.]

Quarto die, (*Octob.* 26. *fer.* 4) Sol, Luna, & reliqua Sidera creata ſunt.

Quinto die, (*Octob.* 27. *fer.* 5) Aquatilia & volatilia animantia producta ſunt; & fœcunditate donata.

Sexto die (*Octob.* 28. *fer.* 6) Terreſtria animalia creata ſunt; tùm Gradientia, tùm Repentia. Demùm verò Homo, ad imaginem Dei in divinâ Mentis ſcientiâ (*Coloſſ.* III. 10) & genuinâ Voluntatis ſanctitate (*Epheſ.* IV. 24) præcipuè conſiſtentem, conditus eſt. Ille ſtatim reliquis animalibus, divinitùs ad ſe adductis, ut Dominus eorum deſignatus, nomina impoſuit. In quibus cùm adjutricem ſibi ſimilem non inveniret;

B

A life's work. Archbishop Ussher's *Annals of the World* drew mixed reviews, but his "biblical chronology" achieved immortality when it was published in Bibles.

THE FIRST BOOK OF MOSES
CALLED

GENESIS

GENESIS is the book of beginnings. It records not only the beginning of the heavens and the earth, and of plant, animal, and human life, but also of all human institutions and relationships. Typically, it speaks of the new birth, the new creation, where all was chaos and ruin.

With Genesis begins also that progressive self-revelation of God which culminates in Christ. The three primary names of Deity, Elohim, Jehovah, and Adonai, and the five most important of the compound names, occur in Genesis; and that in an ordered progression which could not be changed without confusion.

The problem of sin as affecting man's condition in the earth, and his relation to God, and the divine solution of that problem are here in essence. Of the eight great covenants which condition human life and the divine redemption, four, the Edenic, Adamic, Noahic, and Abrahamic Covenants, are in this book; and these are the fundamental covenants to which the other four, the Mosaic, Palestinian, Davidic, and New Covenants, are related chiefly as adding detail or development.

Genesis enters into the very structure of the New Testament, in which it is quoted above sixty times in seventeen books. In a profound sense, therefore, the roots of all subsequent revelation are planted deep in Genesis, and whoever would truly comprehend that revelation must begin here.

The inspiration of Genesis and its character as a divine revelation are authenticated by the testimony of history, and by the testimony of Christ (Mt. 19:4-6; 24:37-39; Mk. 10:4-9; Lk. 11:49-51; 17:26-29, 32; John 1:5; 7:21-23; 8:44, 56).

Genesis is in five chief divisions: I. Creation (1:1–2:25). II. The Fall and Redemption (3:1–4:7). III. The Diverse Seeds, Cain and Seth, to the Flood (4:8–7:24). IV. The Flood to Babel (8:1–11:9). V. From the call of Abram to the death of Joseph (11:10–50:26).

The events recorded in Genesis cover a period of 2,315 years (Ussher).

CHAPTER 1.

The original creation.

In the [a]beginning [1b]God [2]created the heaven and the earth.

Earth made waste and empty by judgment (Jer. 4:23–26).

2 And the earth was [3]without form, and void; and darkness *was* upon the face of the deep. And [c]the [d]Spirit of God moved upon the face of the waters.

The new beginning—the first day: light diffused.

3 And God said, Let there be [4]light: and there was light.

4 And God saw the light, that *it*

B.C. 4004

a John 1:1.
b Deity (names of). Gen. 2:4, 7. (Gen. 1:1; Mal. 3:18.)
c Holy Spirit. Gen. 6:3. (Gen. 1:2; Mal. 2:15.)
d Job 26:13. Psa. 104:30.

[1](1:1) *Elohim* (sometimes *El* or *Elah*), English form "God," the first of the three primary names of Deity, is a uni-plural noun formed from *El* = strength, or the strong one, and *Alah*, to swear, to bind oneself by an oath, so implying faithfulness. This uni-plurality implied in the name is directly asserted in Gen. 1:26 (plurality), 27 (unity); see also Gen. 3:22. Thus the Trinity is latent in *Elohim*. As meaning primarily the Strong One it is fitly used in the first chapter of Genesis. Used in the O. T. about 2500 times. See also Gen. 2:4, *note;* 2:7; 14:18, *note;* 15:2, *note:* 17:1, *note;* 21:33, *note;* 1 Sam. 1:3, *note.*

[2](1:1) But three *creative* acts of God are recorded in this chapter: (1) the heavens and the earth, v. 1; (2) animal life, v. 21; and (3) human life, vs. 26, 27. The first creative act refers to the dateless past, and gives scope for all the geologic ages.

[3](1:2) Jer. 4:23-26, Isa. 24:1 and 45:18, clearly indicate that the earth had undergone a cataclysmic change as the result of a divine judgment. The face of the earth bears everywhere the marks of such a catastrophe. There are not wanting intimations which connect it with a previous testing and fall of angels. See Ezk. 28:12-15 and Isa. 14:9-14, which certainly go beyond the kings of Tyre and Babylon.

[4](1:3) Neither here nor in verses 14-18 is an original *creative* act implied. A different word is used. The sense is, made to *appear;* made *visible.* The sun and moon were *created* "in the beginning." The "light" of course came from the sun, but the vapour diffused the light. Later the sun appeared in an unclouded sky.

Biblical chronology? For centuries, many Bibles utilized Ussher's dating scheme, but today few incorporate his "young Earth" ideas.

Over the next two centuries, Ussher's dates were printed alongside the scriptural text in millions of English-language Bibles, leading generations of Bible readers to assume that Ussher's chronology was the *biblical* chronology.

This comingling of Scripture and chronological interpretation confused at least one reader. "I declare I had fancied that the date was somehow in the Bible," said Charles Darwin.

HOW WE GOT OLD

Today, astronomers say our cosmos is billions of years old, not thousands. But geologists studying our planet—not astronomers studying the heavens—were the first to use emerging scientific disciplines that gradually expanded our ideas about the age of the Earth.

In the 1800s, pioneering geologists studying successive layers of lava flows surrounding Italy's Mount Etna concluded that it had taken seventy thousand to one hundred thousand years for these flows to accumulate. Later, biologist Charles Darwin studied coastal erosion on the cliffs of England and geologist Charles Lyell studied the glacial erosion in Europe's

Earth is getting older! Biologist Charles Darwin and geologist Charles Lyell said coastal erosion in England and Europe proved the Earth was older than previously thought.

deep mountain valleys. Both men concluded our Earth was more than 300 million years old.

In the 1900s, scientists studying the decay rates of uranium deposits developed a new process called radioactive dating. Using radioactive dating methods, researchers concluded our world was more than two billion years old.

Catholic priest and astronomer Georges Lemaître added even more billions to the cosmic timetable in the 1930s with his "Big Bang" theory, embraced by the Roman Catholic Church in the 1950s (see chapter 22).

In recent years, increasing numbers of evangelicals have embraced an old Earth. The BioLogos Foundation states its position on its website: "We believe that God created the universe, the earth, and all life over billions of years."

As scientific evidence for an old Earth piled up, Ussher's chronology faced new scrutiny. Most Bible publishers abandoned Ussher's young-Earth chronology. England's university presses at Oxford and Cambridge removed Ussher's dates from their Bibles in the early 1900s. Most publishers followed suit, although some Bibles continue to feature Ussher's dates, especially the popular Scofield study Bibles.

BACKING INTO A CHRONOLOGICAL CORNER

In the previous chapter we saw what happened after Galileo viewed the heavens through his powerful new telescope, witnessing marvels that forever changed our understanding of the universe.

Unfortunately, the Catholic Church dismissed this new science and dug in, turning against one of its faithful members and investing its power and authority in defense of the mistaken belief that the Sun and planets orbit the Earth. Galileo was found guilty of heresy, put under house arrest for the remainder of his life, and forced to recant his heliocentric views. The church apologized for its actions centuries later.

I'm afraid some Christians today may be following a similar self-defeating strategy when they say the universe was created ten thousand years ago. That was the consensus back in Ussher's day, but things have moved on. To embrace a young Earth today, you pretty much need to ignore many of the amazing discoveries by geologists, biologists, archaeologists, and other scientists over the last few centuries.

When I talk to my young-Earth students, they say a literal, "Christian creationism" approach is the only way to understand the Genesis creation accounts. When the Bible says "day," that means a twenty-four-hour day. No ifs, ands, or buts. To question this young-Earth orthodoxy is heresy.

My students are wrestling with a problem that has bedeviled evangelicals for decades, as historian Mark Noll showed in his influential 1994 book, *The Scandal of the Evangelical Mind*. The book opens with this sad sentence: "The scandal of the evangelical mind is that there is not much of an evangelical mind." Noll said anti-intellectual and anti-science approaches have been a "catastrophe" for the evangelical movement.

Anti-intellectualism isn't a new problem, as St. Augustine showed more than sixteen hundred years ago:

> Usually, even a non-Christian knows something about the earth, the heavens, and the other elements of this world, about the motion and orbit of the stars and even their size and relative positions, about the predictable eclipses of the sun and moon, the cycles of the years and the seasons, about the kinds of animals, shrubs, stones, and so forth, and this knowledge he holds as certain from reason and experience. Now it is a disgraceful and dangerous thing for an infidel to hear a Christian, presumably giving the meaning of Holy Scripture, talking nonsense on these topics; and we should take all means to prevent such an embarrassing situation, in which people show up vast ignorance in a Christian and laugh it to scorn.

UNDERSTANDING GOD'S TIMETABLE

When I see the Great Age Divide opening up before me in my classroom, I'm not thinking about Augustine. I'm praying for students who feel they must defend young-Earth orthodoxy as proof of their faithfulness. I'm asking Christ to grant freedom to these chronological captives. I'm hoping I can show them what it means to be a diligent student of God's two books: creation and revelation.

As a devoted follower of Jesus, I take the Bible as God's holy revelation. I respect its authority. I submit to its teaching. That's why I begin each of my astronomy class sessions by reading a passage of Scripture and discussing it with my students.

Scripture claims authority in matters of faith and practice: "All Scripture is God-breathed and is useful for teaching, rebuking, correcting and training in righteousness" (2 Tim. 3:16). But the Bible never claims such authority when it comes to global timetables. Ussher's "biblical chronology" was an impressive feat, but his effort to transform the Bible into a terrestrial timetable was misguided, and his research has failed the test of time.

When I read the 750 words of the Genesis 1 creation account, I learn about a Creator who made everything "in the beginning." I don't learn about scientific or chronological details, because that wasn't the intention of God's revelation.

God's Word is eternal, but our interpretation of that Word will change as our understanding of the world changes. May God guide us and give us wisdom as we study both of his books. And may we resist the temptation to baptize *any* particular cosmology or declare it the final word about how our Creator created.

One small sip. Before Neil Armstrong walked on the Moon, Buzz Aldrin celebrated Communion in the *Apollo 11* lunar module.

12

GOD, COUNTRY, AND THE SPACE RACE

COMMIES, COMMUNION ON THE MOON, AND CHURCHES THAT ARE OUT OF THIS WORLD

The first man-made satellite to orbit the Earth wasn't much to look at. With a shiny round body the size of a beach ball and four spindly antennae that resembled skinny legs, the device looked like an undersized barbecue grill.

But this primitive little satellite had a huge global impact. Launched into low Earth orbit in October 1957, *Sputnik* circled our planet every ninety-six minutes. Millions of people around the globe went outside to see it pass overhead. Amateur radio enthusiasts tuned in to hear its distinctive *beep, beep* signal.

Now everyone knew the truth. The US had been outmaneuvered by the USSR, its dreaded Cold War foe. The space race was on, and we were playing catch-up. President John F. Kennedy challenged the country to prove itself in a 1961 speech to Congress: "I believe that this nation should commit itself to achieving the goal, before this decade is out, of landing a man on the Moon and returning him safely to the Earth. No single space project in this period will be more impressive to mankind, or more important for the long-range exploration of space; and none will be so difficult or expensive to accomplish."

Kennedy's audacious goal was dramatically realized eight years later when Neil Armstrong walked on the Moon and returned safely home, his journey broadcast on live television for all to see. Science fiction had become science fact. America declared victory in the space race, thanks to the billions of dollars NASA spent developing the cutting-edge technologies needed for dozens of Mercury, Gemini, and Apollo missions.

But more than money and national pride were involved. Another hidden factor served as a major motivator of the many men who risked their lives so we could reach the Moon. That hidden factor was a deep faith in a God who endowed humans with a passion to explore, and who was now asked to bless America's efforts to triumph over its atheistic adversary.

"Many historians have examined the cultural and social impact of the space program, but few have explored the important role of the faith factor," says Princeton doctoral student William J. Schultz. "This faith factor is the untold story of the space race."

PUBLIC PRAISE, PRIVATE WORSHIP

In December 1968, Frank Borman, James Lovell, and William Anders became the first humans to orbit the Moon and see the Earth "rise" over the lunar surface. To celebrate, the three Apollo 8 astronauts delivered a simple Christmas Eve message for everyone back home, taking turns reading the first ten verses of Genesis 1 from the King James Bible: "And God saw the light, that it was good: and God divided the light from the darkness. And God called the light Day, and the darkness he

Merry Christmas from the Moon. A billion TV viewers heard the *Apollo 8* astronauts recite Genesis 1 from their lunar orbit, but one atheist activist was not so merry.

called Night. And the evening and the morning were the first day. . . . And God called the dry land Earth; and the gathering together of the waters called he Seas: and God saw that it was good."

Borman concluded the broadcast with a brief farewell: "And from the crew of Apollo 8, we close with good night, good luck, a Merry Christmas—and God bless all of you, all of you on the good Earth."

From a distance of nearly 240,000 miles, the astronauts reached an estimated one billion TV viewers—the biggest audience ever at the time.

I felt thrilled to see astronauts praising God on TV. My passion to become an astronomer grew even stronger that summer. And my parents were glad to see good news about America after years of coverage of the bloody Vietnam war and violent student protests. Everybody seemed completely over the Moon.

Except for Madalyn Murray O'Hair, the activist atheist whose lawsuit before the US Supreme Court had ended the widespread practice of mandatory Bible reading in public schools. After hearing taxpayer-supported astronauts reciting the Bible from space, she sued the US government for violating the First Amendment. The case was dismissed, but from now on, most Christian astronauts would find quieter ways to express their faith.

Fast-forward to July 1969. Apollo 11's Neil Armstrong and Buzz Aldrin had safely landed their lunar module on the Moon's dusty surface. The next day Armstrong would take his incredible "giant leap for mankind." But first, Aldrin paused to privately thank God for extraterrestrial travel mercies.

Like many astronauts and their families, the Aldrins were committed churchgoers. Buzz served as an elder at Webster Presbyterian Church in Clear Lake, Texas, a congregation known as the "Church of the Astronauts" for its long association with some of NASA's biggest and brightest celebrities, including John Glenn, Jerry Carr, Charlie Bassett, and Roger Chaffee.

Before Aldrin left for the Moon, his congregation provided him with an in-flight communion kit. As he rested in the lunar module that sat upon the Moon's surface, he poured out a few drops of wine. In the Moon's low gravity, the red liquid gracefully curled into the small silver chalice. As Aldrin swallowed the wine and chewed a small piece of bread, he read a passage from the gospel of John that affirmed his complete dependence on God:

Cosmic church. *Apollo 11*'s Buzz Aldrin was an elder at Webster Presbyterian Church, a Houston-area congregation often called the "Church of the Astronauts."

"I am the vine; you are the branches. If you remain in me and I in you, you will bear much fruit; apart from me you can do nothing" (John 15:5).

As Aldrin took Communion on the Moon, back on Earth members of Webster Presbyterian stood together in their church to celebrate the sacrament with their distant brother.

The public remained in the dark about Aldrin's brief lunar liturgy, but he described his feelings about the moment years later. "It was interesting to think that the very first liquid ever poured on the moon, and the first food eaten there, were communion elements," he said.

CHURCHES THAT ARE OUT OF THIS WORLD!

Some churches teach their members to reach out and help people in their local communities. Some focus on service and missionary efforts that reach around the globe. Members of Webster Presbyterian developed a more cosmic conception of their faith.

Decades after one of its members walked on the Moon, the church still celebrates Lunar Communion Sunday every July. Its sanctuary is still beautifully decorated with astronomical improvisations on the standard church furnishings. Stained glass windows portray nebulae, the gigantic clouds of stellar dust and gas that the Hubble Space Telescope is examining. The cross features slices of a Mexican meteorite that NASA astronauts used while training to handle moon rocks.

Webster Presbyterian is one of a handful of churches in

and around Clear Lake, the Houston suburb that was home to NASA's Manned Spacecraft Center. Many NASA scientists, engineers, astronauts, and their families attended these churches, hearing sermons that wrestled with some of the new theological questions raised by the space race of the 1960s and 1970s:

- Do astronauts travel through heaven?
- Are angels extraterrestrial beings?
- What would the discovery of alien life mean for Christianity?
- Did Jesus Christ die to save life on other worlds?
- Could space travel be a sign of the approaching end times?

After the sermons, Clear Lake believers sang hymns like "Bless Thou the Astronauts":

> When first upon the moon man trod,
> How excellent thy name, O God.
> The heavens thy glory doth declare;
> Where-e'r we are, Lo! thou are there.

The Clear Lake–area churches formed a close-knit community. Members comforted loved ones of the three Apollo 1 astronauts who were killed by a fire in their command module during a prelaunch test. They calmed family members of the Apollo 13 astronauts who issued this emergency message: "Houston, we've had a problem here."

Christian fellowship was more than just a Sunday routine for the many NASA workers who regularly attended one of the many informal Bible studies and prayer groups held at the Manned Spacecraft Center throughout the week.

"Religious faith was shared through small groups and interpersonal interactions," says William J. Schultz. "The faith of people involved in the space race was a regular background presence that was never dominant but certainly never absent."

NASA employees attending one of these Manned Spacecraft Center prayer groups founded Gloria Dei Lutheran Church, which once videotaped its Christmas service so NASA could transmit the program to astronauts aboard the International Space Station.

Priests from St. Paul's Catholic Church were among local clergy participating in prayer breakfasts held at the center every Tuesday morning.

The Clear Lake churches continue to serve the NASA community today, long after the glory days of the space race have passed. In 2009, one local congregation reaffirmed its calling: "We at University Baptist Church consider it a privilege to serve Christ in the midst of a community of science and technology."

A LASTING LUNAR LEGACY

The space race slowed down after NASA successfully met JFK's audacious challenge. Manned missions to space continued, but none generated the same kinds of excitement we all felt when we witnessed the first men land on the Moon. By the time of the *Challenger* space shuttle disaster of 1986, TV networks no longer did live broadcasts of NASA launches and landings.

The Apollo program ended in the 1970s, but not before twelve men had visited the Moon during six separate lunar missions. Astronaut James Irwin was the eighth human to walk on the Moon's surface. "I felt an overwhelming sense of the presence of God on the moon," wrote Irwin. "I cannot imagine a holier place."

Irwin and the pastor of one Clear Lake church, Nassau Bay Baptist, cofounded High Flight Foundation, a nonprofit organization that supported Irwin's evangelistic ministry until his death in 1991. "God walking on the earth is more important than man walking on the moon," he told his audiences.

The exciting stories of the space race and humanity's first journeys to the Moon have been told and retold in numerous books and movies, but the faith factor remains largely overlooked, despite the powerful role Christianity played in the lives of astronauts, scientists, and their families.

As Buzz Aldrin wrote at the time, "There are many of us in the NASA program who trust that what we are doing is part of God's eternal plan for man."

Solar system surprises. New missions are helping us learn more about the planets in our neighborhood.

13

A STROLL THROUGH THE NEIGHBORHOOD

MEETING OUR SOLAR SYSTEM'S WEIRD AND WACKY NEIGHBORS

Cities grow up around important features like rivers, railroads, highways, businesses, or mineral deposits. Our neighborhood in space is organized in a similar way: everything has developed around the big central attraction—our Sun.

For most of our existence, humans thought our solar system was everything there was. But centuries' worth of observation and exploration have shown that our cosmic address is a bit humbler. Here is a simple way of showing where we fit into the big scheme of space:

- Earth
- Solar system
- Orion (an arm or spiral of our galaxy)

- Milky Way galaxy
- Local group of galaxies (our Milky Way is part of a group of thirty local galaxies)
- Virgo Cluster or Supercluster (a group of hundreds or thousands of galaxies)
- Universe (see color photo section p. 4)

Even though we may no longer live at the crossroads of the cosmos, we still inhabit a pretty amazing place. Let's take a brief stroll through our neighborhood, sampling its beauty, marveling at its many mysteries, getting to know some of our weird and wacky neighbors, and learning even more about the mind of our Maker.

IN THE BEGINNING

Where did our solar system come from? We're still trying to fill in many details, but the big picture is becoming clearer every day.

Our neighborhood began as a solar nebula, a vast spinning disk of gas and dust. The Sun came together in the center of the cloudy disk. (See chapter 17.) Before long (a hundred million years or so), the eight planets were born in much the same way, taking up their residence elsewhere in the spinning disk. Today, most but not all bodies in the neighborhood still spin in the same direction as that original nebula, orbiting the star that brought us all together.

As our stroll takes us farther and farther away from the Sun, we will see why astronomers divide the solar system's planets into two distinct groups. The four *terrestrial planets* closest to the Sun are small, rocky, and solid, while the four more distant *Jovian planets* are large, gaseous, and surrounded by numerous rings and moons.

Mercury: Hot and Bothered

Earth undergoes extreme temperature fluctuations, from a record high of 136°F to a record low of –126°F. But we've never experienced hot spells and cold chills like those on Mercury, the smallest planet in our neighborhood and the one that orbits closest to the Sun.

This tiny planet may have had its own protective atmosphere once upon a time, but any remnants of that insulating cocoon were broiled away long ago. As a result, temperatures vary wildly, with day time highs soaring to 800°F and nighttime lows plunging to –300°F.

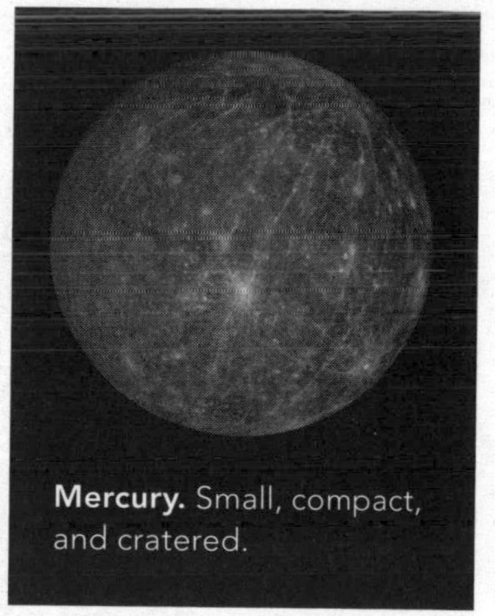

Mercury. Small, compact, and cratered.

Mercury is difficult to study because it's so close to the Sun. I've seen it only five times. NASA launched the *Messenger* mission in 2004 to take a closer look. *Messenger* reached Mercury in 2011 and spent the next four years orbiting and closely studying the planet.

The planet resembles our Moon: small, compact, and marked by many impact craters caused by asteroids and meteoroids. We now know it harbors water ice in shaded craters near its poles. Mercury is also home to volatile elements like chlorine, sulfur, and sodium that astronomers had assumed were burned away long ago.

Messenger concluded its mission in dramatic fashion in 2015, hurling itself toward Mercury's surface and creating a collision so we could study the results. In the process, we added one more crater to the planet's battered surface.

NASA plans to launch its next mission to Mercury in 2017, but we'll need to wait until 2024 for it to reach the planet.

Venus: Simmering Sister

Venus. Greenhouse inferno.

The second planet from the Sun resembles the third in size and density, but that's where similarities to Earth end.

Venus is cloaked in an incredibly dense atmosphere and surrounded by thick clouds that conceal its surface. Scientists describe the planet as a sweltering inferno, superheated by a runaway greenhouse effect. A Soviet spacecraft landed on the planet in 1975 but survived less than an hour before succumbing to Venus's extreme environmental conditions, including temperatures of 1000°F and atmospheric pressures some ninety times greater than on Earth.

Underneath its big blanket of clouds, Venus has a relatively smooth surface, thanks in part to active volcanoes and lava flows.

Unlike everyone else in the neighborhood, Venus rotates backward. This retrograde spin probably began when another heavenly body whacked the planet and altered its rotation.

Earth: Happy at Home in the Goldilocks Zone

Our beautiful blue world and our privileged location seem to fit us just fine. Although our planet has similarities to others in the neighborhood, we are unique in ways that have made us the only life-friendly planet that we know of so far. (See chapter 5.)

Mars: Red and Dead

No planet has excited our imagination more than Mars, and none has been studied so thoroughly. That's why we're devoting the next chapter to our red neighbor.

Jupiter: Stormy Giant

As our stroll takes us across the tracks to the Jovian half of our solar system neighborhood, we can immediately see how different things are out here.

Jupiter is 11 times the diameter of Earth. It has 121 times the surface area and 317 times the mass of our planet. More than fourteen hundred Earths could squeeze into Jupiter.

The planet is a turbulent, gaseous giant with no solid

surface but plenty of activity. On Earth, big storms often develop over bodies of water and gradually calm down once they reach land. But with no landmasses to calm things down, Jupiter is constantly enveloped by intense storms that speed around in vast atmospheric bands that give the planet its striped and mottled appearance.

Jupiter. Massive and moon-blessed.

Making things even more turbulent, Jupiter's immense gaseous surface moves at hyperspeed, rotating on its axis in slightly less than ten hours, faster than on any other planet. This hectic pace means the planet's surface speed is 2,500 mph, only adding to the violence of its stormy winds.

The planet's most tempestuous region is the fabled Red Spot, visible from Earth ever since the invention of the telescope. This horrendous hurricane, about two times the size of Earth, has whirled out of control for centuries and will do so for centuries more, even though NASA says it is slowly shrinking (it was 150 miles smaller in 2015 than it was in 2014).

Galileo shocked the world four centuries ago when he observed four moons orbiting Jupiter. Since then, another sixty Jovian moons have been identified. So far the most interesting is hotheaded Io, the most geologically active object in our entire neighborhood with some eighty active volcanoes. Io's nearest neighbor, Europa, may have deepwater oceans beneath its thick ice crust. Astronomers suspect there may be life in these oceans, and NASA may send a probe to find out more.

Saturn: More Than Pretty Rings

All four of the Jovian planets sport rings around their middles, but Saturn outdoes them all with big, beautiful circular bands that offer some of the most iconic images from space.

NASA's *Voyager* probes analyzed these rings more closely, showing they're actually tens of thousands of narrow ringlets, all of them moving in sync to play their part. These ringlets consist of orbiting debris left over from the planet's creation, as well as pieces of moons that may have ventured too close and been torn apart by Saturn's violent tidal forces.

Saturn and Jupiter share many similarities: they're big, gassy, and surrounded by moons. But Saturn is twice as far away from the Sun, lowering its temperature and stretching out its orbital period to nearly thirty Earth years.

Saturn. Big, gassy, and distant.

So far, astronomers have identified fifty-six moons orbiting Saturn, the most interesting of which are Titan (its hydrocarbon lakes make it the only heavenly body besides Earth known to have significant liquid on its surface) and Enceladus (this icy moon has hydrothermal jets that shoot high into space, possibly indicating the presence of a huge underground lake).

Uranus and Neptune: Mysterious Newbies

The last two planets to be discovered (in 1781 and 1846, respectively) inhabit the outermost reaches of our neighborhood. Their distance explains why they remain two of astronomy's biggest mysteries. Neptune is so far away that it takes 164 years to orbit the Sun. Astronomers only recently saw it complete its first full orbit since its discovery.

Uranus is unique. It seems to have been tipped over sideways on its axis (its North Pole is tipped a whopping 98 degrees to its orbital plane). This anomaly subjects the planet to extreme weather variations.

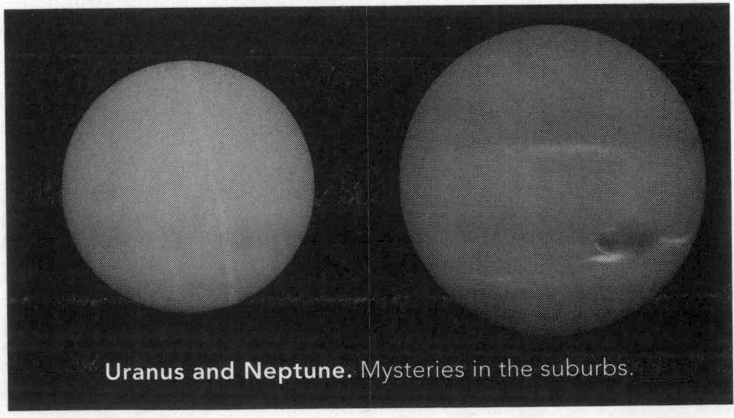

Uranus and Neptune. Mysteries in the suburbs.

The weather is even rougher over on Neptune. Winds continually rake across the planet's gaseous surface at more than 900 mph.

The Pluto Problem

Pluto. Now a trans-Neptunian object?

Back when I studied astronomy in high school, Pluto was considered the ninth planet in our solar system. It was discovered in 1930 by American Clyde Tombaugh (an astronomer I was able to meet at a scientific meeting) and declared a planet soon after. But in a controversial 2006 decision, the International Astronomical Union (IAU) demoted this distant body, with its 248-year solar orbit.

Students at New Mexico State University, where Tombaugh had taught, protested the decision with signs that said, "Size Doesn't Matter." But it apparently does. Pluto is now considered a "dwarf planet," similar to the huge asteroid Ceres. Some astronomers use an even less exciting term to describe Pluto: "trans-Neptunian object."

How did this lonely object some three billion miles from the Sun lose its planetary status? Long story short, when the IAU finally decided it was time to create an official definition of a planet, Pluto met only two of the three astronomical criteria. Yes, it orbits the Sun. Yes, it has been formed and shaped by its own gravitational force. But no, it hasn't "cleared the neighborhood." IAU now says real planets must be massive enough to dominate their immediate neighborhoods, but Pluto isn't big enough to rule its roost.

We may be bidding farewell to planet Pluto, but NASA is keeping a close eye on our distant dwarf. In July 2015, NASA's *New Horizons* space probe became the first satellite to study Pluto up close, passing within eight thousand miles of its surface. Among the surprises:

- Two of Pluto's distinctive mountains might be cryovolcanoes, or ice volcanoes. Instead of ejecting molten rock, NASA says they emit "a somewhat melted slurry of substances such as water ice, nitrogen, ammonia, or methane."
- Pluto's moons behave differently than other moons in our neighborhood. Most moons are in synchronous orbits with their planets. For example, our Moon both rotates on its axis and orbits the Earth in one Earth day. But Hydra, one of Pluto's five moons, rotates a stunning eighty-nine times during each orbit around the dwarf.

WAY OUT IN THE SOLAR SUBURBS

Hundreds of thousands of additional items orbit our Sun, including comets and asteroids. Many of these objects travel together in the Kuiper belt, located just beyond Neptune's orbit. That's where Pluto and the other trans-Neptunian objects hang out.

Even more space stuff floats around in the Oort cloud, located way past the Kuiper belt some 500 billion to 9 trillion miles from the Sun. We currently believe the Oort cloud is populated by icy planetesimals that consist of water, ammonia, and methane. This vast cloud may even be the birthplace of comets, whose nuclei are formed from floating dirt and ice.

These objects are so distant and so small that we know little about them, but astronomers always love a new challenge. In the next few decades, we will reach out to these solar suburbs to find out more about their mysterious movements.

UNIQUE NEIGHBORS

All in all, it's quite a neighborhood. Actually, it's pretty amazing! Sometimes I wonder how our Creator came up with the varied assemblage that *National Geographic* called "our wild, wild solar system."

Each neighbor is unique but all share a common origin story, and all seem to get along just fine as we gather around the one thing that unites us, the energy and gravity of our Sun.

Militant Martians. Mars and its alleged residents have a public relations problem, as we see in this publicity image from the movie *Mars Attacks!* Why have so many worried so much about our neighbor planet?

14

MARS WITHOUT MARTIANS?

WHAT'S COOLER—MARTIAN SCIENCE OR MARTIAN SCI-FI?

Ladies and gentlemen, we interrupt our program of dance music to bring you a special bulletin from the Intercontinental Radio News.

On a quiet Sunday night in 1938, the first news bulletin reported "several explosions of incandescent gas occurring at regular intervals on the planet Mars." Listeners felt no great concern about Martian gas, gladly returning to their music. But as the evening wore on, reports grew increasingly grim.

Ladies and gentlemen, I have a grave announcement to make. Incredible as it may seem, both the observations of science and the evidence of our eyes lead to the inescapable assumption that those strange beings who landed in New Jersey farmlands tonight are the vanguard of an invading army from the planet Mars.

Soon, eyewitness accounts were describing shocking details of Martian invaders and American deaths, scaring millions of listeners out of their wits, some of whom called police stations, organized prayer groups, or started packing suitcases for an escape . . . before realizing everything had been part of an elaborate Halloween hoax.

When the dust settled, a little known twentysomething actor and producer apologized for abusing the public's airwaves and trust. Three years later, the same young man would release his film masterpiece *Citizen Kane*, perhaps the best movie ever made.

This is Orson Welles, ladies and gentlemen, out of character to assure you that "The War of the Worlds" has no further significance than as the holiday offering it was intended to be. . . . We couldn't soap all your windows and steal all your garden gates by tomorrow night . . . so we did the best next thing. We annihilated the world before your very ears.

This wasn't the last time the red planet next door aroused our fascination or phobias. "Mars has become a kind of mythic arena onto which we have projected our earthly hopes and fears," said the late astronomer Carl Sagan.

We Earthlings have long viewed our planetary neighbor through a jumble of fiction and fact. Today, multiple Mars missions are gathering more facts than ever before. We haven't uncovered any Martians so far, but the scientific research we're doing fascinates me more than any science fiction.

PLANETARY PR PROBLEMS

How did Mars get such a bad reputation? The blame game begins with the ancient Babylonians, who called the planet

Masters of Martian mysteries. These four writers shaped our notions about Mars. H. G. Wells gave us *The War of the Worlds*, which Orson Welles dramatized in a shockingly realistic radio drama. Ray Bradbury's *Martian Chronicles* featured beautiful creatures far superior to Earthlings. His friend Gene Roddenberry celebrated cosmic diversity in *Star Trek*.

Nergal after their god of war, pestilence, and destruction. The Romans followed suit, naming the blood-red planet Mars after their own bloody war deity.

Humanity's anti-Mars bias was still going strong in the twentieth century when English composer Gustav Holst wrote his popular orchestral suite, *The Planets*. While most of the suite's seven movements were pleasingly melodic and graced with upbeat titles ("Venus, the Bringer of Peace" or "Jupiter, the Bringer of Jollity"), Holst's Mars movement reinforced the old, negative stereotypes, from its title ("Mars, the Bringer of War") to its harsh, menacing sound.

Holst wrote the Mars movement in a minor key and an unconventional 5/4 time signature driven home by a relentless staccato sound created by violinists whacking their strings with the wooden side of their bows. This percussive Mars movement could serve as marching music for battalions of angry Martian invaders, and the composition sounds even more menacing in hard rock versions by Led Zeppelin and Black Sabbath.

Over time, our negative perceptions of the planet were applied to its presumed residents. Welles based his controversial broadcast on H. G. Wells's powerful 1898 novel, *The War of the Worlds*, which described angry, ugly Martians with immense eyes, quivering mouths, and slithering tentacles. "Those who have never seen a living Martian can scarcely imagine the strange horror of its appearance," wrote Wells, whose novel also served as the basis of a 2005 Steven Spielberg film starring Tom Cruise.

So many cheesy sci-fi books, TV shows, and movies followed Welles's marauding Martian model (*The Three Stooges in Orbit*, anyone?) that director Tim Burton parodied the genre's worst clichés in *Mars Attacks!* In the film, Earth's defeat looks imminent until one enterprising human discovers that the Martians' abnormally large brains explode when exposed to Slim Whitman's recording of "Indian Love Call." Once the song is broadcast around the world, the invasion comes to a gooey end.

IMAGINING OUR FAVORITE MARTIANS

Ray Bradbury did more than any other writer to take science fiction into the cultural mainstream, helping change our negative attitudes with his *Martian Chronicles*, published in 1950. These aliens looked great, with their "fair, brownish skin" and "yellow coin eyes." They sounded good too, with their "soft musical voices."

Bradbury's Martians were intellectually, technologically, and telepathically superior to the lowly Earthlings, who colonized and exploited Mars only after having destroyed their own planet with nuclear bombs. We even took our destructive ways along with us into space, unintentionally wiping out much of the Martian population with chicken pox.

As America embarked upon its space race in the 1960s, Bradbury's good-aliens approach would influence novels, movies, and TV shows like 1963's *My Favorite Martian*, which portrayed interplanetary visitors as average guys who looked and acted just like us. Bradbury's close friend Gene

Roddenberry would enthusiastically celebrate cosmic diversity in his *Star Trek* series.

Christian writer C. S. Lewis added a theological dimension to the good-Martian/bad-human approach in *Out of the Silent Planet*, the first installment in his space trilogy. Lewis portrayed Martians as sinless residents of an unfallen planetary Eden.

Our favorite aliens. TV's *My Favorite Martian* portrayed aliens as good guys just like us.

A big fan of science fiction, Lewis sought to "redeem" the genre by creating a "theologized" approach, using space as a setting to examine humanity's spiritual challenges. Lewis also wanted his science fiction to attack an emerging worldview he called "scientism," with its unshakable faith that technological progress could solve humanity's biggest problems.

Lewis worked on his space trilogy after writing *A Preface to Paradise Lost*, a critical analysis of Milton's epic poem about humanity's original fall from innocence. Imagining what Adam and Eve might have been like if they had never sinned, Lewis created a sin-free planet much different from our own Wounded World.

The concerns Lewis expressed in his fiction informed his view about the space race. "I look forward with horror to contact with the other inhabited planets, if there are such," said Lewis in a 1963 interview with the Billy Graham Evangelistic Association. "We would only transport to them all of our sin and our acquisitiveness, and establish a new colonialism. I can't bear to think of it."

Only a global renewal could counteract the cosmic effects of human sin. "Once we find ourselves spiritually awakened, we can go to outer space and take the good things with us," Lewis said.

FROM FICTION TO FACT

Astronomers do their best to separate fantasy from fact, but Mars has baffled scientists for centuries. In 1877, Italian astronomer Giovanni Schiaparelli observed a series of markings on the Martian surface that he called *canali* (that's Italian for "channels"). In the popular imagination, these *canali* became *canals* supposedly constructed by Martians.

The twentieth-century American astronomer Percival Lawrence Lowell prolonged the canal craze. The founder of the Lowell Observatory in Flagstaff, Arizona, and author of books like *Mars and Its Canals* and *Mars as an Abode of Life*, Lowell enthusiastically promoted his mistaken belief that Martian creatures had reshaped their planet's surface to conserve precious water.

Now, thanks to decades' worth of unmanned missions, we can safely set the record straight:

- No, there aren't any Martians, canals, flying saucers, or marauding armies.

- No, the red planet is not "angry." Like Georgia's red clay, Mars owes its red surface to rusted iron particles.

I've enjoyed my share of Martian movies over the years, but I'm shedding no tears over the death of these perennial fantasies. That's because the reality of Mars is proving to be way cooler than any fantasy we could ever concoct.

CLOSER CONTACT

NASA's *Spirit* and *Opportunity* rovers are still examining and photographing the Martian surface's huge volcanoes, deep canyons, and vast dune fields, years after they were expected to conk out and go cold. Meanwhile, the Mars Reconnaissance Orbiter circles the planet, examining its surface with the most powerful telescopic camera ever used in space.

In 2011, scientists studying some of the orbiter's photos noticed curious streaks on the Martian surface. After four years of study, the verdict was delivered: we had finally found water on Mars. We've long suspected that the planet's distinctive polar ice caps harbor frozen liquid of some kind and that the planet once had huge quantities of this liquid in rivers, lakes, and even oceans. But until 2015 we had never confirmed the presence of a single drop.

We've been studying Mars at close range for a long time. In 2012, NASA landed the *Curiosity* rover on Mars. This ultra-high-tech lab on wheels, powered by a glowing chunk of radioactive plutonium, picks up rocks, drills into their cores, and analyzes their chemical composition.

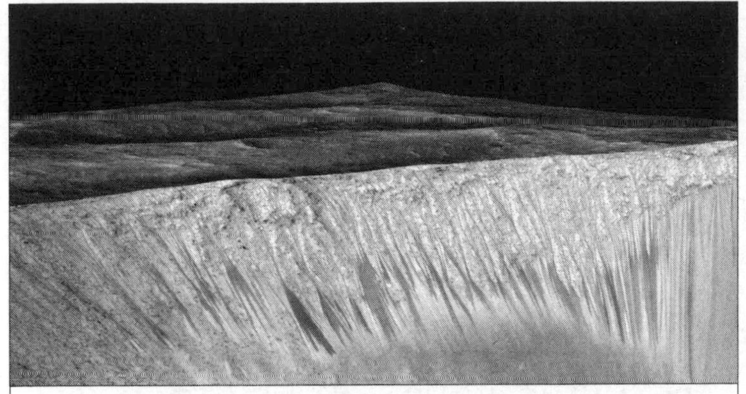

No wait for water. After decades of searching, we finally found liquid water on Mars, but the prospects for life remain dim.

Curiosity discovered nitrogen, one of the building blocks of DNA, in 2015, but no evidence yet exists that such building blocks were ever assembled into an actual Martian life form.

Prospects for Martian life are slim due to the planet's harsh conditions. Billions of years ago, its atmosphere disappeared. The planet, located 50 percent farther from the Sun than we are, froze solid. Scientists say that's when Martian water was locked away in a huge permafrost layer underneath the planet's dry, dusty surface. If Mars ever warms up again, that frozen water could cover its surface to a depth of 30 feet.

Mars exhibits many similarities to Earth and the other terrestrial planets, including its violent, geologic history. The red planet was shaped by hundreds of major volcanoes, including one that's the biggest ever seen in our solar system. That volcano created the solar system's biggest mountain: Olympus

Mons is three times taller than Mount Everest and its base is big enough to cover most of France.

All such activity ceased long, long ago, and today Mars is considered geologically dead. Now, enormous hurricane-speed dust storms scour its surface. Martian storms can last six months or more, and they're famous for playing tricks on astronomers, filling and emptying huge impact craters, and covering and then uncovering major surface landmarks.

PLANNING YOUR JOURNEY TO MARS

Humans have been traveling to Mars for centuries, at least in science fiction. These fantasies may soon become fact if various planned manned missions take off.

NASA's Orion mission is scheduled to take astronauts to Mars in the 2030s. The agency has been busy working out the bugs in its new rocket systems, testing improved materials for the heat shields that protect the flying saucer–shaped command module, and running astronauts through rigorous tests.

Will Congress keep funding Mars research? NASA typically eats up only about 0.4 percent of the federal budget each year, and during its entire history NASA has cost less than the 2008 Wall Street bailouts. But continued funding is necessary. As they say, "No bucks, no Buck Rogers."

Reaching Mars will require a one-way journey of seven to twelve months. How will human bodies and minds adapt to the rigors of long periods spent in space? NASA is studying everything from the impact of low gravity on human eyesight (eyeballs change shape in the weightlessness of space) to the long-term consequences of high-powered radiation on human cells.

NASA has been paying special attention to twins Scott and Mark Kelly. Mark stayed Earth-bound while Scott spent 340 days on the International Space Station—twice the length of a normal stay. (He said it felt like "forever.") After Scott returned to Earth in March 2016, NASA analyzed Scott's body, comparing it with Mark's to see if any important differences showed up.

"Going to Mars is doable," said Scott Kelly at the NASA press conference after his return. The problems he experienced included muscle soreness, fatigue, and burning sensations on his skin, perhaps caused by the fact his skin hadn't touched anything for nearly a year. Kelly also grew an inch and a half taller in the weighlessness of space, but that height gain disappeared upon his return to Earth's gravity.

NASA is also looking into the psychological dimensions of long-term confinement and isolation. That's why six volunteers entered a dome-shaped building on a Hawaiian volcano in 2015 for a yearlong research project.

Russia and China have conducted their own research, locking up a team of six international volunteers for a year and a half in the Mars500 simulator, located in Moscow. "A human journey to the Red Planet is feasible," said French engineer Romain Charles after 520 days in isolation.

Meanwhile, a private company called Mars One says it can do the job sooner and cheaper. Hundreds of volunteers believed them enough to sign up for the one-way trip planned for sometime in the 2020s. (The company doesn't plan to return its passengers to Earth. See chapter 19.)

IMAGINING TOMORROW'S MARTIANS

After centuries of novels and movies about Martians invading Earth, history's first Martians may actually be us invading Mars over the next few decades.

The Martian, a popular 2015 movie adapted from a thrilling sci-fi book of the same name, stars Matt Damon as an American astronaut who gets left behind on the red planet

No walk in the park. Six volunteers from Italy, France, China, and Russia spend 520 days in Russia's Mars500 simulator to study the impact of long-term confinement and isolation.

when a major dust storm forces his crewmates to head back to Earth without him.

After centuries of Martian fantasy and fiction, we're closer than ever to manned missions that will teach us even more about this still-mysterious planet.

But no matter how many facts we gather, I doubt we will ever exhaust our imaginary fantasy life about our next-door neighbor. Fact and fiction about Mars have intersected for centuries, and this tug-of-war will likely continue for centuries more. That's because we humans are created in the image of God. We are as passionate about creating imaginative Martian worlds as we are about creating new technologies and tools that will help us discover more about the actual history and makeup of Mars.

So don't worry. We're saying farewell to the old Mars of fantasy and fiction, but we're gaining new understandings of how our Creator made the cosmos. And everything we're learning about our nearby red neighbor will likely inspire future generations of storytellers to create new kinds of Martian sci-fi.

Desert destruction. A 150-foot-wide meteoroid struck Arizona some 50,000 years ago, unleashing the explosive force of 20 million tons of TNT.

15

INCOMING!

WHO'S KEEPING AN EYE ON 600,000 NEAR-EARTH OBJECTS?

An asteroid the size of Texas is racing our way at 22,000 mph. With only eighteen days until impact, how can we protect our planet from oblivion?

The Americans have an answer. They dispatch a veteran deep-sea oil driller to the speeding rock. He digs a deep hole and deposits a nuclear bomb, destroying the asteroid so the rest of us can live happily ever after. At least that's the way it is in *Armageddon*, 1998's top-grossing movie, which takes its title from the Bible's book of Revelation.

From 1958's *The Blob* to the 2016 TV series *You, Me, and the Apocalypse*, dozens of movies and series have shown objects crashing into Earth, causing massive mayhem and death. But these cinematic bombardments are merely a figment of Hollywood's overly dramatic imagination, right?

Wrong.

Cosmic visitors regularly collide with Earth, and if it

weren't for nifty features that God designed into our Goldilocks planet, it would be scarred by the same kinds of craters and pockmarks that mar the Moon's surface.

Our atmosphere deftly intercepts most space invaders. Every day our powerful atmospheric shield hijacks some 100 tons of small rocks and other pieces of space stuff heading our way, breaking up and incinerating everything before it can hit us.

Even when larger cosmic visitors occasionally slip through our atmospheric defense system, God's sustaining processes of weather, wind and water erosion, volcanoes, and plate tectonics help Earth tidy everything up after we've been whacked. So successful are these planetary scrubbers that only in recent decades have scientists realized how often and how violently we've been struck in the past.

To make sure we don't get blown to smithereens in the future, scientists with NASA's Near-Earth Object Program currently track some six hundred thousand orbiting objects (including an asteroid named after me!), paying closest attention to the fifteen hundred or so objects that are big enough and close enough to cause real damage.

Is Armageddon heading in our direction? Statistically speaking, it's more likely that you will die in an airplane wreck than be killed by an asteroid. But the dangers are real, as history shows.

THE MAN AND HIS CRATER

Today it's common knowledge that cosmic visitors regularly strike planet Earth, but that knowledge was far from common a century ago. One man did more than anyone else to change the scientific consensus: Daniel Barringer, a mining engineer, entrepreneur, adventurer, and explorer who went on hunting trips with US President Teddy Roosevelt.

After striking it rich with silver mines in the Southwest, Barringer heard locals describing an unusual hole in the ground west of Winslow, Arizona. After checking it out, he acquired mining claims to the crater and surrounding land in 1903.

Barringer—never one to suffer from self-doubt—was absolutely convinced of two things.

First, he was certain a meteoroid had dug out his mile-wide crater. But after spending nearly three decades trying to persuade leading geologists that he was right, he died from a heart attack in 1929 without having convinced a single "demented" scientist.

Second, he was certain the meteoroid responsible for his crater still lay buried deep down there somewhere. He blew most of his fortune and the money of several investors drilling dozens of deep holes he said would locate the "millions" (later "tens of millions") of tons of valuable nickel and iron hiding down there just waiting for him. Unfortunately, his theories about mining meteorites proved utterly ridiculous.

Riches from space. Mining engineer and entrepreneur Daniel Barringer believed he could get rich mining an Arizona asteroid.

Only decades after his death did Barringer receive partial vindication. Following years of study, geologists and astronomers finally concluded that his crater was indeed created by a meteoroid impact. This paradigm shift set the stage for a scientific reckoning: hundreds of locations around the world have now been recognized as impact sites.

But where did Barringer's space rock and all its supposed mineral wealth go? Scientists say that when a 150-foot-wide meteoroid struck Arizona some fifty thousand years ago, unleashing the force of 20 million tons of TNT, the meteoroid vaporized upon impact, spreading tiny specks of molten metal across the desert for miles around.

Today, Barringer's descendants still own the crater, and the Barringer Crater Company welcomes thousands of paying guests to view exhibits at a nearby visitor's center and take brief tours along part of the crater rim. During tours, guides show guests where the remains of Barringer's meteoroid went, sticking a small magnetic rod into the soil and holding it up for all to see the tiny specks of metal clinging to the magnet.

A CAST OF COSMIC VISITORS

Ancient astronomers believed that heavenly bodies behaved in simple, elegant, orderly ways. Rogue rocks and icy space invaders have helped us realize how vast and unruly our cosmos can be.

But what are the real differences between *Armageddon*'s asteroids and Barringer's meteoroid? Let's meet our cast of incoming cosmic visitors.

God created

our Goldilocks world so it's "just right" for life. Today he sustains it through powerful processes.

Brother Sun and Sister Moon couldn't be more different, but they collaborate with Earth to form a harmonious celestial trinity.

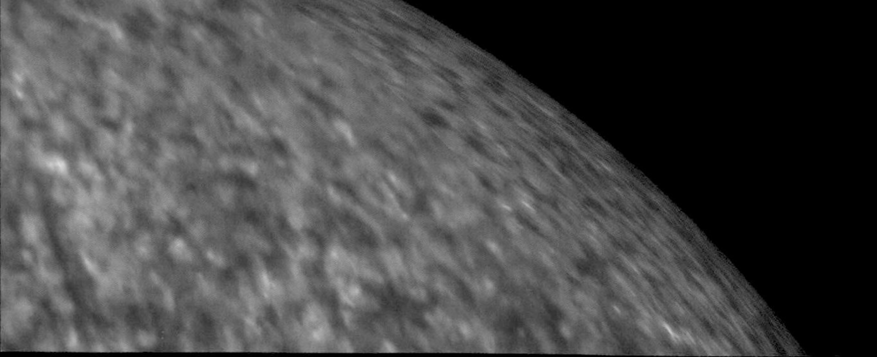

Sun, Earth, and the Moon depicted in their relative sizes.

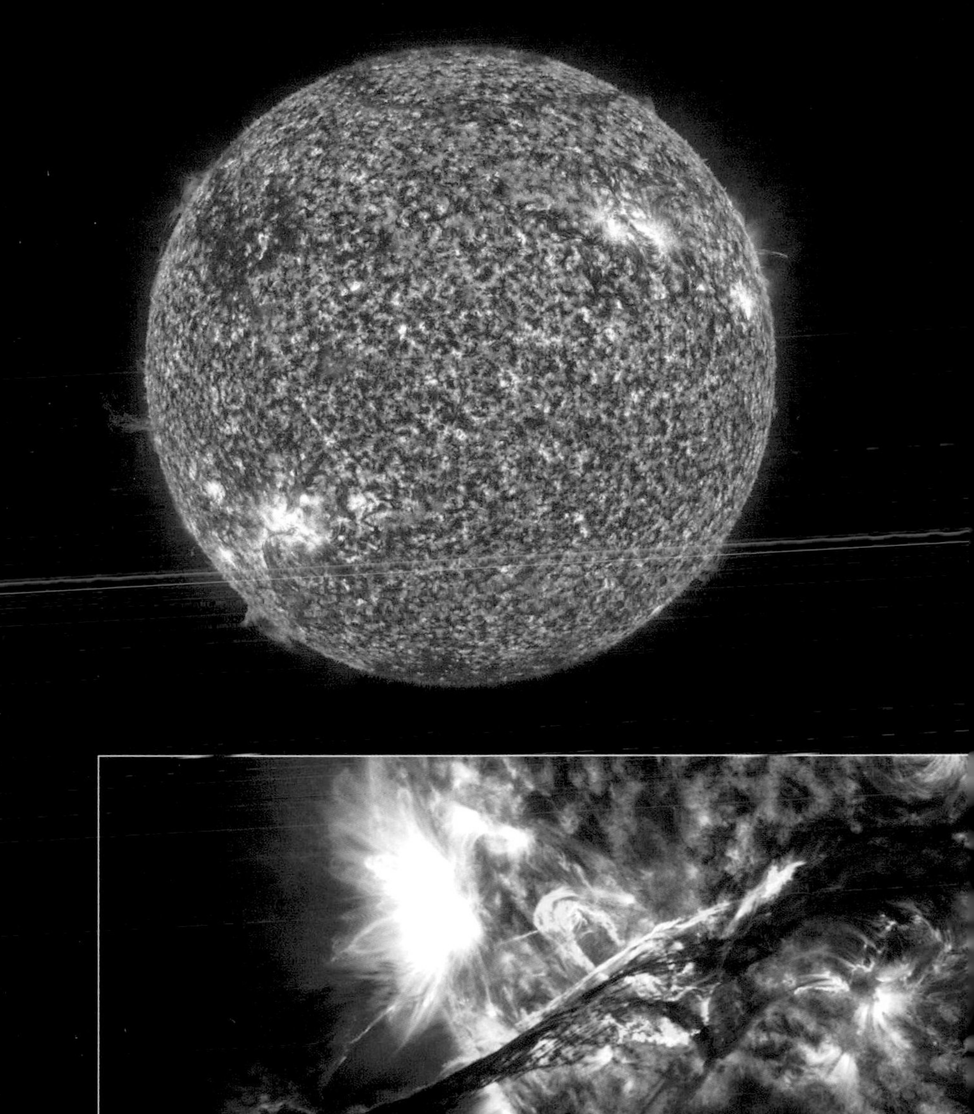

Brother Sun can be wild and explosive. His outbursts and flares disrupt our cell phone calls and produce our northern lights.

Once upon a time we thought we were the center of Creation. Now there may be no center. Things are bigger. We are smaller. And our cosmic address keeps changing.

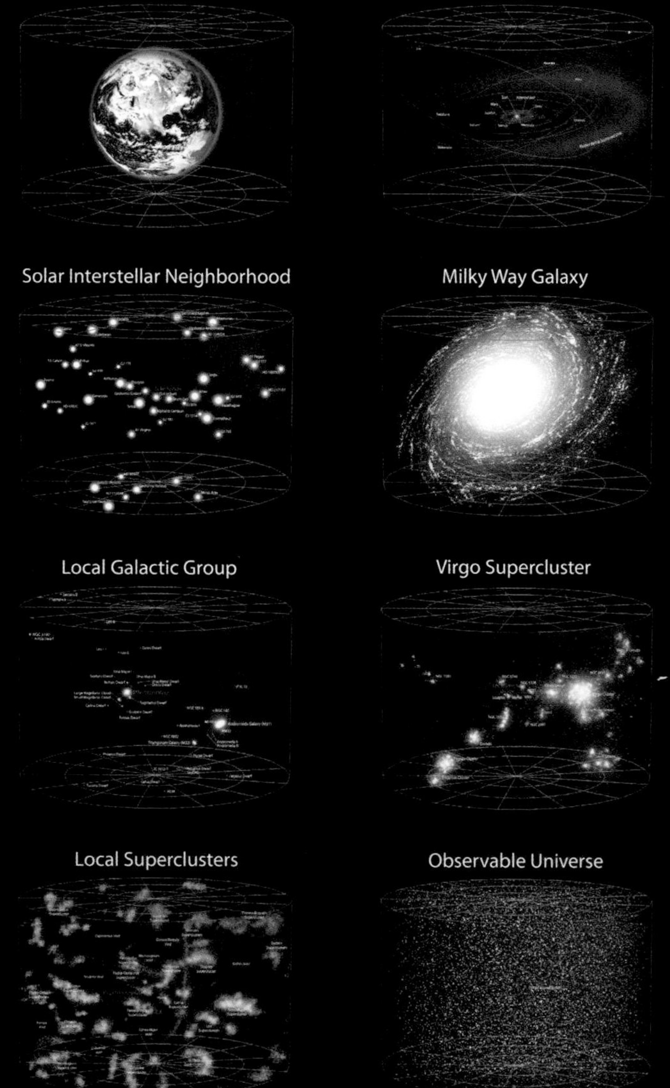

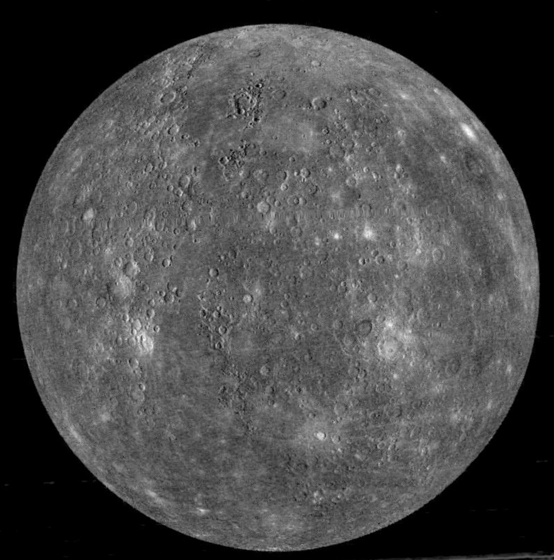

Temperature shifts of 1,000 degrees or more hammer Mercury, our solar system's smallest planet. Meanwhile, Venus is a sweltering inferno that's superheated by a runaway greenhouse effect.

Jupiter's fabled Red Spot is a centuries-old hurricane two or three times the size of Earth. Io, one of Jupiter's fifty-some moons, is the most geologically active object in our solar system.

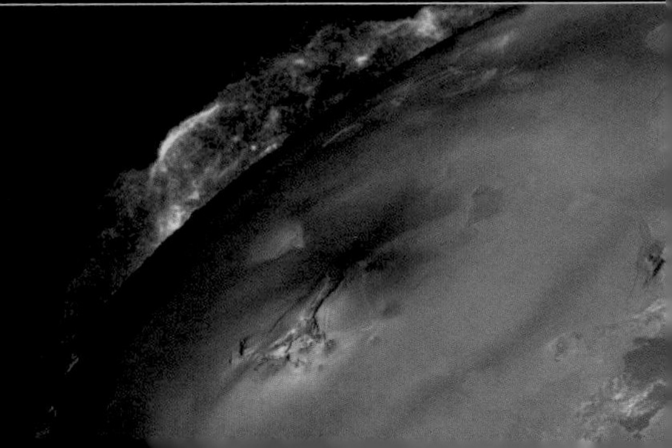

Recent missions show

that Saturn's rings are actually thousands of ringlets made of orbiting space debris. The rings are illumined when the planet eclipses the Sun (bottom).

Pluto once was a planet.

Now it's a lowly trans-Neptunian object.

Rovers and orbiters

unravel Martian mysteries, finding proof of liquid water in 2015.

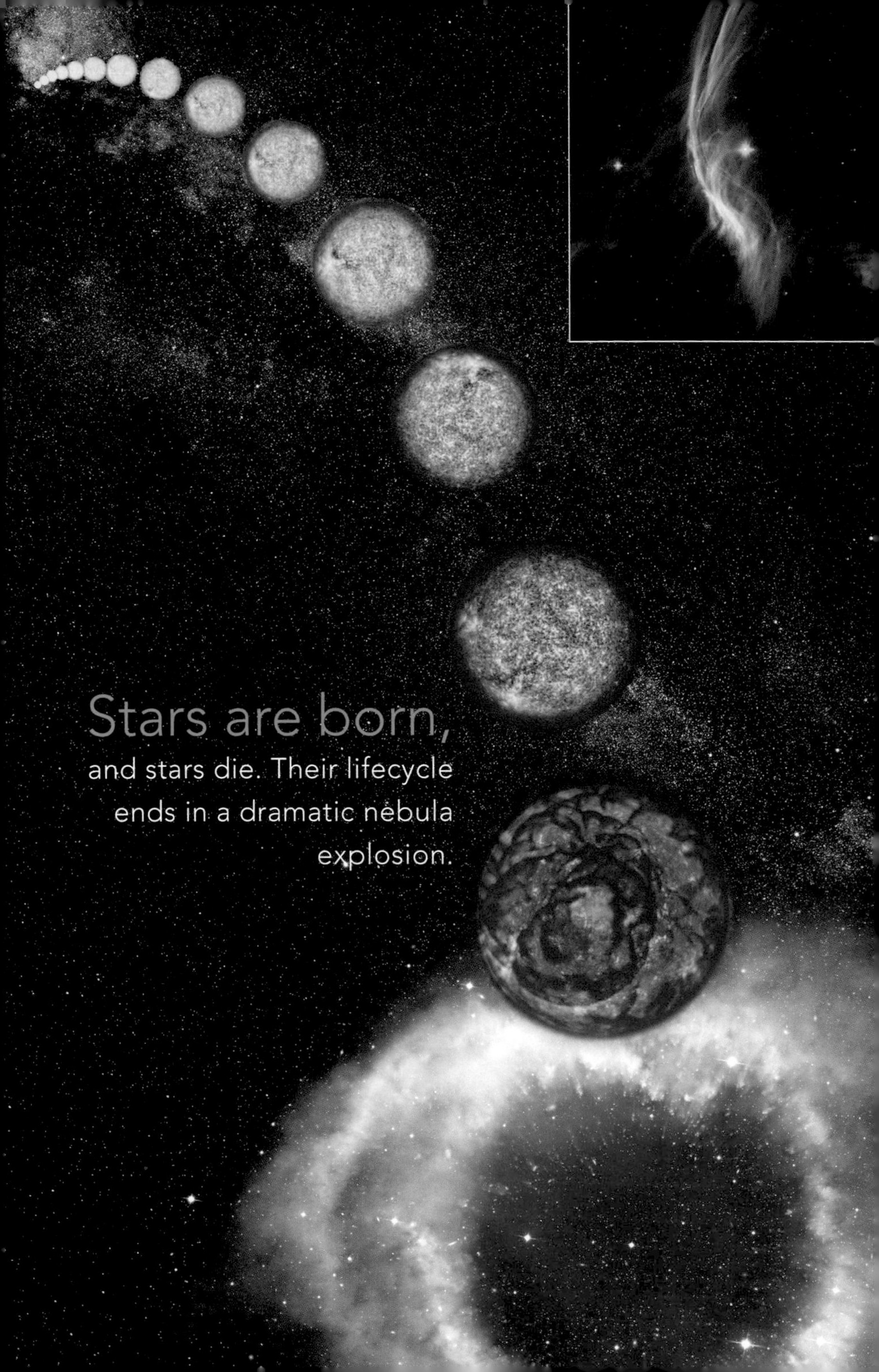
Stars are born,
and stars die. Their lifecycle
ends in a dramatic nebula
explosion.

Most stars are combo packages, like these binary and quad systems. Our solitary Sun is an outlier.

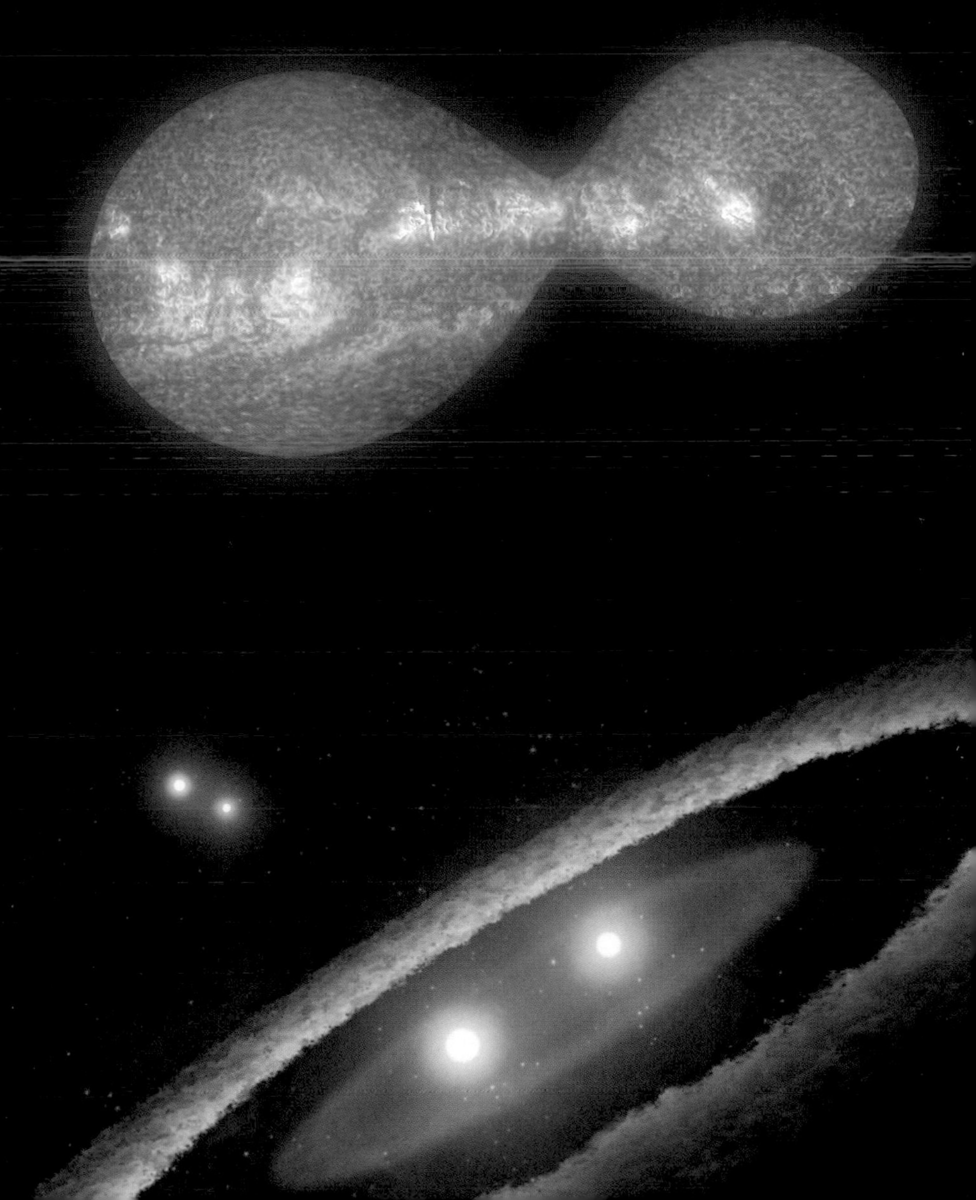

"Pillars of Creation,"
a photo from NASA's Hubble Space Telescope, shows a group of nebulae, massive clouds of dust and gas that stretch across wide expanses of space.

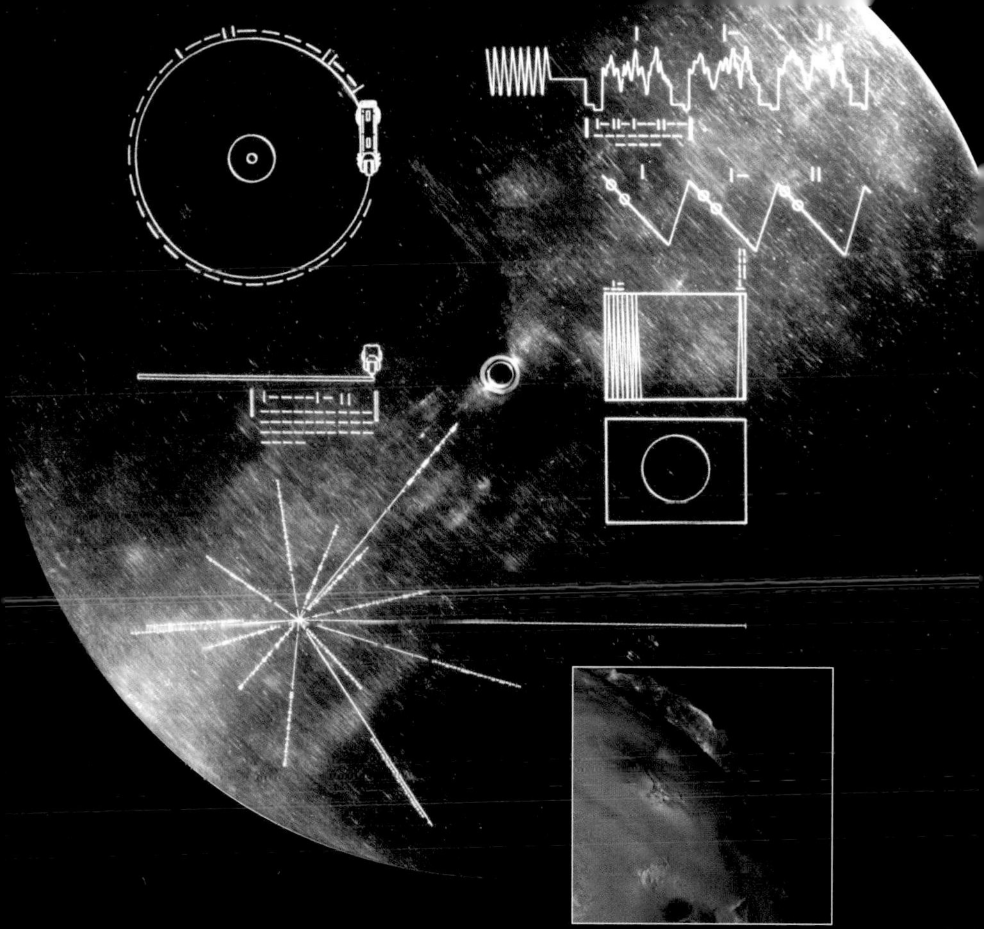

As *Voyager 1* journeys deeper into interstellar space, it carries a Golden Record full of Earth's sights and sounds. On its journey, *Voyager* photographed Jupiter's moon Io, and Neptune.

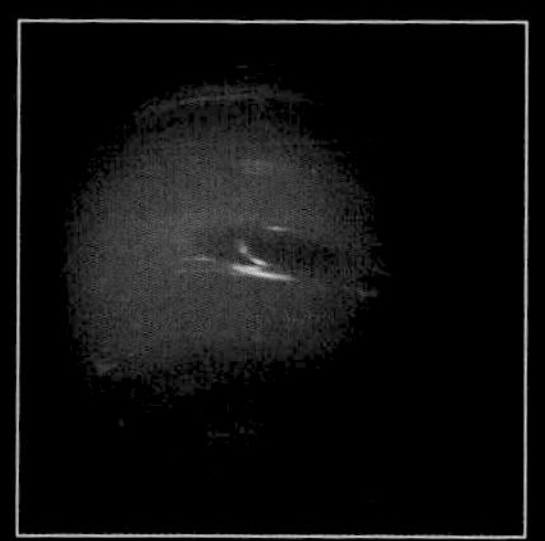

Voyager image of Neptune.

Galaxies are vast star-making factories. Our Creator knows each star by name. The Hubble Space Telescope reveals galaxies at work.

Apollo 11 astronaut Buzz Aldrin (inset photo, right) took Communion in the lunar module. A moon rock is in Washington National Cathedral's stained glass window.

Dirty snowballs with gossamer tails. Comets are big balls of rock and ice. As they speed through space, they leave behind trails of gas and dust.

Comets are flying balls of rock and ice that American astronomer Fred Whipple appropriately called "dirty snowballs." Halley discovered his comet in 1705, tracking its elliptical 1.7-billion-mile, seventy-five-year orbit around the Sun. Today, astronomers divide comets into two groups. *Short term* or *periodic* comets orbit the Sun in two hundred years or less. By contrast, the *long-term* comet West needs 250,000 years to complete its orbit.

The closer comets get to the Sun, the better we can see their long, gossamer tails of dust and gas. These tails always point away from the Sun, pushed into space by powerful solar winds radiating outward from the burning star.

Scientists think of comets as astronomical deep freezers that preserve primeval elements from the creation of our solar system. We had hoped to learn much more about these mysterious visitors from Europe's Rosetta mission, which landed an unmanned probe on the surface of Comet 67P/Churyumov–Gerasimenko in 2014 after a journey of ten years and four billion miles.

Asteroids beget more asteroids. Asteroids have dense cores surrounded by stony and metallic material (top). When two asteroids collide (middle), even more asteroids are created (bottom).

Unfortunately, *Philae*, the mission's unmanned probe, had a rough landing, bouncing around in the comet's weak gravity before finally coming to rest in a shady crater that hides *Philae*'s solar panels in the shade. Its batteries ran down in two days and it lost contact. It powered back up briefly in 2015 before dying once again. In 2016, scientists finally gave up on resurrecting *Philae*. (The Rosetta mission had already discovered oxygen on 67P/Churyumov–Gerasimenko before *Philae* went dead.)

Asteroids are big chunks of rocky and/or metallic material—our solar system's rugged individualists. Guiseppe Piazzi, an Italian astronomer and Catholic priest, first discovered one on New Year's Day 1801 but didn't know exactly what he'd found. "I have announced this star as a comet, but since it is not accompanied by any nebulosity and, further, since its movement is so slow and rather uniform, it has occurred to me several times that it might be something better than a comet. But I have been careful not to advance this supposition to the public."

Piazzi had discovered Ceres, which at 600 miles across is the biggest asteroid of them all (that we know of). In 2015, NASA's *Dawn* robotic spacecraft completed a three-billion-mile journey to Ceres, settling into orbit around the asteroid to conduct our most detailed studies yet of these oddly shaped visitors.

Most of our solar system's asteroids travel together in a huge asteroid belt between Mars and Jupiter, where they repeatedly collide and merge with each other. But like some humans, some asteroids have problems bonding. Perhaps Jupiter's strong, cyclical gravitational influences prevent them from conglomerating into a single planet.

These asteroids are fated to spend their long lives orbiting the Sun, colliding with one another, and suffering all manner of scrapes, scars, and missing bits in the process. That explains why no two asteroids look the same. Some are Ceres-sized monsters, some are tiny pebbles, and many are in between. B-612, the fictional asteroid in Antoine de Saint-Exupéry's *The Little Prince*, was "scarcely any larger than a house!"

Meteors are chunks of interplanetary material that typically burn up when they come into contact with our atmosphere. We call them *meteoroids* when they're floating in space. They're *meteorites* once they land on the ground, as many thousands do every year. And when Earth's orbit takes it through the debris field of a comet orbiting near the Sun, we witness a *meteor shower*. (To find out when you can view one of the half dozen or so most impressive annual meteor showers, visit the NASA.gov website.)

Meteors may actually be the "falling stars" John referred to in Revelation 6:13 ("and the stars in the sky fell to earth, as figs drop from a fig tree when shaken by a strong wind"). I don't think John's falling stars could be actual stars like our Sun. If they were, Earth would be toast. (The Greek word translated as "star" in the New Testament doesn't distinguish between stars, planets, or comets, but refers to any heavenly light-giving body.)

Blown to bits. The Tunguska meteor blast knocked down an estimated 80 million trees across some 800 square miles.

OUR PUMMELED PLANET

In 2013, people watched a 10,000-ton meteoroid streak across Russia's sky. This cosmic visitor exploded miles above the remote town of Chelyabinsk, but the resulting powerful blast still injured sixteen hundred people. YouTube videos show the meteor exploding in a brilliant fireball, generating powerful shockwaves that broke windows, knocked over walls, and brought ceilings tumbling down in thousands of buildings.

A century earlier, Russia's Siberia region was the site of one of the most destructive visitations of modern times. The Tunguska meteor was traveling toward Earth at 40,000 mph when it exploded far above our planet's surface. The blast's force knocked down an estimated 80 million trees across some 800 square miles, instantly turning forests of tall timber into trillions of toothpicks.

If either of these meteors had hit a major city, the results would have been catastrophic. But as big as these visitors were, neither strike compares to the unprecedented collision Earth suffered millions of years ago.

The mother of all impact craters is called Chicxulub (pronounced *chick-shoo-loob*), located on the tip of Mexico's Yucatan Peninsula, where a gigantic asteroid struck some 65 million years ago. Over time, the crater has filled in and smoothed out, but satellite photographs taken in the 1970s by petroleum engineers looking for oil discovered the telltale signs of the crater, more than 100 miles wide and 12 miles deep.

Scientists believe the Chicxulub impact was catastrophically destructive. It broiled the Earth's surface; set off massive shockwaves, earthquakes, and volcanoes; created mega-tsunamis that flooded major landmasses; and spewed out a global dust cloud that darkened the Sun for months, if not years, eventually killing off the planet's dinosaurs and most other living things.

The Chicxulub dust cloud included an element named iridium, extremely rare on Earth but plentiful in meteorites. Geologists around the world think Chicxulub may have been the source of a thin layer of iridium that has turned up between layers of very old rock all around the world.

When will the next big one hit? Nobody knows. But my

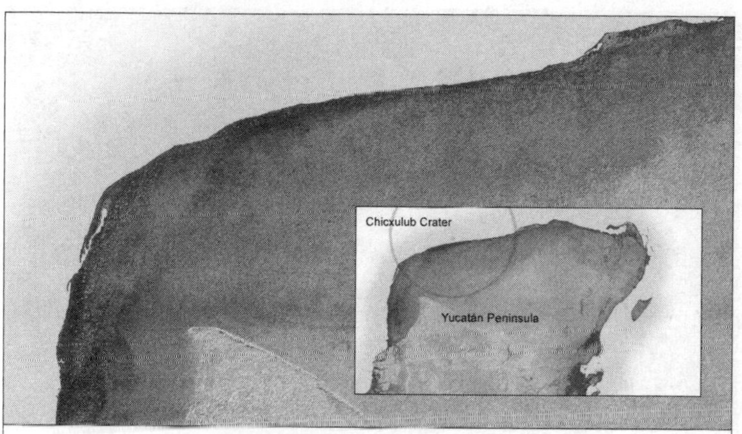

Monster impact. The gigantic Chicxulub asteroid that struck Mexico's Yucatan Peninsula 65 million years ago may have wiped out all life on Earth.

reading of Revelation leads me to believe that God may use an asteroid to fulfill this prophecy: "The second angel sounded his trumpet, and something like a huge mountain, all ablaze, was thrown into the sea. A third of the sea turned into blood, a third of the living creatures in the sea died, and a third of the ships were destroyed" (Rev. 8:8–9).

GOD DOESN'T MAKE JUNK

An Associated Press writer recently described asteroids as "rocky leftovers from the formation of the sun and planets," and the textbook I use in my astronomy classes at Eastern University calls comets and asteroids "solar system debris."

I don't particularly like hearing asteroids described as debris, particularly the one named 5826 Bradstreet.

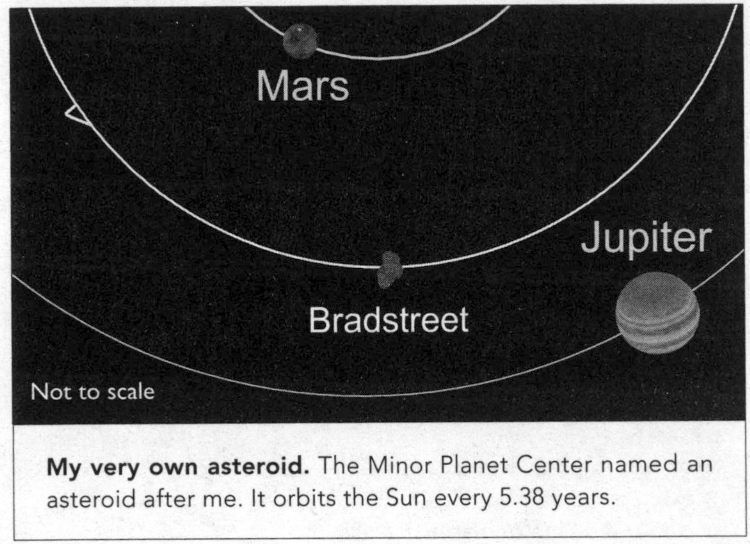

My very own asteroid. The Minor Planet Center named an asteroid after me. It orbits the Sun every 5.38 years.

In October 2014, I was honored to have the Minor Planet Center name an asteroid after me. The honor recognized my teaching at Eastern and the educational resources I've created. *Binary Maker* is a light-curve software program that helps astronomers study binary stars, my astronomical specialty (see chapter 18). Spitz Fulldome Curriculum is a series of presentations and classes used in planetarium settings throughout the world.

We can't tell if "my" asteroid is rocky or metallic. We know only that it travels in the asteroid belt between Mars and Jupiter, orbiting the Sun every 5.38 years.

Some scientists consider asteroids like 5826 Bradstreet space junk, but I think these cosmic visitors are incredibly beautiful and fascinating. I also believe they have real value.

Their financial value could be tremendous if we ever

learn how to mine asteroids and retrieve their nearly limitless supplies of nickel and iron. But now I'm starting to sound like Mr. Barringer! At least for now, transporting tons of ore millions of miles through space remains prohibitively expensive.

There's another reason to appreciate these rocky/metallic visitors. God probably banged some asteroids together when he created the oasis we call Earth. We may even owe some of our DNA to ancient material from this so-called junk.

God doesn't create trash, and whether he is at work here on Earth or in the farthest reaches of space, he often seems to find perfectly good uses for things we consider utterly useless.

Hello? At the National Radio Astronomy Observatory's Very Large Array in Socorro, New Mexico, scientists train twenty-seven huge dish antennae on the heavens in the quest to find life in space.

16

IS ANYBODY OUT THERE?

THE FRUSTRATING QUEST FOR EXTRATERRESTRIAL LIFE

Listening. That's what astronomer Frank Drake has been doing since 1960, using astronomical observatories and telescopes to pick up signs of life in the universe.

More than half a century later, he still hasn't heard a single personal peep or beep from space. The silence has been deafening for Drake, one of the pioneers in SETI (the Search for Extraterrestrial Intelligence) and author of the famous Drake Equation, which argues that since there are so many billions of planets in our cosmos, it makes sense that somewhere between one thousand and 100 million of them should be home to technologically advanced alien civilizations.

It's a logical argument, and it may even be true, but so far SETI hasn't found a single shred of scientific evidence showing that anybody else is out there. Drake, now in his eighties, is still listening, but his frustration is growing.

"Things have slowed down, and we are in bad shape in several ways," a disappointed Drake told science writer Lee Billings in *Five Billion Years of Solitude: The Search for Life among the Stars*. "Most people don't seem to think there is much benefit to it."

For decades, scientists hoped SETI would help us find someone out there somewhere, none more enthusiastically than the late Carl Sagan, who wrote the novel that became the popular 1997 movie *Contact*. In the film, Jodie Foster plays Dr. Ellie Arroway, a scientist who picks up signals from space. Finally, another civilization has reached out with an intelligent radio handshake.

Meanwhile, real-world SETI research keeps coming up empty, except for one tantalizing 72-second-long signal picked up by Ohio researcher Jerry Ehman in 1977. Often called the "Wow!" signal, because Ehman wrote that word on his computer printout, the nonterrestrial signal was never heard again, even though scientists tried to find it again over the coming months and years.

Now, after decades of work and millions of dollars, many scientists are moving on. "The money simply isn't there these days. And we're all getting old," says Drake. "The lack of interest is, I think, because most people don't realize what even a simple detection would really mean. How much would it be worth to find out we are not alone?"

In 2014, SETI scientists pleaded with leaders in Congress to help keep the program going.

"The possibility that life has arisen elsewhere, and perhaps evolved intelligence, is plausible and warrants scientific inquiry," argued one scientist. Another claimed the chances for the existence of extraterrestrial life are "close to 100 percent."

But Yuri Milner isn't waiting for government money. In 2015, the Russian internet billionaire said he would spend $100 million to continue the SETI search, enlisting celebrity astrophysicist Stephen Hawking as part of his team. "In an infinite universe, there must be other occurrences of life," said Hawking.

IS THE TRUTH OUT THERE?

Most Americans think we've got company in the universe, and nearly a third of us believe aliens have visited our planet.

You can find some of these true believers in Roswell, New Mexico, an out-of-the-way town made famous by the controversial "Roswell Incident" of 1947. A local man found something out in the desert. Was this the remains of an alien visitation, or merely a lost weather balloon from a local military base? And where did government officials hide the little green men? (Learn more at Roswell's official-sounding International UFO Museum Research Center.)

Amid growing public concern about Roswell and other mysterious incidents, the US Air Force conducted investigations from 1947 to 1969 to determine if America faced any risks from alien aircraft. Project Blue Book investigated more than twelve thousand alleged UFO sightings, concluding that nearly all the "unidentified" flying objects people had reported were actually fairly easily identifiable human-made objects.

A red-hot piece of metal that reportedly fell out of the sky and landed with a bang on a sidewalk in the Midwest was traced back to the overheated brakes of a delivery truck, not a flying saucer. Other supposed UFOs turned out to be commercial airplanes, clouds, meteors, stars, or other normal objects.

Government reports pooh-poohing UFOs seldom convince true-blue believers to give up hope. Most of us remain thoroughly convinced space is teeming with life despite the fact that no one has ever seen one iota of verifiable evidence for such an idea.

Perhaps we embrace our own version of the Drake Equation: we think a cosmos as big as ours must be home to someone besides us.

ALIENS AMONG US!

Here's my theory explaining why most of us seem to believe alien life forms are out there somewhere: pop culture. Our hearts and minds have been shaped by decades' worth of adorable aliens who've visited us on screens small and large most of our lives. I know these celebrity extraterrestrials have informed my imagination about life in space.

There's Spock, the half-Vulcan, half-human science officer who helped *Star Trek*'s starship *Enterprise* fulfill its mission "to explore strange new worlds, to seek out new life and new civilizations, to boldly go where no man has gone before."

There's *Mork and Mindy*'s Mork from Ork, a comic alien from a planet where humor is forbidden. Robin Williams's

Recurring alien visitation syndrome. Among the adorable pop culture aliens who've appeared on screens small and large over the years are *Star Trek*'s Spock, Mork from Ork, E.T., and a Muppet Martian.

signature "Nah-noo Nah-noo" phrase, along with his hand gesture that echoed Spock's Vulcan salute, are forever etched deep in my memory.

We've even granted these two fictional aliens the same kind of single-name celebrity we lavish upon Elvis, Madonna, and Oprah.

When I think about all the lovable aliens I've met in

movies like *Close Encounters of the Third Kind*, *Cocoon*, *E.T.: The Extraterrestrial*, *Starman*, *Star Wars*, and *Muppets from Space*; in TV series like *The X-Files*; and in countless cable programs on "ancient aliens," it's hard for me to resist the overwhelming verdict of pop culture. Space seems to overflow with life of all kinds, most of it friendly. Why wouldn't we want to reach out and connect with these creatures?

THE QUEST CONTINUES

Traditional SETI is *passive*: we listen for signals. Now a younger generation of SETI researchers says we should do *active* SETI. Instead of waiting for aliens' signals to reach us, we should "join the galactic club" and send out broadcasts of our own so that somebody out there can pick up our signals.

But wait just a minute. What if we run into galactic bad guys like the ones we've been warned about in movies like *Alien*, *Battlestar Galactica*, *The Blob*, *Invasion of the Body Snatchers*, *Men in Black*, *Stargate*, and *They Live*?

Dozens of scientists are concerned enough about evil extraterrestrials that they've signed a petition to prohibit active SETI programs. "We know nothing of ETI's intentions and capabilities, and it is impossible to predict whether ETI will be benign or hostile," says the petition, which has been signed by SpaceX founder Elon Musk and others.

Arguments about active SETI (also known as METI, or Messaging to Extraterrestrial Intelligence) broke out at the 2015 meeting of the American Association for the Advancement of Science.

As these arguments continue, astronomers are developing powerful new tools in the search for alien life. Instead of relying on Earth-based telescopes or radars to connect with extraterrestrials, we're sending telescopes out into space to actively seek out planets where we think the conditions for life look most promising. These efforts have opened an exciting new chapter in our timeless quest to find out if we are all alone.

KEPLER'S QUEST FOR EARTH 2.0

Johannes Kepler was a devout Christian astronomer and forerunner of the scientific revolution (see chapter 8). He felt certain God had created many kinds of life, a concept he explored in his book *Somnium* (*The Dream*), probably the world's first sci-fi novel. Written in 1608, the year before his friend Galileo looked through his telescope and changed the world, Kepler's story imagines a trip to the Moon that provides opportunities to study its plants, its creatures, and its astronomical sights.

We're looking for you! With NASA's *Kepler* space observatory on the prowl, we're no longer passively waiting for aliens to find us.

Four centuries later, Kepler's curiosity about all of God's creatures is honored in NASA's *Kepler* space observatory mission. Launched in 2009, *Kepler* is an orbiting telescope that observes deep space much better than Earthbound instruments can.

If passive SETI is us sitting by the phone waiting for aliens to call us, and if active SETI is us placing calls to space and waiting for someone to answer, *Kepler* faces an even bigger challenge: trying to find a needle in a cosmic haystack. Its mission is to scan a small section of our Milky Way galaxy in search of planets that orbit stars, as Earth does.

There are hundreds of billions of planets in our galaxy, but *Kepler* is searching for only those that most closely resemble our own Goldilocks planet, which has all the essentials that life (as we know it) needs to thrive: a protective atmosphere, moderate temperatures, liquid water, and a symbiotic relationship with our Sun and all its solar energy.

Scientists studying *Kepler*'s data have already found thousands of possible planetary candidates, but they're focusing attention on a thousand or so of the most interesting-looking extrasolar planets—or exoplanets—that *Kepler* has located in more than four hundred of the Milky Way's solar systems.

None of these planetary candidates are exact analogs of Earth, but a dozen or so look intriguing, particularly Kepler 186f (a planet about our size) and Kepler 452b (a planet twelve hundred light-years away, meaning it would take us more than 25 million years to get there traveling on NASA's speediest spaceship).

FROM ASTROBIOLOGY TO ASTROTHEOLOGY

Giordano Bruno made many extraordinary claims. He claimed that life exists on millions of planets. He imagined millions of Christs ministering in these faraway worlds. Because he was a sixteenth-century Dominican friar and not a sci-fi novelist, he was burned at the stake.

Fast-forward to the summer of 1969. As Neil Armstrong prepares to walk on the Moon, the July issue of evangelical magazine *Christianity Today* publishes an interview with NASA scientist Rodney W. Johnson, who acknowledges his anxiety about who or what we might find out there.

"The most frightening thought regarding space exploration is that we might encounter a form of life with a higher intelligence," said Johnson, who worried this could mean that God had "made beings superior to us and didn't tell us about it."

Today astrobiologists are busily searching for traces of life in space. If they ever find anything, we will need astrotheologians to help us connect the dots and figure out how our faith will adapt to the reality of knowing we're not God's only creatures.

Consider some of the questions tomorrow's astrotheologians may ponder:

- Is our Earth unique, or somehow central in God's plans? Or is ours merely one of many inhabited worlds?
- Christ paid the ultimate price. Did his death and resurrection on a cross here on Earth impact only people on our planet? Or did his sacrifice cover the sins of all creatures throughout the cosmos?
- Do people on other planets sin? If so, do they need a Savior like we do? Do other planets have their own gardens of Eden and their own Messiahs?
- Do aliens have blood? If not, how would they understand the necessity of blood sacrifice for the

atonement of sins? And what would be the equivalent atonement for bloodless creatures?

- What if the creatures we encounter in other worlds are disciples of some other religious faith? Should we convert them? Allow them to convert us? Or engage in respectful interfaith/interplanetary dialogue?
- And could Jesus have been talking about aliens (in addition to Gentiles) when he told his disciples: "I have other sheep that are not of this sheep pen. I must bring them also" (John 10:16)?

THE EVEN GREATER COMMISSION

Christ's Great Commission commands believers to go into "all the world" as ambassadors of the faith. Should we now update that command and go into "all the cosmos"?

C. S. Lewis wrestled with such issues in his 1958 essay "Religion and Rocketry." He liked the advice given by a much earlier writer: "If I remember rightly, St. Augustine raised a question about the theological position of satyrs, monopodes, and other semi-human creatures. He decided it could wait till we knew there were any. So can this."

Others are convinced Christ already reached out to creatures on other planets. Pioneering Christian musician Larry Norman suggested as much in his 1971 song "U.F.O.":

> And if there's life on other planets
> Then I'm sure that He must know
> And He's been there once already
> And has died to save their souls.

Novelists have long explored this brave new theological territory. In Robert Heinlein's 1961 classic, *Stranger in a Strange Land* (the title comes from the King James Bible's wording of Exod. 2:22), a human raised on Mars by Martians comes to Earth as a superintelligent Messiah figure who launches a neopagan religious group called the "Church of All Worlds." (Later, a group of California residents created an actual religious group based on the novel's ideas. Can you *grok* it, baby?)

Half a century after Heinlein's neopagan novel, Michel Faber's *The Book of Strange New Things* describes an evangelical missionary who travels to a planet called Oasis to minister to its spiritually hungry natives.

Astronomers also enjoy speculating about salvation in space. "Any entity—no matter how many tentacles it has—has a soul," says Vatican astronomer Guy Consolmagno in his nonfiction book, *Would You Baptize an Extraterrestrial? . . . And Other Questions from the Astronomers' In-box at the Vatican Observatory.*

Vanderbilt University astronomer David Weintraub says historic faiths like Judaism, Christianity, and Islam may be at a competitive disadvantage when competing for souls against newer faiths like Mormonism, Jehovah's Witnesses, and the Baha'i Faith, all of which clearly endorse the concept of extraterrestrial life.

Pope Francis knows how he will respond if aliens come seeking salvation. During a 2014 homily on the family, he stated his intention: "If tomorrow, for example, an expedition of Martians arrives and some of them come to us . . . and if one of them says: 'Me, I want to be baptized!', what would happen?"

The pope plans to follow the model of St. Peter. At a time when most early Christians in Jerusalem believed Christ came to minister only to Jews, Peter believed Christ's gospel offered salvation to all people. His controversial mission to the Gentiles changed the face of faith. As the pope explained: "When the Lord shows us the way, who are we to say, 'No, Lord, it is not prudent! No, let's do it this way.' Who are we to close doors?"

THE GLORIOUS GIFT OF LIFE

I gratefully accept life as a gift that God has bestowed on us humans and our wonderful blue planet. Who am I to complain if our Creator wants to offer this wonderful gift to others?

Astronomer/theologian David Wilkinson agrees. In his book *Science, Religion, and the Search for Extraterrestrial Intelligence*, Wilkinson argues that the same God who has been so extravagantly life-creating here on Earth would likely create life elsewhere as well:

"The Creator God is an extravagant creator who gives us the gift of science to discover more about that extravagance. In addition, I would not be surprised that the God who creates a Universe where the laws of physics and biology lead to such extravagance in the natural world of the Earth takes delight in other life elsewhere in the Universe."

Either there is life out there or there isn't. We may never know. But either way, the alien life question is absolutely mind-blowing.

If this universe teems with extraterrestrial life, that's exciting news with profound implications.

If, on the other hand, we're really the only intelligent, sentient beings in the entire universe, that may be even more astounding news!

Stellar life cycle. Stars like the one shown here are born, mature, and then die.

17

A STAR IS BORN (AND SO ARE WE!)

STARS ARE BORN, GROW, AND DIE, BUT NOT BEFORE PLAYING A VITAL ROLE IN LIFE

I'm not the only astronomer who was star struck as a child. Growing up in rural Arkansas, Jennifer Wiseman felt a powerful connection to the land, its creatures, and the starry heavens spread out above.

"Just about every evening, if the weather was pleasant, my parents and I would take our dogs out for walks up and down our country lane," she says. "I saw stars from horizon to horizon."

Wiseman's childhood curiosity grew more serious in the 1970s after NASA launched two *Voyager* probes to explore the farthest reaches of our solar system.

"These missions were sending back amazing images of exotic, faraway planets in our solar system, and their fantastic moons," she says. "One moon, such as Jupiter's Europa, would be covered by oceans locked away under thick layers of ice. Another moon, like Io, would be a volcanic world with molten surfaces.

"I thought sending these probes to explore the solar system was one of the greatest things human beings had ever done, and from then on I wanted to be a part of the human enterprise to explore these fascinating worlds in outer space."

Some dreams come true. Today Dr. Wiseman (she has a PhD from Harvard) is an astronomer using a variety of telescopes to study the process of star formation. New stars and planets are continually being born and dying. New stars are generated from interstellar gas, which is enriched by dying stars that disperse their elements into space—essential elements all living things need.

Star struck. Astronomer Jennifer Wiseman fell in love with stars as a child, and space exploration fueled her passion to "be a part of the human enterprise to explore these fascinating worlds in outer space."

Dr. Wiseman, who has worked at major observatories and universities, is currently a senior astrophysicist at NASA. I want you to meet her because she's a top-notch astronomer and star expert who serves as a powerful role model for young women, who are sometimes mistakenly told that science is only a "guy thing."

A POWERFUL PERSPECTIVE

Four centuries ago Galileo revolutionized our understanding of the universe when he scanned the skies with his powerful new telescope. Now astronomers utilize a palette of many kinds of far more powerful telescopes, both in space and on the ground.

Some telescopes are sensitive to the same kinds of visible light our eyes can see. Others are able to capture radiation from "colors," or wavelengths of light that our eyes cannot see, such as ultraviolet and infrared light, radio waves, and X-rays.

One powerful telescope that Wiseman uses is the Hubble Space Telescope, named after Edwin Hubble, the twentieth-century astronomer who expanded our concepts about the cosmos (see chapter 21).

Launched into space in 1990, the Hubble telescope orbits the Earth outside our atmosphere, allowing it to see farther and more clearly than Earth-based telescopes. From its privileged vantage point high above clouds and light pollution, Hubble has made more than a million observations, studying the origins and expansion of the cosmos, discovering previously unknown moons of Pluto, and examining the atmosphere of planets far outside our solar system.

Unlike Galileo's telescope, Hubble has no eyepiece for humans to use. Instead, Hubble analyzes light from space using an array of scientific instruments attuned to the different kinds of light emitted by stars and other objects in space (visible, ultraviolet, and infrared).

Hubble has several cameras that capture images, as well

as spectrographs that spread out light like a prism to help us determine the temperature, chemical composition, density, and motion of stars and interstellar gas. These cutting-edge instruments are helping us understand parts of our cosmos previously shrouded in mystery.

Along the way, Hubble has generated hundreds of thousands of stunning images showing the workings of galaxies, black holes, and nebulae. One of NASA's most popular Hubble photos is titled *Pillars of Creation*. The image of the Eagle Nebula shows a group of three fingerlike pillars, massive clouds of star-forming dust and gas that stretch across wide expanses of space. (See color photo section p. 12.)

While Hubble's infrared cameras can "see" within some of these dusty pillars, other kinds of telescopes are needed to peer even deeper within similar interstellar star nurseries. Dr. Wiseman uses radio telescopes to look into deeply buried, dense clumps of gas and dust collapsing under their own gravitational contractions.

If the pressure in the core of one of these dense clumps becomes high enough, the hydrogen gas there gets pressed into a reaction called "fusion," producing helium atoms and releasing light. That's the moment when astronomers can proclaim, "A star is born!" Each dense interstellar gas cloud can generate numerous stars.

Wiseman uses a technique called *interferometry* that enables several Earth-based radio telescopes (including the Very Large Array in New Mexico and the ALMA observatory in Chile) to work in unison with Hubble. Working together, the telescopes provide more detailed analysis of the complex conditions inside deeply embedded clumps of star-forming gas.

Wiseman compares the work of an astronomer using interferometry to study astronomical objects to the work of a conductor who brings together different kinds of music as he directs a symphony orchestra.

"You need many telescopes of different kinds to get a full understanding of what you are studying in space, just like you need different kinds of instruments to make an orchestra," says Wiseman. "Once you put it all together and harmonize everything, you have an unbelievably rich piece of music."

A BEAUTIFUL NEW BUNDLE OF HOT SWIRLING PLASMA

On the way to becoming a star, a baby "protostar" goes through spectacular stages of adolescence over millions of years, including a phase where some of the gas getting drawn into the star gets caught up in magnetic fields surrounding the star and is actually ejected, in the form of fast, outflowing jets from the stellar magnetic poles.

Wiseman has been studying one such amazing protostar system (named 05413-0104) and its accompanying bipolar outflowing jet (named HH212). It might be nicer to give this new star a proper name like other famous stars—Sirius, Betelgeuse, or Polaris—but there are so many stars out there that astronomers need a simple alphanumeric system for keeping track of them all.

"I'm tracking a newbie," Wiseman reports. "The names

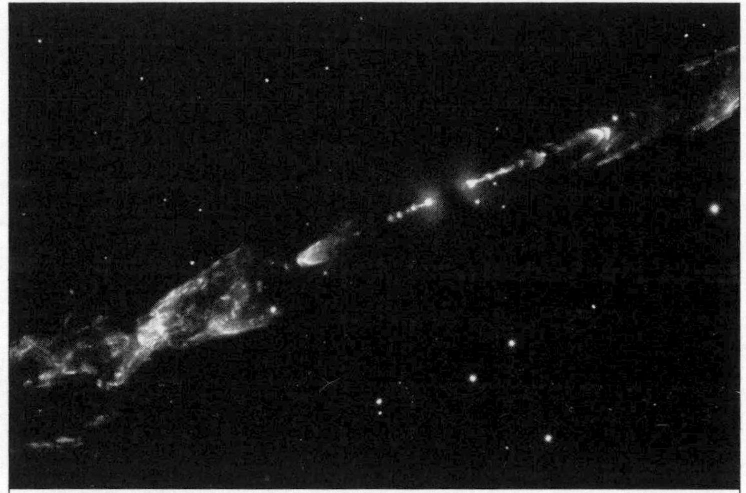

Tracking a newbie. Astronomer Jennifer Wiseman has been observing the formation of a new star named 05413-0104 and its outflowing jet named HH212.

05413-0104 and HH212 aren't very poetic, but this baby star system is my favorite because of its beautiful outflowing jets that show the process of star formation in action.

"What makes the whole process so spectacular is the combination of accretion and venting," says Wiseman. "There's an inflow of materials from the gassy cloud, and an outflow of exhausted material that also transports away some of the angular momentum of the system, allowing the spinning baby protostar to slow down enough to 'turn on.'" These outflowing jets are vast fountains of material that speed away from the star system at several hundreds of thousands of miles per hour, resembling huge torrents of water being shot out of a cosmic fire hose.

"These streams come in pulses that you can measure in real time to determine how long the process has been going on," Wiseman explains. "When you see all this, you can tell a lot about the history of a young forming star. And in the case of HH212, this is a very young one—only a few thousand years old."

Our own Milky Way galaxy is home to more than 200 billion stars. There are more than 200 billion additional galaxies in the cosmos. These galaxies serve as gigantic star factories, each of which has its own 100 to 300 billion stars. Do the math and the numbers are mind-boggling: our Sun is merely one among some 100,000,000,000,000,000,000,000 stars.

Some are about the same size as our Sun, some are giants a thousand times more massive, but about 75 percent of stars are smaller red dwarf stars. Stars differ in color as well as size. Blue stars are hotter than red stars, which have cool outer

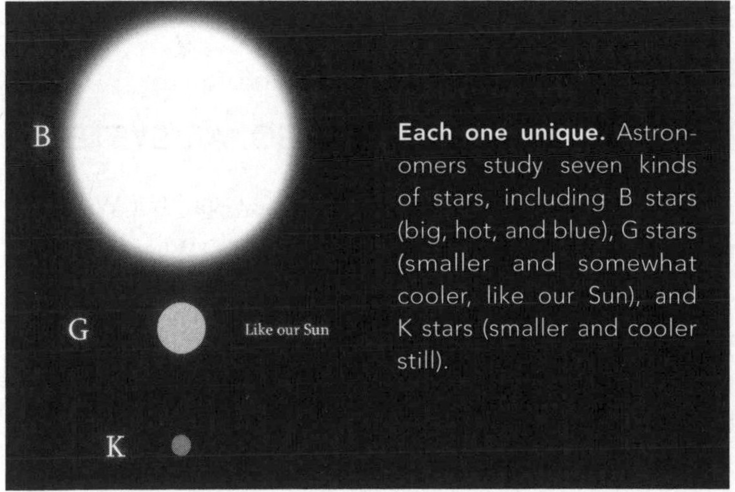

Each one unique. Astronomers study seven kinds of stars, including B stars (big, hot, and blue), G stars (smaller and somewhat cooler, like our Sun), and K stars (smaller and cooler still).

layers. Telescopes help us study stars' differing chemical compositions, which determine the spectra of light they emit.

Even with so much diversity, stars have this in common: each has a beginning and an end. Stars are born and stars die, including our Sun, which is expected to burn out in a few billion years.

Because of the incredibly long times involved, no astronomer can study the entire life cycle of a star. But by examining stars that are going through various stages of this process, we're learning how the whole cycle plays out.

Once born, stars live active, turbulent lives, as we saw in chapter 7. These big churning balls of gas, or plasma, "shine" because of the nonstop process of fusion taking place deep within their cores under extreme gravitational pressures. It's a violent, combustive process that contrasts with the calm, domestic tone set by the popular English lullaby: "Twinkle, twinkle, little star, how I wonder what you are."

"It's part of living in a universe that is dynamic, varied, and changing," says Wiseman.

NEW STARS BEGET NEW SOLAR SYSTEMS

It's exciting to celebrate the birth of a new star, but Wiseman also studies the end of the stellar life cycle. When stars run out of inner hydrogen fuel, they become unstable and begin to release their outer atmospheres in spectacular and often beautiful ways. Eventually, most dying stars simply cool off and become "white dwarfs."

But the biggest stars–those much more massive than our

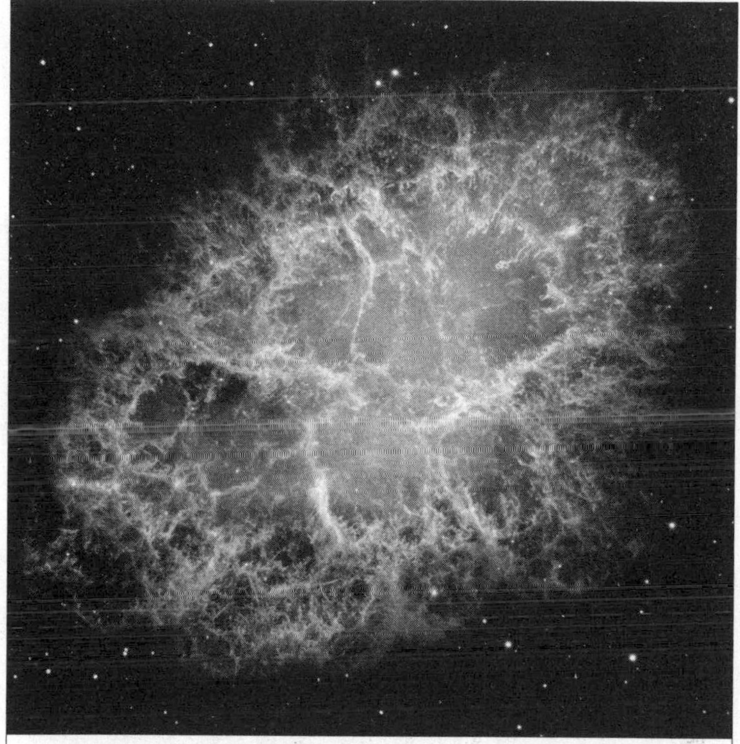

A dramatic finale. Massive dying stars explode in brilliant eruptions called supernovas that light up the heavens.

Sun–become so unstable as they reach the end of their prime that they explode in brilliant eruptions called supernovas that can be a billion times as bright as our Sun. These supernovas also spread stars' elements throughout the universe, including the elements you and I need to live, like carbon, oxygen, and iron.

These dispersed elements also seed the interstellar clouds from which the next generation of stars will be born. This stellar birth process can create a surrounding circumstellar disk of gas and solid materials, and in some cases new solar systems are born from these circumstellar disks.

In fact, our Earth and the other planets in our solar system seem to have been formed in such an environment, thanks to an abundance of heavier elements expelled from previous generations of stars in our Milky Way galaxy.

OUR COSMIC CONNECTIONS

To some people, stars may seem distant, remote, and even irrelevant. But the fact is they are vital to life. No stars, no supernova death explosions. No supernovas distributing stellar elements throughout the cosmos, no life.

Ray Jayawardhana, a professor of physics and astronomy, calls stars "molecular breweries." He described humanity's crucial connection to stars in a 2015 *New York Times* essay titled "Our Cosmic Selves": "The iron in our blood, the calcium in our bones and the oxygen we breathe are the physical remains—ashes, if you will—of stars that lived and died long ago."

Modern telescopes have helped us learn much about our cosmic connections, but the idea that our lives are interconnected with the cosmos has been around for quite a while.

Millennia ago, the author of Genesis wrote, "The LORD God formed a man from the dust of the ground" (Gen. 2:7).

In 1970, Joni Mitchell expressed similar sentiments in her hit song "Woodstock": "We are stardust / Billion year old carbon."

A few years later, Carl Sagan provided scientific support: "We are made of star stuff."

You may not *feel* connected to the stars, but you *are* connected whether you feel it or not. Ponder that the next time you walk under a brilliant starry sky.

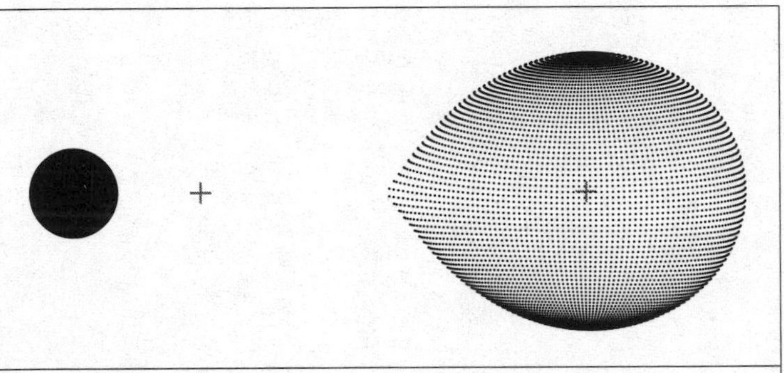

Power in pairs. Most of the stars in our universe are multiples, not singles like our Sun.

18

TWO ARE BETTER THAN ONE

OUR SUN IS SOLO, BUT MOST STARS ARE COMBO PACKAGES

In Jane Austen's day, the English elite met to eat at the Grand Pump Room, the most elegant dining spot in the town of Bath. During the 1770s, diners enjoyed entertainment by the Pump Room Band featuring multi-instrumentalist William Herschel and his singing sister Caroline.

Like many professional musicians, William worked on many projects to make ends meet. His main job was playing organ at the Octagon Chapel, an upscale church that Austen and other luminaries attended. He also composed church music, concertos, and symphonies, some of which are available today on CD.

Behind the scenes, William and Caroline pursued a more powerful passion: astronomical research. Neither had any formal training, but that didn't stop them from working together for decades as they searched the skies for undiscovered heavenly bodies.

William was a self-taught expert at making the big mirrors required for powerful new telescopes. In 1781, he used one of his new telescopes to make history and enlarge our understanding of our universe. Herschel had discovered the distant Uranus, the first new planet anyone had seen in more than two thousand years.

Suddenly, the world celebrated Bath's low-profile astronomers, and our cosmos was shown to be bigger and more changeable than we had ever imagined.

Their work received mixed reactions. Thomas Hardy was among contemporary thinkers who declared Herschel's more complex universe "frightful." But fellow composer Joseph Haydn, who visited Herschel at his observatory, welcomed these new discoveries as exciting reasons to praise our Creator. Haydn's visit with Herschel even helped inspire Haydn's famous oratorio, *The Creation*.

Herschel was a Lutheran but felt hesitant to offer theological interpretations of his astronomical research. "My feeble understanding is not capable of pushing so far into the secrets of the Almighty," he wrote.

But as he and Caroline looked deeper into space than anyone had done before, they sensed in the cosmos the same kinds of harmony and balance they experienced in music. "If one observes the whole Natural World as one, one finds everything in the most Beautiful Order," said William.

King George III named Herschel his court astronomer—a comfy position that allowed William to finally devote himself

Making music, scanning the heavens. William and Caroline Herschel were professional musicians, but it was their work as amateur astronomers that made the brother-sister duo famous.

to astronomy full-time. He and Caroline moved to a larger house close to Windsor Castle and began building even more powerful telescopes.

In time, this sibling duo became worldwide experts in an interesting area of astronomy that most people know nothing about, but that I absolutely love: double stars and multiple-star systems.

TWINKLING TWINS AND TRIOS

A surprising thing happened when Herschel trained one of his new telescopes on Polaris, also known as the North Star, or the Pole Star, because it appears to be positioned directly above our Earth's North Pole. Herschel could see that this famous star that navigators had relied on for centuries was actually *two* stars.

Before they finished, William and Caroline would discover hundreds of previously unknown double and multiple stars, demonstrating that many of the brilliant spots of light we see far, far away are not individual stars but multiples engaged in beautiful, complex stellar dances.

Today, most scientists agree that 60 percent to 80 percent of all the stars in the cosmos are in multiple-star systems. Our solo Sun is not the norm, but a solitary outlier.

We saw in the previous chapter that stars are created in clusters within interstellar clouds of gas and dust known as nebulae. More often than not, these star-making clouds give birth to twins, triplets, and other multi-sibling systems.

For decades I've studied the twins, known as binary stars. Most students tell me they've never heard of binaries, but I know millions of people have seen one. In the Star Wars movies, Luke Skywalker's planet of Tatooine is watched over by a pair of shining binaries. This makes for some beautiful double sunsets! Recently, NASA's *Kepler* space telescope found a pair of planets orbiting binary stars, showing that Tatooine's binaries aren't so far-fetched after all.

As with just about everything else in our amazing cosmos, no two binaries are the same. Some pairs are millions of miles apart, with the smaller (or companion) star taking a few decades or even a few centuries to orbit the larger (or primary) star. Most of my research focuses on close binaries, with orbits of only a few hours or days.

Some binaries get even closer than that. Over time, many multiple star systems coalesce into a single star that incorporates all the energy and mass of the original multiples. For all we know, our own Sun may have started out as a multiple.

DOUBLE THE INSIGHT

The life cycle of a star can stretch across billions of years. That's why no one has witnessed the entire process from start to finish. The best we can hope for is to watch the behavior of various star systems as they make their way through the stages of their stellar life cycles. After we observe how they interact at these moments in time, we can combine the moments to gain a better understanding of the entire stellar evolution process.

I've studied binaries ever since my undergraduate work in astronomy at Villanova University, and I've created a specialized computer program called *Binary Maker* that lets astronomers and students experiment with hundreds of different sample binary star systems. The program allows users to tweak various eccentric and asynchronous orbits to see how these impact the dual stars.

Astronomers love binaries because their subtle interplay helps us find out what they're made of. We can learn so much more from the ways multiples interact than we can from a solitary star. This interplay helps astronomers determine the mass and chemical composition of heavenly objects. If all stars were single, we wouldn't know the mass of most of the stars we've discovered over the centuries.

Did the Creator give us binaries so we could read his book of nature with greater clarity? I don't know, but I thank him for creating them anyway.

Binaries are also beautiful. I love it when I can observe a pair of close binaries doing their dance. When two stars orbit relatively close to each other, each can feel the tug and pull of its companion, as well as the force of its gravity. The closer the binaries are, the more these gravitational (or tidal) forces distort the stars into unusual shapes. Our solo Sun is relatively round and spherical, but binaries can become lopsided or teardrop-shaped or take on other strange and wonderful configurations.

What's most exciting is to watch close binaries finally come together and touch each other. The clouds of dust and gas flowing between these super-close pairs seem lost. They can't figure out which star they belong to. The gravitational pull is equal from both stars, and even the slightest nudge from one star can send these molecules fleeing into the hot embrace of the other.

The more stars participating in the dance, the more complicated the moves. You can see what I mean by looking at the photo of the quadruple star system on page 11 of the color section of this book.

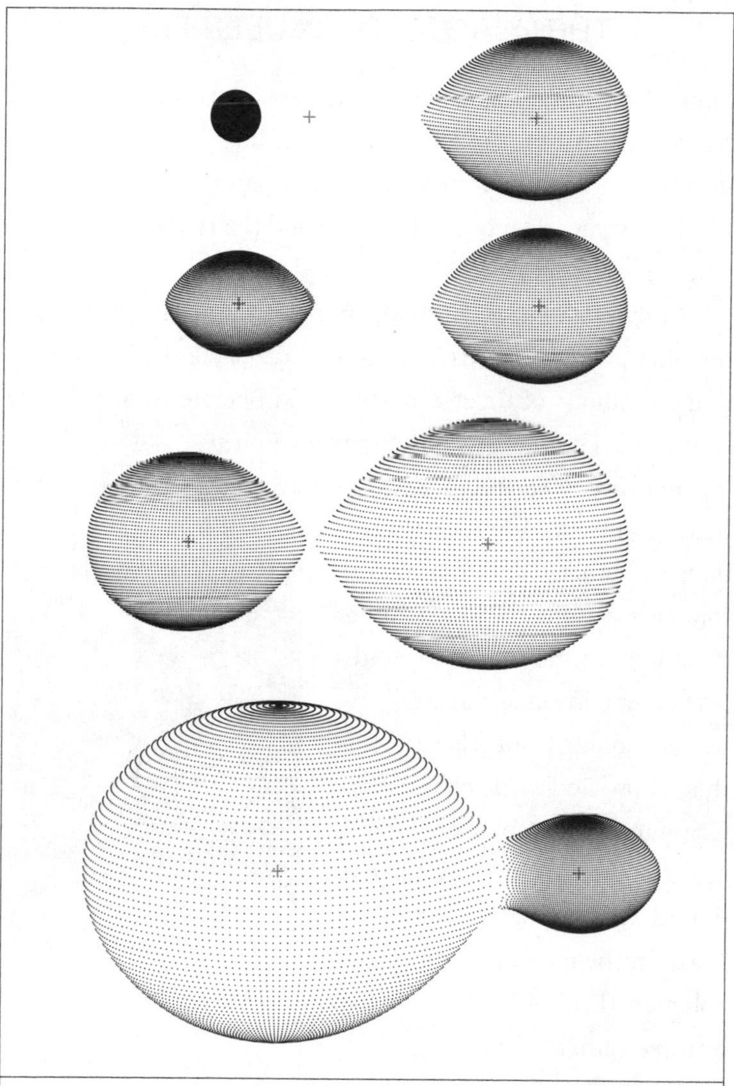

Mutual attraction. Close multiple-star systems impact the shape of the stars, while distant binaries cause less disturbance.

THE MAGIC OF MULTIPLES

Many Americans like their movie heroes strong, silent, and solitary. Whether it's John Wayne riding his trusty horse into the horizon or Tom Cruise eliminating bad guys in the *Mission: Impossible* movies, fans applaud the rugged individual who takes matters into his own hands.

Individualism is fine for movie characters, but it's a horrible way to organize a cosmos. God made the heavens so that its zillions of diverse parts would operate harmoniously together in community and complementarity.

In space, it seems that two—or even a few—are typically better than one. We witness this basic truth not only in the dance of binary stars but also in the connections between other common cosmic pairs: asteroids, galaxy systems, and pulsars.

Two are better. The beauty that poet (and my distant relative) Anne Bradstreet saw in a loving marriage is the same beauty I see in binary stars.

It shouldn't surprise us that this is how God made our cosmos. Community and complementarity are the same principles he embraced when he made you and me. "Two are better than one," wrote Solomon (Eccl. 4:9). "Where two or three gather in my name, there am I with them," said Jesus (Matt. 18:20).

A distant relative of mine praised pairs centuries ago in her most famous poem. Anne Bradstreet was born in England in 1612 and sailed to America on a ship with fellow Puritans. By the time she died at age sixty, she was being hailed as one of the New World's top poets, and her "To My Dear and Loving Husband" was one of her most popular poems.

I sometimes think of her opening line when I'm studying a pair of close binaries: "If ever two were one, then surely we."

Billionaire space race. Jeff Bezos (Amazon), Richard Branson (Virgin Atlantic), Larry Page and Eric Schmidt (Google), Elon Musk (PayPal and Tesla Motors), and moviemaker James Cameron (*Avatar* and *Titanic*) are at the forefront of a new commercial space race.

19

YOUR TICKET TO THE STARS

MEET THE BILLIONAIRES COMPETING TO BRING YOU SPACE 2.0

We humans are persistent creatures, as we have demonstrated by our tireless efforts to overcome gravity's powerful grasp. The ancient Chinese experimented with kites that could briefly lift a man up into the air. Many inventors leapt off cliffs or tall towers, futilely flapping strapped-on wings. Others tried gliders designed to ride the wind. Multiple bones and lives were sacrificed along the way.

Our first real liftoff came in 1783, when France's Montgolfier brothers sent test pilots into the sky over Paris in their huge new balloon. American ambassador Benjamin Franklin was among the tens of thousands of Parisians looking heavenward as pioneering "aeronauts" dared to take longer and higher flights.

For the next century, slow-moving and difficult-tomaneuver balloons, blimps, and zeppelins—all of them pumped full of dangerous, explosive gases—would remain our primary means of getting airborne.

We finally earned our wings in 1903, when Orville and Wilbur Wright, two brothers who ran a bicycle shop in Dayton, Ohio, successfully flew their homemade airplane at Kitty Hawk, North Carolina. The air race had begun, even though many remained skeptical about the practical benefits of flight.

"The public has greatly overestimated the possibilities of the airplane, imagining that in another generation they will be able to fly over to London in a day," said one pessimistic Harvard expert. "This is manifestly impossible."

Despite the doubters, commercial aviation took off. Now, slightly more than a century after the Wright brothers first flew, some eight million of us take to the skies every day. That's three billion commercial passengers each year.

Battling gravity. Balloons took to the sky over France beginning in 1783. In 1903, the Wright brothers flew their homemade airplane at Kitty Hawk.

HELLO, SPACE 2.0

It took us thousands of years to fly, but only a few decades more to reach space.

The first Earthling in orbit wasn't even human. Laika the Soviet space dog died on *Sputnik* 2 in 1957, instantly becoming our planet's first real-life space hero.

Since then fewer than six hundred humans have traveled to space, including more than two hundred who have visited the International Space Station. None of these people could have done it without expensive government missions costing multiple millions or billions of dollars.

That was Space 1.0. Are you ready for Space 2.0? Then say farewell to the days when governments dominated space exploration. NASA's current budget is half what it was in the go-go 1960s. Now, dozens of private companies plan to write the next chapter in the space race.

Some companies are already lining up to compete for the lucrative luxury travel market. Others want to mine asteroids, and thanks to the US Congress, they're entitled to mine all the celestial platinum they can find. It says so right there in the 2015 SPACE Act: "Any asteroid resources obtained in outer space are the property of the entity that obtained such resources, which shall be entitled to all property rights thereto, consistent with applicable provisions of Federal law."

Other companies plan to focus on setting up colonies on other planets, enabling at least a few of us to survive anticipated environmental degradation or catastrophe here on Earth.

We may be entering an exciting era in human history, one that makes the centuries-old exploits of European explorers look like walks in the park.

Will space travel become as common in the twenty-first century as air travel became in the twentieth? And will journeying through space be part of your future travel plans? It all depends on whether a new generation of entrepreneurs can fulfill their grand schemes.

THE BILLIONAIRE SPACE RACE

The Wright brothers funded years' worth of airplane experiments with profits from their Dayton bicycle shop. Costs of entry are much higher for those seeking to compete in the twenty-first-century space race.

For decades, big aerospace companies have created most of the rockets, astronaut modules, and scientific devices used in government space missions. Many of these companies remain major players, but the members of a new billionaires' club are crashing the party.

Jeff Bezos made his billions from Amazon, the humongous online retailer. The goal of Blue Origin, the aerospace company he founded in 2000, is to allow "anybody to go into space."

BLUE ORIGIN

Bezos has enthusiastically promoted space tourism since his high school valedictory speech, but it has been slow going for Blue Origin, which initially said it would start offering "aspiring astronauts" brief rides into space in 2010 (then in 2011, then in 2012, and most recently in 2018). The company's six-passenger *New Shepard* space vehicle passed its first test flight in 2015. If such good news continues, the company plans to sell tickets for rides that will carry passengers more than sixty miles into space, allowing them to experience weightlessness and take stunning photos of Earth through the vehicle's huge windows.

British billionaire Richard Branson made his money making and selling records (Virgin megastores sold albums by Culture Club and the Sex Pistols, who recorded for Virgin Records), running an airline (Virgin Atlantic), and pursuing other ventures (pay phones, comics).

Since unveiled in 2004, Virgin Galactic has sold more than 700 tickets for space travel at prices ranging from $200,000 to $250,000. Among the takers are celebrities Leonardo DiCaprio, Justin Bieber, and Angelina Jolie.

Flights were supposed to take off as early as 2009 from Spaceport America, the huge $200-million facility built with funding from the state of New Mexico. But Virgin Galactic has experienced numerous technological challenges and accidents. A 2014 test flight of Virgin's *SpaceShipTwo* ended in disaster when the vehicle crashed in the Mojave Desert, killing one of its test pilots. Branson pledged his company will work out the bugs and said he and his family still plan to travel on *SpaceShipTwo*'s maiden passenger flight.

Google billionaires Larry Page and Eric Schmidt are driving forces behind Planetary Resources, "the Asteroid Mining Company." Its website makes its mission clear: "Asteroids will play a key role in the development of a space economy and be the main driver in allowing humanity to become a flourishing multi-planetary species."

First, the company plans to launch a telescope into orbit so it can search out potentially profitable asteroids to mine. Once a promising chunk of rock is located, a robotic spacecraft will be dispatched to do the digging.

The current leader in the billionaire space race is Elon Musk. The South African who made his fortune from PayPal owns other forward-looking companies, including Tesla Motors (electric cars) and SolarCity (solar energy).

While some private space ventures have burned through piles of investor cash only to accomplish very little, Musk's SpaceX (or Space Exploration Technologies Corporation) is building an impressive track record ferrying supplies to the International Space Station. (NASA says paying SpaceX for transport services is cheaper than maintaining its own fleet of space shuttles.)

Colonizing Mars is Musk's long-term goal, but first the company must develop the reusable rocket engines, launch vehicles, and space capsules required to take humans to the

Martian surface and bring them safely back to Earth. SpaceX hopes its Mars Colonial Transporter will be operational by the 2020s.

Musk and Page (along with *Avatar* and *Titanic* moviemaker James Cameron) serve as trustees of the XPrize Foundation, which encourages "radical breakthroughs for the benefit of humanity" by staging competitions that challenge scientists to solve pressing problems. All you need to do if you want to win the $20 million Google Lunar XPrize is land a rover on the Moon, make it travel more than 500 meters, and transmit images and video back to Earth!

XPRIZE

PLANETARY POLICEMEN

With dozens of companies and countries jostling for their place in space, who's going to enforce law and order? That's the mission of the US Space Command, created in 1985 to police the skies.

One of Space Command's biggest worries is satellites. Right now, some one thousand artificial (or human-made) satellites orbit the Earth, monitoring our weather, processing our credit card payments, beaming us our favorite cable TV programs, feeding geographic information to our GPS systems, and conducting military reconnaissance.

Unfortunately, these satellites are "orbiting ducks." Not only are they defenseless and vulnerable to attack, they also emit electronic signals that make them very easy to locate.

AIR FORCE SPACE COMMAND

China has been testing anti-satellite weaponry since at least 2007, scoring one direct hit that instantly created thousands of new chunks of space debris.

"That is a bad thing for the United States," General John Hyten told the news program *60 Minutes*, "a bad thing for the planet." Military experts say the ability to destroy satellites would enable an enemy to "blind" America's eyes in the sky as a possible first step in an all-out attack. Without satellites, America's defense systems would be paralyzed, rendering them incapable of anything more than a World War II style of "industrial age warfare."

Among the high-tech tools Space Command is developing to protect vulnerable satellites are *new satellites*! These models may be able to monitor, damage, disable, or jam enemy satellites.

All of this makes me wonder about our future in space. Will everyone be able to agree on rules governing their conduct, or will the heavens become a new battleground for our earthly conflicts?

Will the commercialized space race create a Wild West–style frontier where anything goes? If so, will this require us to militarize space?

Or will saner minds create a more peaceful world up there than the world we've created down here?

So far, cooperative efforts to rein in humanity's astronomical aspirations have been weak. The Outer Space Treaty of 1967 prohibits nations from claiming ownership of heavenly bodies, but doesn't mention private companies or space-obsessed billionaires. The Moon Treaty of 1979 reaffirms the prohibition against ownership of celestial bodies, but the United States, Russia, and China never signed it.

EXIT EARTH

According to some entrepreneurs, space travel won't be a *choice* for future Earthlings. It will be a *necessity*.

What will you do if Earth's atmosphere grows increasingly toxic and our planet's farms lose the ability to feed our population? That's the challenge in the 2014 movie *Interstellar*. Knowing that something must be done, a former NASA pilot named Cooper (Matthew McConaughey) volunteers to attempt something new, taking off for another solar system in the hopes of finding a new home for the human race.

We've been hearing tales about human colonies in space for ages. In the 1950s, German-American scientist and engineer Wernher von Braun told *Collier's* magazine that establishing colonies on Mars was merely a matter of time. "Will man ever go to Mars?" asked von Braun. "I am sure he will—but it will be a century or more before he's ready."

Elon Musk hopes Martian colonies can happen sooner, and his Mars Colonial Transporter may just be the vehicle that makes it possible. "I think it is actually very important that we start making progress in extending life beyond Earth and we start making our own existence a multi-planetary one," says Musk.

SpaceX plans to take humans to Mars and back. Another company is trying to simplify things by offering *one-way* rides to the red planet. Mars One says it plans to begin establishing its human settlements on Mars in 2026, but the company is not developing any return vehicles—an approach that Neil deGrasse Tyson calls "Pilgrim style" because of its similarity to the one-way rides that brought European settlers to the New World. Many customers have already signed up, even though the company's website acknowledges the plan has significant risks, including cost overruns and loss of life. Something tells me these travelers won't be listening to David Bowie's 1969 hit "Space Oddity": "Can you hear me, Major Tom?"

Space 1.0 isn't extinct. NASA still plans to send more astronaunts into space. When the agency announced it was looking for a few good space men and women, some 18,300 people applied for the fourteen positions. Some of this new group may be the first to land on Mars.

But going to Mars is one thing. Reaching another solar system, as Cooper did in *Interstellar*, remains a distant dream. If scientists can't find a wormhole like Cooper discovered, tomorrow's long-distance astronauts will need a fountain of youth. The journey to the nearest solar system will take some seventeen thousand years.

EXTENDING OUR REACH

Every time we humans develop new modes of transportation, critical voices sound the alarm: The end of civilization draweth nigh.

Moralists warned that bicycles allowed young people to escape the scrutiny of parents; neglect important duties such as farmwork, homework, and prayer; and pursue unsupervised sexual shenanigans.

Far worse fears accompanied the emergence of the automobile, which some preachers called a big bed on wheels.

Are you ready for the warnings about space travel and exploration? One young-Earth creationist offered this fusillade: "The search for extraterrestrial life is really driven by man's rebellion against God in a desperate attempt to supposedly prove evolution!"

That's news to me!

A study in the journal *Space Policy* found that evangelicals—my beloved brothers and sisters in Christ—know less about space, care less about space exploration, and are less supportive of government space policies than other Americans.

I share some of my fellow Christians' concerns and uncertainties, but we can't stop the future. People are getting ready to head into space like never before. I would love to go myself, but I don't have an extra quarter-million dollars in my travel budget right now.

After millennia of looking and studying and wondering, humanity is about to enter a bold new chapter in our relationship with the cosmos. Let us pray for God's guidance as we venture forth, striving to be wise stewards of this unprecedented historical opportunity.

Big galactic drains? We can't see black holes, which gobble up everything nearby, including light. This artist's rendering shows a black hole near the Large Magellanic Cloud.

20

DARK STUFF

WE CAN'T SEE BLACK HOLES OR DARK MATTER, BUT WE KNOW THEY'RE OUT THERE

You are relaxing by your favorite pond when movement suddenly disturbs the calm. A series of ripples spreads across the water. You can see the circles on the mirrorlike surface, but their cause remains invisible. Did a fish come up to snag a bug and set things in motion?

Similar mysteries confront astronomers trying to figure out what is going on in our cosmos. Everywhere they look they detect ripples in space. Things move and pulse—mainly gravitational fields that indicate something big and powerful is going on—but the causes remain hidden in deep darkness that not even our best telescopes have been able to penetrate.

A century ago, Albert Einstein's theory of general relativity opened up a tantalizing theoretical possibility: if a celestial object has enough mass, it can drastically deform the contours of space and time, creating something called a *black hole*. So far, no one has been able to see one, only the ripples they cause in space. But right now a team of international scientists is trying to change that, using the largest telescope in history to boldly see where no human has ever seen before.

Black holes are far from the only dark, mysterious things out there waiting to be explored and understood. Astronomers are also on the lookout for *dark matter* particles, which are "believed to be ubiquitous but have yet to be observed," according to *National Geographic* writer Timothy Ferris: "Dark matter's aloofness makes it challenging for experimenters to catch even if, as some scientists estimate, dark matter particles are so commonplace that billions of them pass through every human being every second."

Others search for something called *dark energy*, which is supposedly everywhere but so far remains unseen, leading one scientist to call it the "most profound mystery in all of science." Ferris acknowledges that at present, the term *dark energy* is little more than a "general label for what we do not know about the large-scale properties of our universe."

Why should we even care about all these dark, mysterious entities? Because they may add up to 80 to 90 percent of everything that's out there. If so, we've seen only a narrow slice of our cosmos so far.

Our days of groping in the dark for all this dark stuff may soon be coming to an end as a new generation of scientists, a network of powerful telescopes, and emerging scientific disciplines like supersymmetric quantum physics help us extend our view into some of the most powerful yet most elusive forces in our cosmos.

No one is sure what we'll find when we figure out how to

adjust our goggles just right and discern these unseen things. But it's already crystal clear that space is not really *space*—if by space we mean vast expanses of empty nothingness. Instead, space seems to be full to the brim with all manner of mysterious objects and forces, many of which have apparently escaped our notice since the beginning of time.

When we are able to see into these mysteries, we will need to rewrite our astronomy textbooks once again!

MYSTERIOUS COSMIC CHARACTERS

Black holes—so far as we know—are celestial phenomena (possibly the remains of dying stars) that compress vast amounts of matter and energy into a very small space, unleashing gravitational forces so strong that they suck in everything nearby, including light waves, which explains why they're so black.

Some people describe black holes as giant vacuum cleaners that travel around sucking up planets and energy like so much space dust. It's probably more accurate to describe them as big, galactic bathtub drains. Open your bathtub drain and you can see the dirty water swirling around and going down. It's similar with black holes, except we never see the drain itself, only space stuff swirling around and disappearing. We can't tell where everything is going, nor do we know if the standard laws of physics apply within their mysterious boundaries.

We may not be able to see what happens inside black holes, but we have heard one singing. In 2003, NASA detected massive sound waves speeding away from a supermassive black hole in the Perseus cluster of galaxies. Translated into a musical note, these sound waves were the equivalent of a B flat that's fifty-seven octaves below middle C on the typical seven-octave piano. Humans can't actually *hear* these sound waves, which are a billion times lower than the sounds our ears can pick up, but our instruments can detect them, declaring the Perseus song the deepest note ever received from space.

"The Perseus sound waves are much more than just an interesting form of black hole acoustics," said researcher Steve Allen of the Institute of Astronomy in an article on NASA's *Science News* website. "These sound waves may be the key in figuring out how galaxy clusters, the largest structures in the Universe, grow."

If you're a sci-fi fan, you know a clear boundary exists between the visible and invisible parts of a black hole, called the event horizon. At this "point of no return," the black hole exerts such a powerful gravitational pull that nothing can escape it. If you and I were to cross over the event horizon, no one would be able to see us going or hear us screaming as we got stretched past the breaking point by these powerful forces.

Mysteries abound when we talk about black holes, but some of these mysteries may finally be solved over the next few years if a team of international scientists is successful.

SEEING THE UNSEEN WITH THE WORLD'S BIGGEST TELESCOPE

When God endowed his creatures on Earth with the gift of sight, he gave us two eyes, not one. That's because each eye sees the world from its own perspective, and only when these two perspectives are combined do we see a three-dimensional image of the world with visual depth. This process is called binocular vision.

More than one hundred scientists from twenty international institutions and government agencies have put this principle to work in creating the world's biggest telescope. But they're using more than two eyes to search the skies.

They started with existing telescopes in Arizona, California, Hawaii, Mexico, Chile, Spain, and Antarctica. Then they linked all of these telescopes together and synchronized

World's Biggest Sky Scanner. The Event Horizon Telescope links censors around the world to see deeper into space.

them using atomic clocks accurate within one second every 100 million years.

After all this linking and syncing, voila! You now have the world's biggest sky scanner, which scientists have named the Event Horizon Telescope. For the last few years, scientists have been training this gigantic eyeball on a fascinating location called Sagittarius A in the center of our Milky Way galaxy.

Ripples in space indicate that Sagittarius A—more than twenty-five thousand light-years distant—may be harboring a monster, a supermassive black hole. Frankly, we're not really sure what's out there. All we know is we've observed stars speedily orbiting a superdense but unseen host. By measuring the speed and trajectories of these fast-moving stars, we've been able to measure the invisible mass that *must* be there to cause these stars to orbit like they do. We estimate that the mass of this monster is a whopping four million times the mass of our Sun!

In order to see to the event horizon and peer deeper into the mysterious workings of Sagittarius A, scientists tune their radio telescopes to shorter wavelengths to penetrate the haze. They hope these shorter radio waves, combined with the added resolution achieved by linking various telescopes around the world into one massive supertelescope, will enable them to cut through the cosmic clutter for the first time.

If successful, we will be treated to sights no human eyes have ever seen. "We can see a black hole eat in real time," project veteran Sheperd Doeleman told *New York Times* science writer Dennis Overbye in his fascinating article, "Hunt for the Star Eaters."

LET THERE BE LIGHT (JUST NOT TOO MUCH!)

When God said, "Let there be light," the illumination appeared immediately. The human race required thousands of years to create the kinds of artificial light we all depend on today. It has been a long, smoky journey from candles to whale blubber to gas to electricity.

Unfortunately, we now create so much artificial light that it blots out the beauties of the heavens. "For many people, light pollution is now so pervasive that it obliterates any chance they may have to observe the night sky," writes Jane Brox in her book *Brilliant: The Evolution of Artificial Light*.

Some two-thirds of our planet's population suffers significant light pollution, and about a fifth of us can't even see the Milky Way. Our nights are increasingly illumined by "sky glow," a condition resulting from our planet's electric lighting being reflected back to Earth by our atmosphere.

Sky glow has been especially hard on astronomers, gradually surrounding and drowning out once-powerful astronomical observatories in Los Angeles, Chicago, and Toronto.

"Those of us who live in or near cities might live and die without ever seeing things that were as familiar to our great grandparents as the sun and moon," writes a grieving Chet Raymo in *An Intimate Look at the Night Sky*.

The good news: light pollution is easier to reverse than other forms of pollution. As human-made light encroaches on the universe's darkness, we can do two things to help resurrect the darkness.

Bye, bye nighttime sky! "Sky glow" and other forms of human-made light-pollution darken the heavens for two-thirds of the Earth's population.

First, we need to put a lid on it. We unintentionally create much light pollution by poorly designing lights that direct as much brightness up into the sky as they send down to the ground. Using smarter light fixtures, we can illuminate the areas we want to without lighting up everything else in sight.

Second, we should cherish the remaining darkness while we can. Darkness, like silence, is a valuable but dwindling resource here on busy planet Earth. I'm not an alarmist, but I am deeply concerned.

There's no better time than the present to look to the heavens, because tomorrow may be too late for many of us! And if you really want to see the splendor and beauty of the cosmos our Creator designed, head to one of the world's dozens of Dark Sky Parks (there are more than twenty in the United States), where you will be able to see the heavens in all their brilliant glory.

EMBRACING THE MYSTERY

When confronted with complex scientific mysteries, astronomers try to figure things out. That's what science is all about: studying the book of Creation. But for now, many chapters of this book seem closed to us. Space's deepest mysteries remain dark to us for now.

We face many spiritual mysteries too. Jesus told his disciples, "You do not know on what day your Lord will come," and "The Son of Man will come at an hour when you do not expect him" (Matt. 24:42, 44).

Here Jesus seems to suggest that we focus on living our lives in a continual state of readiness for his promised return, not on figuring out dates and clear signs.

Both astronomers and followers of Jesus may wish everything could be black and white, but as we wander through gray uncertainties, let's appreciate God's mysteries for what they are, marveling at the infinite wisdom of God.

A universe of galaxies. When Edwin Hubble studied nebulae, he discovered that these clouds were galaxies.

21

GALAXIES, SPACE, AND TIME

ONCE EDWIN HUBBLE'S CLOUDS BECAME GALAXIES, EVERYTHING WAS SUDDENLY MUCH BIGGER AND OLDER

The cloudy wisps of space stuff always floated around up there in the heavens, but nobody knew what they were or where they came from.

Ancient Greeks blamed Heracles (Hercules to the Romans), the god of strength, sports, and heroic deeds. As the infant Heracles suckled at the breast of the goddess Hera, she pushed him away and her spurting milk created the Milky Way (in Greek, *kyklos galatikos* means "circle milky," the origin of our word *galaxy*).

Aristotle offered a more mundane explanation for these heavenly clouds: they were gaseous excretions that had risen up from Earth.

Only when Galileo pointed his powerful telescope at

these nebulous formations did they give up their secrets, as he excitedly explained in his 1610 book, *The Starry Messenger*: "I have observed the essence or substance of the MILKY WAY circle . . . the GALAXY is nothing else but a mass of innumerable stars planted together in clusters. Upon whatever part of it you direct the telescope straightway a vast crowd of stars presents itself to view; many of them are tolerably large and extremely bright, but the number of small ones is quite beyond determination."

As clouds suddenly became stars, the heavens suddenly were much bigger and busier than anyone had ever imagined.

Centuries after Galileo, most people still assumed the Milky Way contained everything that existed. This assumption was tested in the 1920s when a great debate broke out over the size of the universe.

Some astronomers supported the island universe theory ("Our Milky Way is merely one of many galaxies spread throughout the universe"), while others argued for the nebular hypothesis ("Our Milky Way is the entire universe and contains everything there is"). After years of heated back-and-forth, the scientific community remained divided. Who could settle the great debate?

MORE THAN MEETS THE EYE

Edwin Hubble fell in love with astronomy as a child, but his father wanted him to be a lawyer. The dutiful son obeyed, studying law until his father died. Then Hubble returned to his first love, making up for lost time during three decades of work at Mount Wilson Observatory near Los Angeles.

Using Mount Wilson's new 100-inch-diameter telescope—then the world's largest—Hubble studied cloudy wisps of space stuff farther out in space. Were these nebulae made up of Milky Way stars that Galileo and others had not been able to see, or were they something completely different?

After years of studying the Great Andromeda Nebula, Hubble published his findings: Andromeda was its very own galaxy, and there were plenty more galaxies lurking out there.

The news appeared in a brief article in the November 23, 1924, edition of the *New York Times*. "The results are striking,"

Man and machine. Edwin Hubble used Mount Wilson's powerful telescope to scan the skies for galaxies.

said the article. "Spiral nebulae, which appear in the heavens as swirling clouds, are in reality distant stellar systems, or 'island universes.'"

Hubble transformed our understanding of the universe even more profoundly than Galileo had done. Galileo looked at the clouds and found innumerable stars. Centuries later Hubble looked at clouds much farther away and found galaxies.

Now the Milky Way wasn't everything. Our galaxy was just one among multitudes. Earth was no longer at the center of things, but in a remote galactic suburb of an unbelievably vast metropolis. Out there was an immense cosmos. The era of cosmology and extragalactic astronomy had begun.

But Hubble was just getting started. Even though he began his astronomy career late in life and his work was interrupted by years of volunteer service in World Wars I and II, he would soon announce another game-changing discovery: the many galaxies he had discovered were speeding away from us and from each other.

Old notions of a small, static universe now seemed quaint. Our gigantic universe was growing still larger. As astrophysicist Stephen Hawking wrote in *A Brief History of Time*, Hubble's "discovery that the Universe is expanding was one of the great intellectual revolutions of the 20th century."

BIGGER THAN BIG

Even card-carrying astronomers like me struggle to comprehend the baffling bigness of our cosmos.

The sunlight you see outside your window right now took

8.3 minutes to get here, traveling 186,000 miles a second over a distance of 93 million miles. The next closest star, Alpha Centauri, is so far away (about 25 trillion miles) that its light needs 4.3 years to reach us. (That means Alpha Centauri is 4.3 light-years away.)

Right now roving telescopes are reaching out and conducting close-up examinations of celestial objects billions of light-years away. A writer for *Wired* magazine struggled to put cosmic bigness into human perspective:

"To try imagining how big, place a penny down in front of you. If our Sun were the size of that penny, the nearest star, Alpha Centauri, would be 350 miles away. . . . At this scale, the Milky Way galaxy would be 7.5 million miles across."

Now try to imagine that penny expanding to the size of our Sun, and our Milky Way swimming among billions of other galaxies. These mind-blowing concepts give me a new appreciation for the questions God asked Job.

> Who marked off its dimensions? Surely you know!
> Who stretched a measuring line across it? . . .
> while the morning stars sang together
> and all the angels shouted for joy?
> —Job 38:5, 7

FARTHER THAN FAR

So how do astronomers actually figure out how far we are from all these distant, hazy blobs? Determining distances has always been a challenge. Over the centuries astronomers have created a kind of distance "ladder" that builds on the "rungs" or methods that earlier scientists developed. Here are three of the main methods we use.

Rung 1: The Reach of Radar

Radar beams are a foundational or "bottommost rung" method that astronomers have used to measure distances. Because radar beams are radio signals that travel at the speed of light, we can bounce these beams off of planets, see how long it takes for them to travel back to us, and precisely calculate the distance covered.

For example, scientists used radar to determine that the distance between the Earth and the Sun averages out to 93 million miles. Astronomers call this distance the *astronomical unit* (AU), and we use the AU as a yardstick to measure vast distances in space.

If we didn't know our distance from the Sun, we would be unable to accurately measure the distances to the nearest stars, which we do with the help of the next rung of the ladder, stellar parallax.

Rung 2: The Power of Parallax

Stargazers have used stellar parallax to measure distances since 1839. The process may sound complicated, but it's actually fairly straightforward. In fact, you rely on this method to determine distances in your daily life. If you can eat dinner without stabbing your face with your fork, you have already mastered parallax. Let's see how it works.

Hold one of your fingers about 12 inches in front of your

nose. Now look at your finger with only your left eye, and then only your right eye. See how your finger appears to jump back and forth? Now bring your finger in closer and try looking again. See how your finger appears to jump back and forth even more? The distance of these jumps is called the parallax angle.

Astronomers use parallax to precisely measure relatively close stars, which appear to shift positions in the sky as the Earth orbits the Sun.

If you could hold your finger a mile in front of your nose, the parallax angle would be much smaller. It shrinks even more if you're trying to examine stars trillions of miles away. That explains why the parallax method doesn't work so well with distant stars.

One solution is to send up a satellite to gain a better perspective far above the Earth's soupy, smudgy atmosphere. The European Space Agency launched *GAIA* in 2013, and today this supersophisticated satellite is measuring the parallaxes of a billion stars in our Milky Way. That may sound like a lot of stars, but it's actually less than 1 percent of the stars in our galaxy. Still, this fantastic set of measurements will give us the most complete 3D map yet of many stars.

Rung 3: Flashes of Distant Light

Our Creator chose to spice up space by sprinkling around stars that brighten and dim like lights on a Christmas tree. Each pulsating Cepheid star has its own unique *period* (some

God's Christmas lights. The pulsations of Cepheid variables help astronomers accurately estimate stellar distances.

blink slowly, others rapidly) and *luminosity* (some go from very dim to very bright; others vary less dramatically).

God made it so the biggest, brightest stars pulse the slowest, and the smallest, faintest ones pulse the fastest. (That pattern mirrors heartbeats in animals. While elephant hearts beat around 30 times per minute, hummingbird hearts beat some 900 times per minute!)

The first Cepheid variable was discovered in 1754, but not until 1911 did Henrietta Leavitt of Harvard Observatory help us unlock the puzzle of these stars. She found that the stars' period-luminosity relationship, when properly calibrated, allows astronomers to infer the distance to a Cepheid by measuring its pulsation period, which can be observed across great distances. Studying Cepheids has helped us get a better handle on the size of our Milky Way and calculate distances to remote galaxies millions of light-years away.

BIGGER BY THE MILLISECOND

You are stopped at a traffic light as a police car speeds by, siren blaring, in pursuit of a bad guy. You can hear the siren's pitch rise as the car approaches and fall as it speeds into the distance. You've just experienced the Doppler effect.

The Doppler effect that helps coaches determine the speed of a pitcher's fastball also helps traffic cops determine the speed of your car. A speed gun sends out radar waves of a known frequency. These waves bounce off a baseball, which reflects a different frequency depending on its speed. The speed gun calculates the difference between the two frequencies to determine the speed of the ball.

The Doppler effect. Sound and light travel in waves, which can be measured with radar waves. In space, the Doppler effect reveals the expansion of the universe.

Light travels in waves, too, and its behavior mirrors the behavior of sound waves coming from a police siren. The color of light shifts to a shorter wavelength (becoming bluer) when a light source is approaching us, and the color shifts to a longer wavelength (becoming redder) when the light source moves away from us.

Edwin Hubble put light's Doppler effect to work as no one had before, carefully studying nearby galaxies to measure their velocities based on the spectra of light they emitted. Everywhere he looked he saw *redshifts*. In 1929 he concluded these galaxies seemed to be racing away from us. I just hope it's not something we said!

You can see a miniature version of what Hubble saw by baking a loaf of raisin bread in your oven. As the loaf expands, all the raisins move farther away from each other.

Hubble's claim that the universe is expanding shocked many but did not surprise Albert Einstein. Einstein's 1913 theory of general relativity had predicted an expanding universe. But this prediction contradicted the widely held "steady state" theories that claimed the universe had no beginning. So Einstein backtracked, adding in a theoretical fudge factor he called the "cosmological constant," a decision he later called "the greatest blunder" of his life.

Astronomical theory will continue to change as new discoveries both challenge old concepts and suggest new ideas about how the cosmos works. "We live in a changing universe," said acclaimed science writer Timothy Ferris in his 1997 book, *The Whole Shebang: A State-of-the-Universe(s) Report*, "and few things are changing faster than our conception of it."

MYSTERIES OF SPACE AND TIME

NASA and the European Space Agency jointly launched the orbiting Hubble Space Telescope in 1990 to take a closer look at some of the galaxies Edwin Hubble had discovered. One of the beauties this mission photographed (or "imaged") is called Arp 237, featured on the cover of this book.

Arp 237 is made up of two galaxies (UGC 1810 and UGC 1813) crashing into each other. Such galactic collisions are huge, violent, and beautiful. They occur fairly frequently but develop very, very slowly. Whenever two galaxies weave themselves together, their intergalactic dances can play out over many millions or billions of years.

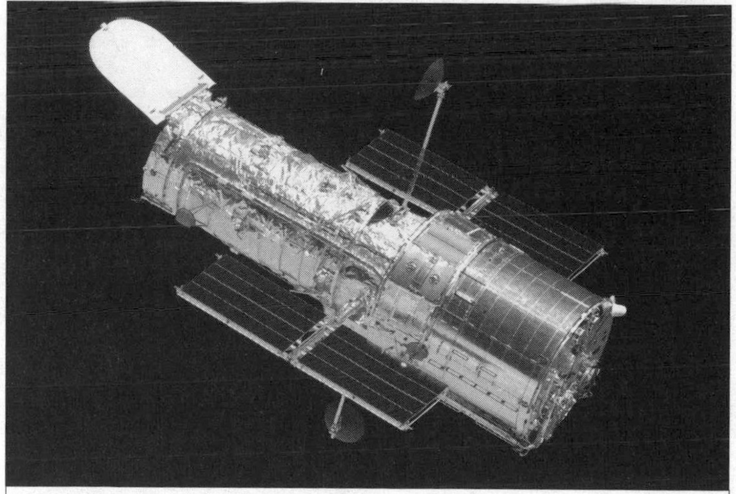

Viewing space and time. The Hubble Space Telescope is finding more galaxies in space. How many more galaxies exist out there?

All this is happening some 300 million light-years away. Or perhaps I should say it *was* happening some 300 million years ago. We have no idea what's happening in Arp 237 today because today's light will take another 300 million years to reach us.

Which leads us to the final mystery of this chapter: time. Telescopes help us see across space while also taking us back in time.

Quasars—the brightest and most distant objects in the universe—illustrate this space/time mystery. The first quasars (the name means "quasi-stellar radio sources") were discovered in the 1950s, but it took decades and repeated observations with Hubble to figure out that these superbright lights are actually galaxies in the process of being born. We are able to see these birth pangs because quasars are one hundred times brighter than our own Milky Way.

If we were able to perform a magical switcheroo, instantaneously traveling to one of these quasars so we could look back in our direction, we would see the exact same thing in reverse. From our new vantage point way out there, we would look back to see a distant quasar—our Milky Way—being born.

No one ever sees any nearby quasars, which means there are no young quasars. All of them seem to have originated in the earliest phases of our universe's birth, back when things were totally different. Apparently the conditions necessary for galaxies to be born are long gone.

Hubble recently captured the most distant galaxy ever identified. GN-z11 is 13.4 billion light years away, meaning this galaxy was born only 400 million years after the cosmos was created.

All kinds of other space stuff may be out there somewhere, but we don't know about it because there hasn't yet been enough time for its light to reach us. As Timothy Ferris explains in *The Whole Shebang*, we'll need to wait and see:

"In actuality, we can see only those galaxies that lie close enough to us for their light to have reached us at the present time: These galaxies, the ones at 'lookback times' less than the age of the universe, inhabit the observable universe. In all feasible expanding universe models, the observable universe is but a fraction of the whole."

Discoveries we're making today will likely increase the size and age of our cosmos even more. It's enough to make a person feel small. Does the vastness of space and time ever make you feel like a tiny speck in an endless sea? Then join David in embracing a bit of cosmic humility:

> Show me, LORD, my life's end
> and the number of my days;
> let me know how fleeting my life is.
> You have made my days a mere handbreadth;
> the span of my years is as nothing
> before you.
>
> —PSALM 39:4–5

When geniuses meet. Albert Einstein originally rejected Georges Lemaître's theory of cosmic origins before accepting it and calling it "beautiful."

22

THE GOD BEHIND THE BIGGEST BANG

HOW A PRIEST'S CONTROVERSIAL THEORY BECAME THE CONSENSUS ON COSMIC ORIGINS

Who hasn't heard of *The Big Bang Theory*? Of course, I'm talking about the TV sitcom about Caltech theoretical physicist Sheldon Cooper and his equally geeky friends who work in aerospace and astrophysics.

The popular show—which features cameo appearances from celebrities of both science (Stephen Hawking) and sci-fi (*Star Trek*'s Leonard Nimoy)—finds humor in Sheldon's many idiosyncrasies. A former child prodigy who graduated from college at age fourteen, Sheldon has the IQ of a genius but the emotional intelligence of a third grader.

Less successful are attempts to wring laughs from the cliché "war" between faith and science. Sheldon's mother, Mary, is a card-carrying evangelical Christian young Earther who uses old-school interpretations of the Bible to dismiss her son's scientific pursuits. The now-atheistic Sheldon returns the favor, dismissing his mother's beliefs as "pre-Enlightenment mythology."

I have an important announcement for Sheldon and Mary. The war is over. As one news site put it: "Atheists, devout Christians, you might want to sit down for this: The Big Bang theory was first proposed by a Roman Catholic priest."

That priest, Father Georges Lemaître, pursued science in the service of God and humanity, emerging as one of the most intriguing scientific thinkers in twentieth-century cosmology and theology. He saw scientific inquiry as a holy calling, as he told the *New York Times*:

"Here we have this wonderful, this incessantly interesting and exciting universe. When we try to learn more about it, learn how it began and how it is put together, to find what it is all about, as you say in America, what are we doing? Only seeking the truth. And is not truth seeking a service to God?"

In this chapter of our journey, I will introduce you to this fascinating man, who follows in the footsteps of earlier Christian astronomers like Kepler and Galileo. I will also try to help you grasp his complex and confounding theory, which was initially rejected as preposterous by many but now reigns as the scientific consensus on cosmic origins.

THE PRIEST AND HIS "COSMIC EGG"

Georges Lemaître was ordained a Catholic priest in his native Belgium in 1923, but he would not serve a local parish, conduct weekly Mass, or hear people's confessions. His parish would be the world of science, his calling to serve God and humanity by enlarging our understanding of our cosmos.

Four years later he published his game-changing theory: "a homogeneous Universe of constant mass and growing radius accounting for the radial velocity of extragalactic nebulae." But few people read the *Annals of the Scientific Society of Brussels*.

Figuring it out. Einstein called theoretical astronomer Georges Lemaître's "Big Bang" theory "beautiful."

Albert Einstein read the priest's paper but was not impressed, calling Lemaître's physics "abominable." Only after Edwin Hubble provided astronomical evidence that our universe was expanding did Einstein change his tune and praise Lemaître's work. "Very beautiful," he said, "very beautiful indeed."

Nonscientists heard about Lemaître's ideas after the *New York Times*' brief 1931 article: "Lemaître Suggests One, Single, Great Atom, Embracing All Energy, Started the Universe."

"We could conceive the beginning of the universe in the form of a unique atom, the atomic weight of which is the total mass of the universe," explained Lemaître, who also called his unique atom "the Cosmic Egg exploding at the moment of the creation."

The question Lemaître tried to settle was logical and straightforward: If we hit the rewind button on the universe and play the program back to the beginning, what will we see? His theory provided a simple but counterintuitive answer: Our astoundingly vast universe that has been expanding for billions and billions of years began its existence as one incredibly small and amazingly compact atom.

People struggled to describe the theory, and over the years the *Times* used a variety of terms: the explosion theory, the evolutionary theory, the Lemaître theory, the Initial Explosion, or "that theoretical bursting start of the expanding universe 10 billion years ago."

Finally, the English cosmologist Fred Hoyle, a vehement critic, provided the name that stuck. "Big Bang" fits a theory that claims *everything* that now exists—matter and radiation alike—originally existed in one single point of enormously high temperature and density, until it suddenly exploded, instantly giving birth to mass, energy, space, and time.

Before this event there was no space, no time, no energy, no anything; only a mysterious "formless and empty" state (Gen. 1:2).

Lemaître called this explosive episode a *singularity*, a once-in-eternity event that has no precedent or parallel. The bang happened before time or laws of physics existed; therefore, no theories currently exist to help us penetrate the singularity's mysteries.

Such ideas were radical and revolutionary, requiring

decades to catch on. Even now, my astronomy students say the theory ties their brains in knots. I sympathize. Astrophysics specializes in esoteric theories about the behavior of quarks, hadrons, bosons, and other quirky, infinitesimally small particles that seem to be everywhere.

But these ideas weren't radical enough to prevent the Catholic Church from embracing them.

THEOLOGY AND SCIENTIFIC THEORY

Four centuries after the Catholic Church condemned Galileo as a heretic for upsetting the traditional astronomical apple cart, Pope Pius XII praised Lemaître's revolutionary theory, claiming, "Modern science has confirmed . . . the world came forth from the hands of the creator."

The pope deeply regretted the whole Galileo affair and worked to open the church to fresh winds of scientific discovery. Lemaître certainly appreciated the pope's warm embrace, but he was concerned the pontiff was confusing matters.

Yes, the Big Bang theory opened the door to the possibility of a creator. But no, the church should not adopt any one particular scientific explanation of cosmic origins, even if it is a faith-friendly Big Bang theory authored by a Catholic priest.

"God cannot be reduced to the role of a scientific hypothesis," said Lemaître.

Just as Kepler and Galileo had used different approaches to study God's two books—nature and revelation—Lemaître wanted to distinguish between *natural truth* (which responds

The pope's cosmologist. Scientist Georges Lemaître served the Catholic Church and its leader, Pope Pius XII.

to "the capacities of our intelligent nature") and *supernatural truth* (which "never could have been reached by ourselves, and it was necessary that it would come down to us").

Ultimately, both types of truth owe their existence "to One Who has said: 'I am the Truth,' One Who gave us the mind to understand him and to recognize a glimpse of his glory in our universe which he has so wonderfully adjusted to the mental power with which he has endowed us," wrote Lemaître in his 1927 paper.

Scientific knowledge is limited. Science isn't designed to answer theological questions, and scientists shouldn't weigh in on theological issues like creation. "The question if it was really a beginning or rather a creation, something started from nothing, is a philosophical question which cannot be settled by physical or astronomical considerations," said Lemaître.

The priest would continue to advise bishops and popes until his death in 1966, successfully persuading Pope Pius to stop claiming the Big Bang theory "proved" divine creation.

EVIDENCE AROUND US AND IN US

Shortly before he died, Lemaître was finally able to see his theory confirmed by observational verification.

Scientists had long said that if the Big Bang really happened there should be evidence of the explosion throughout the cosmos. In 1965 they finally found that evidence—cosmic microwave background radiation—quite by accident, while trying to solve an unrelated problem.

Fifty years ago we knew nothing about microwaves. Today we know they're everywhere. We harness these waves of electromagnetic radiation to transmit our cell phone calls and TV signals, determine how fast automobiles or baseballs are traveling, and warm leftovers in our microwave ovens.

Microwaves don't affect the plastic and glass containers that hold your leftovers, but they stimulate atomic vibrations in the water in your food. The violent friction of these highly agitated water molecules is what heats your potatoes and pasta.

Arno Penzias and Robert Wilson, two scientists working at Bell Telephone Laboratories in New Jersey, stumbled across microwaves when trying to figure out why the sensitive new radio receiver they were designing always picked up so much static from every possible direction.

After ruling out pigeon droppings and other potential culprits, the scientists concluded the microwave radiation they were picking up had originated with the Big Bang. Penzias and Wilson won the 1978 Nobel Prize in Physics for their discovery. Suddenly, Lemaître's theory was more than an esoteric idea: it was an observable phenomenon.

A GOD WHO'S BIGGER THAN BIG

Father Georges Lemaître was a man of science and a man of faith, and he saw no conflict between these two ways of knowing. And while only one way of knowing is essential for salvation, the other way of knowing provides powerful blessings for life here on Earth:

"Does the Church need Science? Certainly not. The Cross and the Gospel are enough. However, nothing that is human can be foreign to the Christian. How could the Church not be interested in the most noble of all strictly human occupations, namely the search for truth?"

I wish all Christians shared Lemaître's commitment to learning from both of God's books: revelation and nature. But there are many believers who, like *The Big Bang Theory*'s Mary, close their minds, unintentionally limiting their understanding of our Creator.

It's a problem British clergyman and Bible scholar J. B. Phillips pointed out more than half a century ago.

"The trouble with many people today is that they have not found a God big enough for modern needs," wrote Phillips in his 1961 book, *Your God Is Too Small*.

"While their experience of life has grown in a score of directions, and their mental horizons have been expanded to the point of bewilderment by world events and by scientific discoveries, their ideas of God have remained largely static."

I pray for believers who try to navigate the challenges of modern life with an outdated, Sunday school comprehension of science. That's why I challenge my students to learn as much science as they can rather than fearfully hiding from scientific discovery.

Phillips warned that having a closed mind can lead to a weak, vulnerable faith:

"It is obviously impossible for an adult to worship the conception of God that exists in the mind of a child of Sunday-school age, unless he is prepared to deny his own experience of life. If, by great effort of will, he does do this he will always be secretly afraid lest some new truth may expose the juvenility of his faith. And it will always be by such an effort that he either worships or serves a God who is really too small to command his adult loyalty and cooperation."

The God behind the Big Bang is anything but small. I still struggle to understand the implications of Lemaître's revolutionary theory, but these struggles have only deepened my faith, enlarged my capacity for awe and wonder, and intensified my praise of our all-powerful Creator.

Bad times coming. Albrecht Durer's portrayal of the four horsemen of the Apocalypse hints at horrors to come.

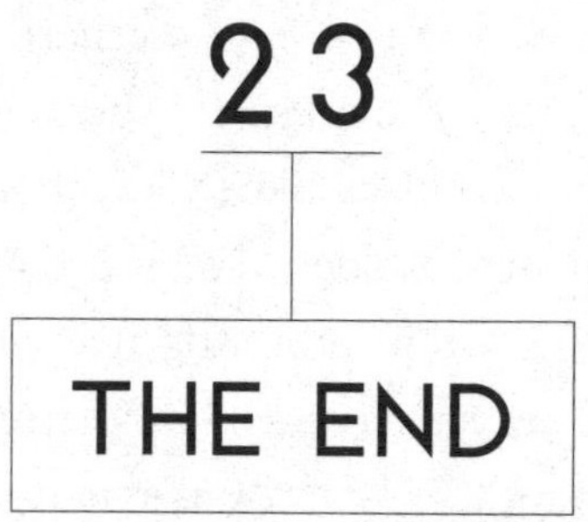

23

THE END

BANG, WHIMPER, CRUNCH, CHILL, OR NEW JERUSALEM?

How do you think the world will end? One online opinion survey found that people's answers to that question often reflect their political affiliations. Among Republicans, nuclear war was seen as the most likely cause of the apocalypse. Among Democrats, climate change ranked as the most likely cause.

Both of these end-time scenarios are compatible with some of the vibrant, nonpartisan pictures Scripture paints. Isaiah uses powerful visual imagery and striking metaphorical language to prophesy horrible things for our Goldilocks world:

> The earth reels like a drunkard,
> it sways like a hut in the wind . . .
> The moon will be dismayed,
> the sun ashamed . . .
>
> —Isaiah 24:20, 23

Revelation's imagery is even more harrowing, as we see after an angel opens the sixth seal: "There was a great earthquake. The sun turned black like sackcloth made of goat hair, the whole moon turned blood red, and the stars in the sky fell to earth, as figs drop from a fig tree when shaken by a strong wind. The heavens receded like a scroll being rolled up, and every mountain and island was removed from its place" (Rev. 6:12–14).

Other angels of doom blow trumpets that usher in destructive astronomical events. After one trumpet is blown, "something like a huge mountain, all ablaze, was thrown into the sea." After another trumpet sounds, "a great star, blazing like a torch, fell from the sky on a third of the rivers and on the springs of water." Following the next trumpet, "a third of the sun was struck, a third of the moon, and a third of the stars, so that a third of them turned dark" (Rev. 8:8, 10, 12).

Christian astronomers ponder how these end-time scenarios will play out on Earth and in the heavens above. Could the huge mountain that was thrown into the sea be a massive asteroid? Could the great blazing star that fell from the sky be a once-distant Sun that may strike the Earth as our Milky Way collides with a neighboring galaxy?

Will God's judgment fall only on our sinful planet, or will our solar system also be destroyed? Or do biblical prophecies speak of a much broader galactic—or even cosmic—destruction to come?

Peter says "the heavens" will be destroyed by fire, but he doesn't explain how far that destruction will reach.

Meanwhile, Peter offers encouragement, for in God's grand scheme of things, the end is not really the end: "Since everything will be destroyed in this way, what kind of people ought you to be? You ought to live holy and godly lives as you look forward to the day of God and speed its coming. That day will bring about the destruction of the heavens by fire, and the elements will melt in the heat. But in keeping with his promise we are looking forward to a new heaven and a new earth, where righteousness dwells" (2 Peter 3:11–13).

I have no idea how God is going to end things, so we can add this question to our long list of mysteries that are beyond our comprehension. But I do know this. He promises to establish his people in "a new heaven and a new earth, where righteousness dwells" (2 Peter 3:13). This promise fills me with tremendous hope.

As a Christian, I know that Jesus could return any minute. As an astronomer, I can see how our universe could continue on for many billions or even trillions of years.

Now, as we near the end of our journey through space, I want to take you on a brief tour of some potential end-time scenarios scientists have sketched out for our cosmos. Let's start with our Sun and travel outward from there.

WHEN THE SUN TURNS BLACK

Each star has a life cycle, including our Sun, the current ruler of our solar system. But this bright, shining star is getting along in years and is already experiencing its share of senior moments.

The Sun is a big furnace that runs on hydrogen fuel. In time that fuel will run out, setting in motion a process that astronomers have witnessed taking place on thousands of other stars. As fuel starts to run low, the Sun will burn up any available energy at an even faster rate as it gradually grows much hotter and bigger.

Eventually the Sun will expand into a red giant some 250 times its current size. Then, its energy mostly spent, it will blow off its weakened atmosphere into an expanding shell called a planetary nebula. The super-dense, Earth-sized, burned-out remnant of the Sun's core will become what we call a white dwarf. After even more cooling, it will become a black dwarf that emits no light or radiant energy.

The Sun's final act is a death-and-resurrection show. What little remains of our Brother Sun will fall apart and be given up into space, where it will float around until summoned to join in assembling a brand-new star.

We don't need to worry yet. None of this is going to happen next Tuesday. The Sun should probably have enough hydrogen fuel to sustain it for another billion years before it begins to go seriously senile and threaten Earth's biosphere.

PLANETS IN PERIL

The Sun's death spiral will impact the whole solar system. Mercury and Venus will be the first to go, incinerated and gobbled up by the much bigger, hotter Sun.

Then, as the Sun shrinks and the power of its gravitational pull weakens, the orbits of planets and moons will expand and

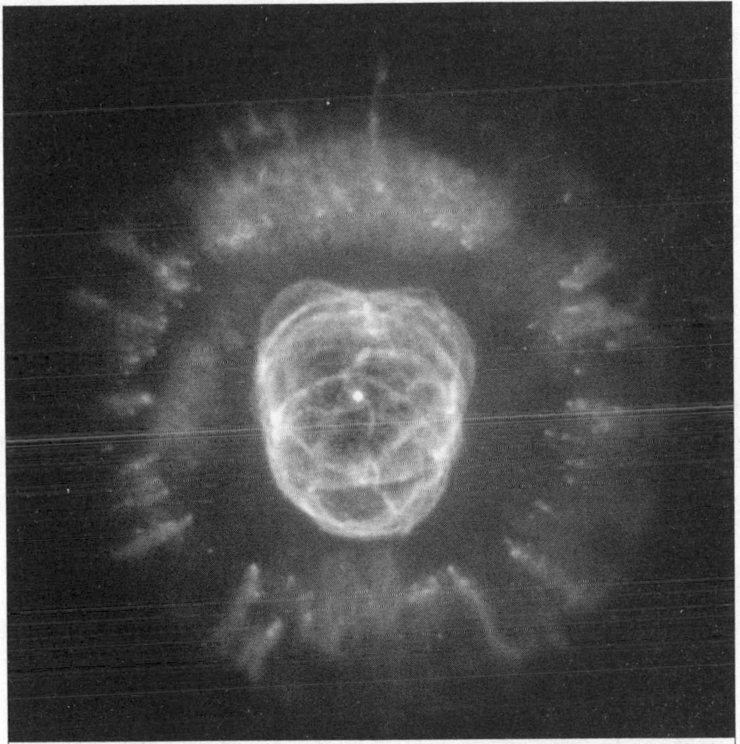

Sign of a dying star. As our Sun nears death, it will blow off its weakened atmosphere, creating a beautiful nebula.

grow more eccentric. Right now the Earth and Sister Moon are linked in a synchronous orbit, but this delicate dance will become less harmonious, forever changing our planet's tides, seasons, and beneficial lateral tilt on its axis.

Sooner or later we too will go the way of Mercury and Venus. Earth temperatures will steadily rise, liquid water will evaporate, our hospitable atmosphere will melt away, and life on Earth will become extinct.

Meanwhile, conditions may actually become more hospitable on Mars. If the red planet does go green, our lost atmosphere may help it generate a new protective layer of its own.

GREETINGS FROM MILKOMEDA!

Galaxies are always on the move. Not only do they spin and rotate, but they travel through space. Right now, our Milky Way appears to be on a collision course with Andromeda, our

Heading our way. The Milky Way is on a collision course with Andromeda, our nearest major galactic neighbor.

nearest major galactic neighbor. The crash will happen in four billion years or so.

When galaxies collide, it's less like a wreck on the highway and more like the delicate dance pictured on this book's cover. The Milky Way and Andromeda will likely flow and merge together, resulting in something astrophysicist Avi Loeb called "Milkomeda."

Galaxies are so big and roomy that most astronomers don't predict too many direct collisions between stars or planets. The merger will undoubtedly fill the sky with some amazing light shows, but nobody will be alive here on Earth to see them.

BANG, WHIMPER, CRUNCH, OR CHILL?

Like a doctor checking a patient's temperature with a thermometer, nearly one hundred scientists from around the world collaborated in 2015, gathering data from dozens of telescopes to measure the universe's current energy level.

The diagnosis was worrisome. "The Universe is slowly dying," read the report from astronomer Simon Driver and his team, who found that today's universe is radiating only half the energy it was putting out two billion years ago.

"The universe has basically sat down on the sofa, pulled up a blanket and is about to nod off for an eternal doze," said Driver.

CNN succinctly summarized the report: "Goodbye, universe. You came in with the biggest bang ever, but now, you're on your way out with a drooping fizzle."

Back in 1925, T. S. Eliot offered two options for how the world would end in his poem "The Hollow Men." Would it be with a bang or a whimper? (Eliot favored whimper.) Today, cosmological theory offers four major endgame scenarios.

Scenario 1: The Big Crunch. Can the universe continue expanding forever? Many astronomers think not. They say gravity eventually will reassert itself, step in, and halt the expansion. Some say this change will initiate a process of contraction that will culminate in "the big crunch." In this scenario, everything that exists will squish itself into a single point that resembles the singularity that existed before the Big Bang suddenly expanded everything. After the big crunch, space and time will be no more.

Scenario 2: The Big Chill. Another scenario sees things going in the opposite direction: Everything keeps expanding forever, until gravity and radiant energy get stretched so far that they become diluted and weakened. The contents of the cosmos will spread out ever farther. Heavenly lights will vanish from the heavens above the Earth as our Sun and other stars grow more distant. Everything gets cooler and cooler until it ends in "the cold death."

Scenario 3: The Big Rip. Chaos and cacophony reign in this scenario. Everything continues to expand at an ever-increasing rate, eventually tearing apart galaxies, solar systems, and even atoms.

Scenario 4: A Sequel for the Ages. The Bible and current cosmological theory seem to agree on this: our world as we know it is headed for a rough future. That may fill some people with dread, but I'm not worried.

I've spent a lifetime examining the cosmos. I've seen the fingerprints of God in the wonders of Creation. I've witnessed his sustaining power holding everything together and making it all work. Why should I worry about how he's going to bring down the closing curtain? I'm sure he will do just fine.

I'm more interested in the next chapter of the story. Millennia ago, God revealed his long-term plans to the prophet Isaiah: "See, I will create new heavens and a new earth" (Isa. 65:17).

More recently, the beloved disciple had a brief glimpse: "Then I saw 'a new heaven and a new earth,' for the first heaven and the first earth had passed away" (Rev. 21:1).

Our cosmos has been a pretty cool home, and every day we're learning more about exactly how cool it is. But a sequel is coming, and something tells me the new world will be even cooler than the old one.

Bon voyage! We launched *Voyager 1* on September 5, 1977. Decades later, it became the first human object to enter interstellar space.

EPILOGUE

EMISSARY TO THE GREAT BEYOND

HI! WE'RE FROM THAT LITTLE BLUE PLANET WAY OUT THERE

Voyager 1 and *Voyager 2* took off from Cape Canaveral, Florida, in 1977, capitalizing on an unusual planetary alignment that happens once every 175 years and offers easier access to our most distant solar system neighbors.

For the next five years, the twin robotic probes worked on the first phase of their mission: speeding by and closely examining Jupiter and Saturn, our neighborhood's two largest planets. We looked more deeply into Saturn's beautiful ring systems and witnessed monstrous volcanoes rattling Io, one of Jupiter's dozens of moons.

The *Voyagers* still had enough propellant to keep them going in the right direction and enough electrical power to keep all systems running, so scientists from Pasadena's Jet

Propulsion Laboratory reprogrammed the two craft, sending each its own way for the next phase of the mission.

Voyager 2 left Saturn to start the next phase of its solar system assignment: a seven-year deployment to study Uranus and Neptune, the most distant planets in our solar system.

Voyager 1, meanwhile, got an early start on the Voyager Interstellar Mission to boldly go where no Earth-based spacecraft had ever gone before. Finally in August 2012, after a journey of thirty-five years and more than 10 billion miles, *Voyager 1* earned a cherished place in history, becoming the first human-made object to leave our solar system and cross over into interstellar space.

At a time when average Americans hang on to their automobiles for a decade, these pioneering space probes are still going strong nearly forty years after liftoff. NASA already has praised *Voyager* as its "most scientifically productive mission ever," and the agency says the two probes will likely have enough juice to remain fully operational through 2025.

Sooner or later, though, power will fail and systems will begin to shut down. *Voyagers 1* and 2 will go quiet and dark, losing their ability to investigate space and relay findings back to scientists on Earth. But they'll still be out there, floating ever deeper into space.

"The *Voyagers* are destined—perhaps eternally—to wander the Milky Way," says NASA.

Some forty thousand years from now, *Voyager 1* is expected to draw closer to AC+79 3888, a "nearby" star in the Camelopardalis constellation. A quarter-million years or so later it will pass by Sirius, the brightest star in the sky.

President Jimmy Carter dedicated the *Voyagers* before liftoff, suggesting they could "survive a billion years into our future . . . when our civilization is profoundly altered and the surface of the Earth may be vastly changed."

A PLANETARY FAMILY ALBUM

The *Voyagers'* closing act may be the most exciting yet. Even after the two craft cease their labors as scientific probes, they will continue their work as cosmic ambassadors, reaching out to any forms of extraterrestrial life they may encounter during their journeys.

If creatures from one of our Creator's other planets ever retrieve one of these *Voyagers*, they will find messages of greeting from us Earthlings, along with an invitation to get to know us better by browsing a multimedia family album featuring iconic sights and sounds from our planet.

These treasured memories are stored on two Golden Records, one on each probe. We were even thoughtful enough to provide a stylus so aliens can "play" the record, and a handy user's guide showing them how to set up the whole thing and how fast to rotate the disc.

The late Carl Sagan, a cheerleader for the search for extraterrestrial life, headed up a small committee that selected the songs, photographs, diagrams, and nature sounds featured on the gold-plated copper discs.

While some people have criticized Sagan and NASA for potentially providing bad-guy extraterrestrials with a road map to Earth, I think it's pretty wonderful that we have reached out to our potential neighbors.

"The spacecraft will be encountered and the record played only if there are advanced spacefaring civilizations in interstellar space," said Sagan. "But the launching of this bottle into the cosmic ocean says something very hopeful about life on this planet."

GOING BEYOND BEYOND

At every step of *Voyagers 1*'s long journey, the scientific community has watched this pioneering craft soar past milestone after milestone.

Think of our solar system as a big bubble. (Its technical name is the *heliosphere.*) Here inside the bubble, conditions are largely shaped by the light and radiant energy of the Sun. Solar wind, or plasma, speeds away from the surface of the Sun at over a million miles an hour, maintaining the bubble's internal pressure against the pressure of space.

Outside the bubble, the *interstellar medium* rules. Space is not empty, but full of space stuff. In between our solar system and the other solar systems out there are matter and energy, gas and dust, radiation and cosmic rays.

The boundary between our heliosphere and the vastness of interstellar space is the *heliopause*. This is an in-between place where the power of the solar wind subsides and the power of the interstellar wind picks up. NASA tracked each step of *Voyager 1*'s unprecedented progress through the heliopause.

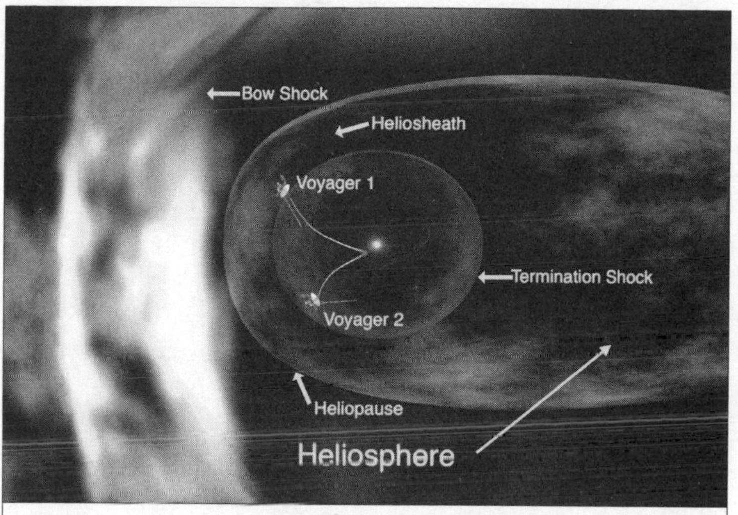

Still boldly going, and going, and going. *Voyager 1* has journeyed where no other human craft has ventured.

- In December 2004, *Voyager* crossed the *termination shock*, where the movement of the solar winds suddenly slows, from more than a million miles an hour to a gentle breeze.
- By August 2007, *Voyager* had reached the *heliosheath*. This is the edge of the heliosphere bubble, a transition zone where solar and interstellar forces interact.
- By August 2012, *Voyager*'s instruments had detected a telltale sudden increase in cosmic rays. The craft had finally crossed over into the interstellar medium, leaving our solar system behind.

Both intrepid *Voyagers* will continue passing milestones in space until someone or something stops them.

EARTH'S GREATEST HITS

Will anyone out there ever play the *Voyager*'s records and see Earth's family album? If so, what will alien life-forms make of the varied sights and sounds from our tiny blue planet circa 1977, the year New York City went dark and the first Apple computer went on sale:

- *Greetings* in more than fifty languages, from Akkadian, a language spoken in Mesopotamia thousands of years ago, to Wu, a Chinese dialect;
- *Compositions* by Bach, Beethoven, Mozart, and Stravinsky; a chant by Navajo Indians; an initiation song sung by pygmy girls in Zaire; songs by Australian aborigines; and Chuck Berry's "Johnny B. Goode";
- *Earth sounds*, including crickets, frogs, wind, rain, thunder, crashing surf, and exploding volcanoes;
- And more than one hundred *color images*, including a map showing our cosmic address; diagrams of the DNA structure and human anatomy; Ansel Adams photographs of California's Golden Gate Bridge and the Snake River winding through the Grand Tetons; and two contrasting residences, India's luxurious Taj Mahal and a humbler dwelling in America's Amish country.

"We cast this message into the cosmos," wrote President Carter in a message included on the Golden Records: "This is a present from a small distant world, a token of our sounds, our science, our images, our music, our thoughts, and our feelings. We are attempting to survive our time so we may live into yours. We hope someday, having solved the problems we face, to join a community of galactic civilizations. This record represents our hope and our determination, and our good will in a vast and awesome universe."

THE QUEST CONTINUES

For thousands of years, we humans have been gazing into the heavens. We're still doing the same thing today, but in different ways and from different vantage points. Instead of standing on Earth and looking into space with our naked eyes, we are exploring space through the images sent back to us by sophisticated spacecraft equipped with the most powerful telescopes ever.

Once upon a time, we had to content ourselves with wondering what's out there. People cooked up elaborate theories and authors devised imaginative sci-fi worlds to fill in the gaps in our knowledge. Today, we're having a hard time keeping up with the flood of scientific data many missions are currently gathering.

It's an exciting time to be an astronomer, and I've been grateful to be able to share some of my joy with you in this book, but I hope this isn't the end of your journey through space.

I pray you continue to follow what's happening with some of the fascinating missions I've highlighted. By learning about the new things astronomers are finding out, you can join with Johannes Kepler and Christian astronomers throughout the ages in the utterly enjoyable activity of "thinking God's thoughts after Him."

It would warm my heart to see some of you become astronomers yourselves. More of us will be needed in the coming years as the private space industry takes off. Perhaps you might even discover some new universal law that reveals in new ways God's creative genius and unsurpassed love for us.

There's one other thing that would make me happy. I would love to see you take a minute or two out of your multitasked life every once in a while, take a deep breath, look up at the heavens above, and take in God's handiwork.

For the longest time, God has broadcast his power and glory through his Creation, but often we fail to tune in. The heavens are an ever-changing image of his omniscience, omnipresence, and omnipotence. Who wouldn't want to look, to watch, and to wonder?

ACKNOWLEDGMENTS

The authors thank:

- John Sloan, our editor at Zondervan, who conceived this project and graciously led it to completion.
- Tony Campolo of Eastern University, our mutual friend, for bringing us together.
- Steve Sanders, Observatory Administrator at Eastern University, for being our art editor and gathering the images.
- Bob Hudson, Zondervan Senior Editor-at-Large, for expert guidance on matters of style and grammar.
- Kim Tanner, Zondervan Senior Visual Content Editor, for help with photos.
- Denise Froehlich, Zondervan Graphic Designer, for the nifty design.
- Brian Phipps, Zondervan Senior Editor, for making all the words and images work together in harmony.

Dave thanks:

- Colleen Bradstreet for her love and unflagging support throughout my life and especially during the hectic times experienced while writing this book.
- Dr. Peter Barker of the University of Oklahoma and

Dr. Ted Davis of Messiah College for steering us to the original reference of an important Kepler quote.

- My dad, Arthur, who has always completely supported my endeavors and was excited throughout this project, always asking how things were going and encouraging me during the challenging times.
- My late mom, Roberta, who, despite our family's limited means when I was growing up, never said no to purchasing a book for me. Her tender love of people and love of learning about everything have always been strong motivators. I felt her soft hand on my shoulder many times during the writing of this book.
- The constant prayers of my in-laws, the Reverend Jesse and Wilma Dourte, that God would be glorified through this book.

Steve thanks:

- Lois Rabey for her sustaining love, encouragement, support, and patience.
- Phil Rabey, my ever-inquisitive brother, for critically reviewing the manuscript.
- Dean Nelson, award-winning author, inspiring journalism professor, and friend, for encouragement and guidance on this project.
- Al, Brian, C.J., Gene, and Scott for walking with me through the process.

NOTES AND SOURCES

After class, students often ask me to explain something I said in class, or to help them track down a resource they can use to dig deeper into topics we've covered. We're doing the same thing in this section, providing you with a bit more background, sources for quoted material, and recommended resources.

CHAPTER 1: STAR STRUCK

19. Mark Twain's " unaccountable freaks" quote comes from Albert Bigelow Paine's *Mark Twain: A Biography* and is used frequently; see https://www.pbs.org/marktwain/scrapbook/09_mysterious_stranger/page4.html.
19. For information and updates on the European Space Agency's Rosetta mission to Comet 67P/Churyumov–Gerasimenko, visit the official Rosetta site: http://www.esa.int/Our_Activities/Space_Science/Rosetta.
23. For information on Eastern University's Bradstreet Observatory, see http://www.eastern.edu/academics/programs/astronomy-and-physics-department/history-bradstreet-observatory.

CHAPTER 2: EARLY ASTROLOGERS

27. Recommended resource: Michael Hoskin's *The History of Astronomy: A Very Short Introduction* (Oxford, 2003) packs a ton of information into its 122 pages. The quote on the sky and Egyptian religions is on page 7.
32. Recommended resource: We are grateful to James Herrick for allowing us to briefly summarize portions of his book *Scientific Mythologies: How Science and Science Fiction Forge New Religious Beliefs* (IVP Academic, 2008).

CHAPTER 3: OUR COSMIC CREATOR

35. The Ebenezer reference is explained in 1 Samuel 7:12, where Samuel erects a stone monument to the Israelites' victory over the Philistines.
35. Stuart K. Hine, "How Great Thou Art" (Hope Publishing Company, 1953).
37. "The extravagant gesture": Annie Dillard, *Pilgrim at Tinker Creek* (Harper's Magazine Press, 1974), 9.
38. Recommended resource: The Martin Gorst quote comes from page 4 of his book *Measuring Eternity: The Search for the Beginning of Time* (Broadway, 2001).
39. Carl Sagan's whopper is found on page 4 of *Cosmos* (Random House, 1980). Recommended resource: Everyone ought to see at least one episode of *Cosmos*, the world's most widely watched PBS series.
39. The Lucretius quote is on page 91 of the Penguin Classics edition of *On the Nature of Things* (1951).
42. "Subcreators," J. R. R. Tokien, "Tree and Leaf: On Fairy Stories," in *The Tolkien Reader* (Ballantine Books, 1966), 54.
42. Chet Raymo describes the benefits of stargazing on page ix of the preface to his book *The Soul of the Night: An Astronomical Pilgrimage* (Hungry Mind, 1992). He discusses his loss of faith on page 56, saying, "I can't say exactly when it was that the God of my youth took to the upland rains."
43. "Science is great as science": Guy Consolmagno, *Brother Astronomer: Adventures of a Vatican Scientist* (McGraw Hill, 2000), 92.

CHAPTER 4: CREATION, CONTINUED

45. Bart's deistic invocation: "Two Cars in Every Garage, Three Eyes on Every Fish," *The Simpsons*, episode 701.

47. Yancey's quote comes from the preface to his first book with Dr. Paul Brand, *Fearfully and Wonderfully Made* (Zondervan, 1980). Yancey adds that we "have cleaved nature from the supernatural."

48. "He had entered into a servicing contract": Michael Hoskin, *The History of Astronomy: A Very Short Introduction* (Oxford, 2003), 69.

49. "If you think you're seeing the same show": Frederick Buechner, "Creation," in *Wishful Thinking: A Theological ABC* (Harper & Row, 1973), 18.

CHAPTER 5: OUR GOLDILOCKS WORLD

53. *The Privileged Planet*, directed by Lad Allen (Illustra Media, 2010), DVD; available from the Discovery Institute at http://www.privilegedplanet.com.

54. Recommended resource: Bill Bryson's *Short History of Nearly Everything* offers a wonderfully written guided tour of our universe and the scientific discoveries that have helped us understand it better. The atoms quote is from page 2 of the 2004 Broadway Books paperback edition.

59. For more on the water cycle, see *Water Falls*, produced by Michael Starobin (NASA/Goddard Space Flight Center, 2014), DVD; available at http://pmm.nasa.gov/water-falls.

59. "[Plants] allow us to eat sunlight": Douglas Tallamy, "The Chickadee's Guide to Gardening: In Your Garden, Choose Plants That Help the Environment," *New York Times*, March 11, 2015, http://www.nytimes.com/2015/03/11/opinion/in-your-garden-choose-plants-that-help-the-environment.html.

62. "Continents Drift" is found on Bruce Hornsby and the Noisemakers' album *Levitate* (Verve Records, 2009).

62. The Anders *Earthrise* material is from https://en.wikipedia.org/wiki/Earthrise.

63. Try reading at least the introduction to Pope Francis's *Laudato si'* encyclical at http://w2.vatican.va/content/francesco/en/encyclicals/documents/papa-francesco_20150524_enciclica-laudato-si.html.

65. For more on Oklahoma's fracking-related earthquakes, see Michael Wines, "Oklahoma Recognizes Role of Drilling in Earthquakes," *New York Times*, April 21, 2015, http://www.nytimes.com/2015/04/22/us/oklahoma-acknowledges-wastewater-from-oil-and-gas-wells-as-major-cause-of-quakes.html.

CHAPTER 6: COSMOLOGICAL CONFUSION

70. We thank Bible scholar Kyle Greenwood for letting us summarize some of his ideas and quote portions of his book *Scripture and Cosmology: Reading the Bible between the Ancient World and Modern Science* (IVP, 2015). The "best scientific evidence of their time" quote is from page 101; "small, flat and round" from 158; and "poetic in nature" from 121.

71. "The Greek intellectual world": Nicholas Nicastro, *Circumference: Eratosthenes and the Ancient Quest to Measure the Globe* (St. Martin's Press, 2008), 31.

73. The Flat Earth Society's "Whole World Deceived" headline: https://en.wikipedia.org/wiki/Modern_flat_Earth_societies.

74. Martin Luther's "upside down" quote: Lewis W. Spitz, *The Renaissance and Reformation Movements* (Rand McNally, 1971), 586.

75. John Calvin's "some who are so deranged" quote: Arnold Huijgen, *Divine Accommodation in John Calvin's Theology: Analysis and Assessment* (Vandenhoeck & Ruprecht, 2011), 222.

75. Philipp Melanchthon's "impudence of mind" quote: https://en.wikipedia.org/wiki/Nicolaus_Copernicus.

76. "We are tucked away": Carl Sagan, *Cosmos* (Random House, 1980), 7.

76. "Just a chemical scum": Stephen Hawking, in a 1995 radio interview, https://en.wikiquote.org/wiki/Stephen_Hawking.

76. "Our cosmic mediocrity": Chet Raymo, *The Virgin and the Mousetrap: Essays in Search of the Soul of Science* (Viking, 1991), xvii.

CHAPTER 7: BROTHER SUN AND SISTER MOON

82. Francis's "Canticle of Brother Sun" can be found at this Franciscan site: http://www.franciscanfriarstor.com/archive/stfrancis/stf_canticle_of_the_sun.htm.

82. Desert Sunlight Solar Farm: Josh Sanburn, "A Burst of Energy" *Time*, March 9, 2015.

85. "Nested in the life of the Sun": Judy Cannato, *Radical Amazement: Contemplative Lessons from Black Holes, Supernovas, and Other Wonders of the Universe* (Sorin, 2006), 119.

86. Steve Rabey tells the story of Francis and the Moon in chapter 3 of *The Lessons of St. Francis*, the book he wrote with John Michael Talbot (Dutton, 1997; Plume/Penguin, 1998).

91. Blood moon news headline: Sarah Pulliam Bailey, "Christian Pastors Warn 'Blood Moon' Is an Omen of Armageddon and Second Coming of Christ," *Huffington Post*, April 15, 2014, http://www.huffingtonpost.com/2014/04/15/blood-moon-armageddon_n_5154043.html.

93. Umbraphiles: Ryan Bradley, "Chasing the Sun into Darkness," *Fortune*, May 19, 2014.

CHAPTER 8: THE CALLING OF A CHRISTIAN SCIENTIST

96. Francis Bacon's "two books" quote is from his book *The Advancement of Learning* (1605).

    Recommended resource: Most of the Kepler quotes are from Carola Baumgardt's wonderful *Johannes Kepler: Life and Letters* (Philosophical Library, 1951).

    Recommended resource: Some of the Kepler quotes are from Daniel J. Boorstin, *The Discoverers: A History of Man's Search to Know His World and Himself* (Random House, 1983).

97. "I wanted to become a theologian": ibid., 309.

98. "Always be ready": Baumgardt, *Kepler*, 129.

98. "Those laws": ibid., 50.

98. "Now nothing can keep me back": Boorstin, *The Discoverers*, 312.
100. You can follow NASA's Kepler mission at http://kepler.nasa.gov.
101. Carl Sagan on Kepler's *Somnium*: *Cosmos* (Random House, 1980), 65.
101. "I have been made priest": Baumgardt, *Kepler*, 122–23.
101. U2's struggles with Shalom are discussed in chapter 3 of Steve Stockman, *Walk On: The Spiritual Journey of U2* (Relevant, 2001).
103. Francis S. Collins, "Why I'm a Man of Science—and Faith," *National Geographic*, April 2015.
103. "Science keeps religion from sinking": Martin Luther King Jr., *The Words of Martin Luther King Jr.* (Newmarket, 1983), 63.
103. "If we study science without Scripture": Timothy Jennings, *The God-Shaped Brain* (IVP, 2013), 11–12.

CHAPTER 9: THROUGH THE TELESCOPE

Recommended resource: Our primary source for Galileo is Dava Sobel, *Galileo's Daughter* (Walker, 1999). Also helpful is Giorgio de Santillana, *The Crime of Galileo* (Time, 1962).

106. "This grand book of the universe": Sobel, *Galileo's Daughter*, 16.
109. "I render infinite thanks to God": ibid., 6.
109. "Until the invention of the telescope": Michael Hoskin, *The History of Astronomy: A Very Short Introduction* (Oxford, 2003), 48.
111. The material about Hans Lipperhey and the history of glass comes from chapter 1 of Steven Johnson's bestselling *How We Got to Now: Six Innovations That Made the Modern World* (Riverhead, 2014) and the companion TV series on PBS.
111. "One of the most versatile and transformative materials": Johnson, *How We Got to Now*, 14.
112. "Within 100 years": Johnson, ibid., 22.
112. "The greatest, most expensive and ambitious spree": Dennis Overbye, "More Eyes on the Skies," *New York Times*, July 22, 2014.

CHAPTER 10: HERO OR HERETIC?

116. "Holy Scripture and Nature": Galileo, quoted in Dava Sobel, *Galileo's Daughter* (Walker, 1999), 64.

118. "Until the telescope": Daniel J. Boorstin, *The Discoverers: A History of Man's Search to Know His World and Himself* (Random House, 1983), 324.
119. "May God forgive Galileo": Pope Urban VIII, quoted in Giorgio de Santillana, *The Crime of Galileo* (Time, 1962), 235.
120. "Though Scripture cannot err": Galileo, quoted in Sobel, *Galileo's Daughter*, 63.
120. Baronius is quoted on page 159 of Arthur Berry, *A Short History of Astronomy* (Dover, 1961), and in many other sources.
120. "Tragic mutual incomprehension": Pope John Paul II, quoted in Sobel, *Galileo's Daughter*, 11.

CHAPTER 11: SHOWING OUR AGE

This chapter relies heavily on Martin Gorst, *Measuring Eternity: The Search for the Beginning of Time* (Broadway, 2001).

127. "The lack of agreement": ibid., 16.
128. "He has thought fit": James Ussher, quoted in ibid., 36.
128. "Fantastically precise misconception": H. G. Wells, quoted in ibid., 1.
130. "I declare I had fancied": Charles Darwin, quoted in ibid., 172.
132. "All life over billions of years": BioLogos, "What We Believe," https://biologos.org/about-us.
133. Mark Noll's critique of evangelical anti-intellectualism in *The Scandal of the Evangelical Mind* (Eerdmans, 1994) features a relevant chapter, "Thinking about Science." Noll's declaration that evangelical efforts to find a thoughtful way to balance knowledge of Scripture with knowledge of the world have been a "catastrophe" is found on page 178. Noll continues: "Creation science has damaged evangelicalism" by "undermining the ability to look at the world God has made and to understand what we see when we do look" (196), fostering "a stunted ability to perceive the world of nature" (197). Noll says the legacy of fundamentalism's influence on evangelical attitudes toward science is that "reflection on the Christian meaning of nature remains in a retarded state among evangelicals" (229), resulting in an approach that is "but a shadow of what God, nature, and the Christian faith deserve" (233).
134. "Usually, even a non-Christian knows something": Augustine, quoted in John Hammond Taylor, *St. Augustine*, vol. 1, *The Literal Meaning of Genesis* (Ancient Christian Writers, Paulist, 1982), 42–43.

CHAPTER 12: GOD, COUNTRY, AND THE SPACE RACE

The authors thank William J. Schultz for letting us·ransack his paper, "God and Man at NASA: Religion and the State in the Space Age" (research paper, Princeton University). Quote from interview with author, July 30, 2015.

138. John F. Kennedy, "I believe that this nation should commit itself": https://www.nasa.gov/vision/space/features/jfk_speech_text.html#.ViqykqIzw9s.
138. "Many historians have examined": interview with Schultz, July 2015.
140. Frank Borman, "And from the crew of Apollo 8": https://en.wikipedia.org/wiki/Apollo_8_Genesis_reading.
142. "The very first liquid ever poured on the moon": Buzz Aldrin, quoted in Schultz, "God and Man at NASA," 1.
143. "Bless Thou the Astronauts." Lyrics by Ernest Krikor Emurian, copyright 1969 (*Book of Worship for United States Forces*, 1974).
144. "Religious faith was shared": Schultz, "God and Man at NASA."
145. "I felt an overwhelming sense": James Irwin, quoted in ibid., 14.

CHAPTER 13: A STROLL THROUGH THE NEIGHBORHOOD

We used tons of sources for this chapter. Recommended resource: "Chasing Pluto," directed by Terri Randall, aired July 15, 2015; available from *Nova*, the PBS science series, http://www.pbs.org/wgbh/nova/space/chasing-pluto.html.

CHAPTER 14: MARS WITHOUT MARTIANS?

160. The "War of the Worlds" radio transcript is available at http://www.sacred-texts.com/ufo/mars/wow.htm.

160. Carl Sagan, "Mars has become a kind of mythic arena": https://en.wikipedia.org/wiki/Mars_in_culture.

162. H. G. Wells, "Those who have never seen a living Martian": https://www.fourmilab.ch/etexts/www/warworlds/b1c4.html.

163. "Fair, brownish skin": Ray Bradbury, *The Martian Chronicles* (Bantam, 1951), 2.

164. Insight into C. S. Lewis's science fiction comes from Martha C. Sammons, *A Guide through C. S. Lewis' Space Trilogy* (Cornerstone, 1980), specifically "redeem" (16); "scientism" (20).

165. "I look forward with horror": C. S. Lewis, *God in the Dock: Essays on Theology and Ethics* (Eerdmans, 1970), 267.

166. You can follow the exploits of the Mars Reconnaissance Orbiter at http://mars.nasa.gov/mro.

168. For information on NASA's funding, see Lee Billings, "Mission Aborted," *New York Times Book Review*, December 13, 2015, p. 21.

168. "No bucks, no Buck Rogers": see Kenneth Chang, "Seeing Obstacle-Filled Path to Mars," *New York Times*, June 9, 2014, http://www.nytimes.com/2014/06/10/science/space/seeing-obstacle-filled-path-to-mars.html.

169. Experiments involving Scott and Mark Kelly are described in Jeffrey Kluger, "Mission Twinpossible," *Time*, December 29, 2014/January 5, 2015.

169. See more about the Mars500 simulator at http://www.space.com/13500-mock-mars-mission-mars-500-ends.html.

CHAPTER 15: INCOMING!

175. Information about Daniel Barringer comes from the authors' visits to Meteor Crater, Arizona, and from Nancy Southgate and Felicity Barringer, *A Grand Obsession: Daniel Moreau Barringer and His Crater* (Barringer Crater Company, 2002).

179. Giuseppe Piazzi, "I have announced this star as a comet": https://en.wikipedia.org/wiki/Giuseppe_Piazzi.

180. "Scarcely any larger than a house!": Antoine de Saint-Exupéry, *The Little Prince* (Harcourt, 1943), 9.

183. "Rocky leftovers": Associated Press, "Spacecraft Drops In on Dwarf Planet," March 7, 2015.
183. "Solar System Debris" is the title of chapter 14 of Eric Chaisson and Steve McMillan, *Astronomy Today*, 6th ed. (Pearson/Addison Wesley, 2008).

CHAPTER 16: IS ANYBODY OUT THERE?

188. "Things have slowed down": Lee Billings, *Five Billion Years of Solitude: The Search for Life among the Stars* (Current/Penguin, 2014), 9–10.
188. "The money simply isn't there these days": Frank Drake, quoted in ibid., 10.
189. "The possibility that life has arisen elsewhere": Dominique Mosbergen, "Aliens Are Almost Definitely Out There, SETI Astronomers Tell Congress," *Huffington Post*, May 22, 2014, http://www.huffingtonpost.com/2014/05/22/aliens-congress-seti-astronomers_n_5370315.html.
189. "In an infinite universe": Steven Hawking, quoted in Dennis Overbye, "Stephen Hawking Joins Russian Entrepreneur's Search for Alien Life," *New York Times*, July 20, 2015, http://www.nytimes.com/2015/07/21/science/yuri-milner-russian-entrepreneur-promises-100-million-for-alien-search.html.
189. Project Blue Book information from Steve Rabey, "UFOs: The Arguing Goes On," *Dayton Journal Herald*, October 25, 1980, p. 23. See also Debbie Siegelbaum, "Project Blue Book: US Air Force UFO Documents Revealed," *BBC News*, January 26, 2015, http://www.bbc.com/news/magazine-30943827.
192. "We know nothing of ETI's intentions": see the online petition at https://setiathome.berkeley.edu/meti_statement_0.html.
195. "The most frightening thought": Rodney W. Johnson, quoted in Robert S. Ellwood, *The '60s Spiritual Awakening* (Rutgers, 1994), 308.
196. C. S. Lewis's "Religion and Rocketry" can be found in *The World's Last Night and Other Essays* (Mariner, 2002) and at https://archive.org/stream/worldslastnighta012859mbp/worldslastnighta012859mbp_djvu.txt.
196. Larry Norman recorded "U.F.O." on *In Another Land* (Solid Rock Records, 1976) and other albums.

197. "Any entity—no matter how many tentacles it has": Guy Consolmagno, quoted in "Pope's Astronomer Would Baptize Aliens," *Fox News*, September 21, 2010, http://www.foxnews.com/tech/2010/09/21/popes-astronomer-baptize-aliens.html.

197. Information on astronomer David Weintraub's insights: Megan Gannon, "Would Finding Alien Life Change Religious Philosophies?" *Space.com*, October 10, 2014, http://www.space.com/27410-religion-extraterrestrial-life.html.

198. "An expedition of Martians": Pope Francis, quoted in Adam Withnall, "Pope Francis Says He Would Baptise Aliens: 'Who Are We to Close Doors?'" *Independent*, May 13, 2014, http://www.independent.co.uk/news/world/europe/pope-francis-says-he-would-baptise-aliens-9360632.html and http://time.com/97695/pope-francis-would-baptize-martians.

198. See also Dennis Overbye, "Finder of New Worlds," *New York Times*, May 12, 2014, http://www.nytimes.com/2014/05/13/science/finder-of-new-worlds.html.

198. "The Creator God is an extravagant creator": David Wilkinson, *Science, Religion, and the Search for Extraterrestrial Intelligence* (Oxford, 2013), 173.

CHAPTER 17: A STAR IS BORN (AND SO ARE WE!)

Our thanks to Jennifer Wiseman for her help in writing this chapter. You can learn more about her work here:

"A 25th Anniversary Q&A about Hubble with NASA's Jennifer Wiseman," *NASA*, April 28, 2015, http://www.nasa.gov/feature/goddard/a-25th-anniversary-qa-about-hubble-with-nasas-jennifer-wiseman.

Her chapter, "What Do We Learn about the Creator from Astronomy and Cosmology?" in *Not Just Science: Questions Where Christian Faith and Natural Science Intersect*, ed. Dorothy F. Chappell (David C. Cook, 2005), 97–108.

Her chapter with Deborah Haarsma, "An Evolving Cosmos," in *Perspectives on an Evolving Creation*, ed. Keith B. Miller (Eerdmans, 2003), 97–119.

210. "Molecular breweries": Ray Jayawardhana, "Our Cosmic Selves," *New York Times*, April 3, 2015, http://www.nytimes.com/2015/04/05/opinion/sunday/our-cosmic-selves.html.
211. "We are made of star stuff": Carl Sagan, *Cosmos* (Random House, 1980), 233.
211. Readers may also be interested in Louie Giglio's YouTube video, *The Star Maker*, https://www.youtube.com/watch?v=rRiIWL04po8.

CHAPTER 18: TWO ARE BETTER THAN ONE

Recommended resource: Material on William and Caroline Herschel comes from Richard Holmes's fascinating book *The Age of Wonder: How the Romantic Generation Discovered the Beauty and Terror of Science* (Vintage, 2010).

213. Recordings of Herschel's music include *Music by the Father of Modern Astronomy* (Newport Classics, 1995), a sampler of symphonies and concertos.
214. Thomas Hardy's "frightful" quote: Holmes, *Age of Wonder*, 118.
214. Haydn's *Creation*: ibid., 199.
214. "My feeble understanding": William Herschel, quoted in ibid., 73.
214. "The most Beautiful Order": William Herschel, quoted in ibid., 73.
217. You can buy your very own copy of *Binary Maker* at http://www.binarymaker.com.

CHAPTER 19: YOUR TICKET TO THE STARS

Information for this chapter came from websites operated by private space firms. See also William J. Broad, "Billionaires with Big Ideas Are Privatizing American Science," *New York Times*, March 15, 2014, http://www.nytimes.com/2014/03/16/science/billionaires-with-big-ideas-are-privatizing-american-science.html.

224. "The public has greatly overestimated": William Pickering, quoted before the preface to Sam Howe Verhovek, *Jet Age: The Comet, the 707, and the Race to Shrink the World* (Penguin, 2010).

225. For more on Laika, see Dana Jennings, "Strays Leading the Soviets into Space," *New York Times*, November 3, 2014, http://www.nytimes.com/2014/11/04/science/soviet-space-dogs-tells-the-story-of-canine-cosmonauts.html.

225. See the 2015 SPACE Act at https://www.congress.gov/bill/114th-congress/house-bill/2262.

Official Notice: If you learned about the XPrize here, please make sure you share your award with the authors!

230. "That is a bad thing for the United States": John Hyten, interview with *60 Minutes*, August 2, 2015, http://www.cbsnews.com/news/rare-look-at-space-command-satellite-defense-60-minutes-2.

231. "Will man ever go to Mars?": Matt Novak, "Wernher von Braun's Martian Chronicles," *Smithsonian.com*, July 30, 2012, http://www.smithsonianmag.com/history/wernher-von-brauns-martian-chronicles-9845747.

231. "I think it is actually very important": Elon Musk, quoted in Sam Howe Verhovek, "Not a Flight of Fancy: Space Tourism Isn't Frivolous, or Impossible," *New York Times*, November 3, 2014, http://www.nytimes.com/2014/11/04/opinion/space-tourism-isnt-frivolous-or-impossible.html.

233. In *The Wright Brothers* (Simon & Schuster, 2015), David McCullough writes, "Bicycles were proclaimed morally hazardous" (24).

233. "The search for extraterrestrial life": Ken Ham, "We'll Find a New Earth within 20 Years," *Ken Ham Blog*, July 20, 2014, https://answersingenesis.org/blogs/ken-ham/2014/07/20/well-find-a-new-earth-within-20-years.

233. For more on the *Space Policy* article, see Jonathan Merritt, "Why Christians Should Get On Board with Space Exploration," *Jonathan Merritt on Faith & Culture*, November 18, 2014, http://www.jonathanmerritt.com/christians-get-board-space-exploration.

CHAPTER 20: DARK STUFF

Timothy Ferris contributes to this chapter with items old and new, including his book *The Whole Shebang: A State-of-the-Universe(s) Report* (Touchstone, 1997) and one of his many articles in *National Geographic*.

236. "Believed to be ubiquitous": Ferris, "A First Glimpse of the Hidden Cosmos," *National Geographic*, January 2015, http://ngm.nationalgeographic.com/2015/01/hidden-cosmos/ferris-text.

236. "Most profound mystery in all of science": ibid.

236. "General label for what we do not know": ibid.

238. "The Perseus sound waves": Steve Allen, quoted in "Black Hole Sound Waves," *Science News*, September 9, 2003, http://science.nasa.gov/science-news/science-at-nasa/2003/09sep_blackholesounds.

240. "We can see a black hole eat in real time": Sheperd Doeleman, quoted in Dennis Overbye, "Black Hole Hunters," *New York Times*, June 8, 2015, http://www.nytimes.com/2015/06/09/science/black-hole-event-horizon-telescope.html.

241. "Light pollution is now so pervasive": Jane Brox, *Brilliant: The Evolution of Artificial Light* (Houghton Mifflin Harcourt, 2010), 283.

241. "Those of us who live in or near cities": Chet Raymo, *An Intimate Look at the Night Sky* (Walker, 2001), x.

243. For Dark Sky Parks see http://darksky.org/idsp/parks.

CHAPTER 21: GALAXIES, SPACE, AND TIME

246. "I have observed the essence or substance": Galileo Galilei, *Sidereus Nuncius*, based on the version by Edward Stafford Carlos (Rivingtons, 1880), newly edited and corrected by Peter Barker (Byzantium, 2004), 36.

248. Hubble's "discovery that the Universe is expanding": Stephen Hawking, *A Brief History of Time* (Bantam, 1988), 39.

249. "To try imagining how big": Adam Mann, "How to Picture the Size of the Universe," *Wired*, December 6, 2011, http://www.wired.com/2011/12/universe-size.

254. "We live in a changing universe": Timothy Ferris, *The Whole Shebang: A State-of-the-Universe(s) Report* (Touchstone, 1997), opening sentence.

257. "GN-z11 is 13.4 billion light years away": http://www.cnn.com/2016/03/04/us/farthest-galaxy-ever-seen/index.html.

257. "We can see only those galaxies": ibid., 78.

CHAPTER 22: THE GOD BEHIND THE BIGGEST BANG

We relied on these two *New York Times* stories from the 1930s:

"Lemaître Suggests One, Single, Great Atom, Embracing All Energy, Started the Universe," May 19, 1931.

Recommended resource: "Lemaître Follows Two Paths to Truth," February 19, 1933.

260. "Atheists, devout Christians": Edgar B. Herwick III, "Big Bang Theory: A Roman Catholic Creation," *WGBH News*, March 20, 2014, http://wgbhnews.org/post/big-bang-theory-roman-catholic-creation.

260. "Here we have this wonderful": "Lemaître Follows Two Paths."

261. Albert Einstein's "abominable" and "very beautiful indeed" quotes: https://en.wikipedia.org/wiki/Georges_Lema%C3%AEtre.

263. "Modern science has confirmed": Pope Pius XII, quoted in Joseph R. Laracy, "The Faith and Reason of Father George Lemaître," *CatholicCulture.org*, https://www.catholicculture.org/culture/library/view.cfm?recnum=8847.

263. "God cannot be reduced": Georges Lemaître, quoted in ibid.

264. "Natural truth" and "supernatural truth": ibid.

264. "To One Who has said: 'I am the Truth'": Georges Lemaître, quoted in ibid.

265. "The question if it was really a beginning": Georges Lemaître, quoted in Herwick, "Big Bang Theory," http://wgbhnews.org/post/big-bang-theory-roman-catholic-creation.

266. "Does the Church Need Science?": Georges Lemaître, quoted in Laracy, "Faith and Reason."

266. J. B. Phillips, *Your God Is Too Small* (Collier/Macmillan, 1961), 7.

CHAPTER 23: THE END

269. You can find the end times opinion poll at http://www.vox.com/2015/3/12/8194903/apocalypse-causes-poll.

275. Avi Loeb's "Milkomeda": Robert Irion, "From Cosmic Dawn to

Milkomeda, and Beyond," *Science*, April 12, 2013, https://www.cfa .harvard.edu/~loeb/Science.pdf.

275. "The Universe is slowly dying": Ben Brumfield, "The Universe Is Slowly Dying, Study Shows with Unprecedented Precision, *CNN*, August 11, 2015, http://www.cnn.com/2015/08/10/us/universe-dying/index.html.

EPILOGUE: EMISSARY TO THE GREAT BEYOND

279. You can follow the journeys of the two *Voyager* crafts at http://voyager .jpl.nasa.gov.
280. "Most scientifically productive mission ever": http://voyager.jpl.nasa .gov/faq.html.
280. "The *Voyagers* are destined": http://voyager.jpl.nasa.gov/mission/ interstellar.html.
281. Jimmy Carter's "survive a billion years" quote: http://www.presidency .ucsb.edu/ws/?pid=7890.
281. Find out more about the Golden Records at https://en.wikipedia. org/wiki/Voyager_Golden_Record; http://voyager.jpl.nasa.gov/ spacecraft/goldenrec.html.
282. Carl Sagan, "The spacecraft will be encountered": http://voyager.jpl .nasa.gov/spacecraft/goldenrec.html.

ART AND PHOTO CREDITS

COLOR PHOTOS

Page 1

Earth (top image): NASA, public domain

Top of the Atmosphere (bottom image): by NASA Earth Observatory, public domain

Convection Chaparral Supercell (top inset): public domain

Lava Lake (middle inset): by User:Cai Tjeenk Willink (Caitjeenk), own work, CC BY-SA 3.0

Water, Lake Nyon (bottom inset): public domain

Page 2

Neil Armstrong on the Moon (inset): NASA, public domain

Sun, Moon, Earth image (bottom image): Steve Sanders, Eastern University

Page 3

The Sun (top image): NASA, public domain

Giant Prominence on the Sun (inset): by NASA/SDO/AIA/Goddard Space Flight Center

Page 4

Earth's Location in the Universe: by Andrew Z. Colvin, own work, CC BY-SA 3.0

Page 5

Mercury (top image): NASA, public domain

Venus (bottom image): NASA, public domain

Page 6

Jupiter and Io (top image): by NASA/JPL/USGS, public domain

Io (bottom left image): by NASA/JPL/USGS, public domain

Pele (bottom right image): by NASA/JPL/USGS, public domain

Page 7

All images of Saturn are by NASA/JPL/USGS, public domain

Page 8

Neptune (top image): by NASA/JPL/USGS, public domain

Pluto (bottom image): NASA, public domain

Page 9

Curiosity Rover (middle image): NASA/JPL, Caltech/MSSS

Red Mars Surface (top image): by NASA/JPL/Cornell, modified from original by Tablizer at en.wikipedia

Mars from Space (bottom image): NASA/JPL, Caltech/Univ. of Arizona

Page 10

Zeta Ophiuchi (inset): NASA, JPL, Caltech, Spitzer Space Telescope

The Life of Sunlike Stars (background image): by ESO/S. Steinhöfel, ESO, CC BY 4.0

Page 11

Binary Star (top image): Steve Sanders and Dr. David Bradstreet, Eastern University

Quad System (bottom image): by NASA/JPL, Caltech/T. Pyle (SSC), public domain, artist's impression

Page 12

Eagle Nebula: NASA, public domain

ART AND PHOTO CREDITS

Page 13

Golden Record (top image): by NASA/JPL, public domain

Pele (top inset): by NASA/JPL/USGS, public domain

Neptune (bottom inset): by NASA/JPL, public domain

Page 14

Hubble Deep Field (background image): by NASA/JPL, public domain

Crab Nebula (top inset): by NASA/JPL, public domain

Veil Nebula (bottom inset): NASA, ESA, Hubble Heritage Team

Page 15

Hubble Deep Field (background image): by NASA/JPL, public domain

Galaxy Cluster (left inset): by NASA, ESA, and the Hubble SM4 ERO Team, public domain

Galaxy (top right inset): by ESA/Hubble, CC BY 3.0

Galaxy (bottom right inset): by NASA Headquarters, Greatest Images of NASA (NASA-HQ-GRIN), public domain

Page 16

Buzz Aldrin on the Moon (background image): by NASA, public domain

Cathedral Window (top inset): NASA, public domain

Crew of Apollo 11 (bottom inset): by NASA, NASA Human Space Flight Gallery, NASA photo ID: S69-31739, public domain

BLACK AND WHITE PHOTOS

16. Comet 67P/Churyumov–Gerasimenko: by ESA/Rosetta/NAVCAM, CC BY-SA IGO 3.0

18. Bayeux Tapestry: public domain

21. Dave's Journal: by Dr. David Bradstreet, Eastern University

24. Stonehenge: by Mavratti, public domain

27. All Gizah Pyramids: by Ricardo Liberato, licensed under CC BY-SA 2.0

30. Temple of Bel (Baal) in Palmyra: by Bernard Gagnon, licensed under CC BY-SA 3.0

32. Applewhite: YouTube screenshot image, Oct. 14, 2015, link: https://www.youtube.com/watch?v=AqSZhwu1Rwo
32. Hubbard: publicity photo
34. Separation of Light from Darkness Panel of Sistine Chapel: by Michelangelo, public domain
37. Vaso Popol Vuh: public domain
39. Carl Sagan: public domain
39. Lucretius: public domain
44. Ancient of Days: by William Blake, public domain
49. Clouds: NASA, Feburary 5th, 2008, taken from the ISS
49. Fault Lines: by Ikluft, own work, licensed under GFDL
52. Blue Marble: by NASA/Apollo 17 crew, public domain
55. Illustration of Tilted versus Straight Earth: Eastern University
56. Convection Process, "Oceanic Spreading": by Surachit, CC BY-SA 3.0
58. Water Cycle: public domain
60. "Earth Poster": by Kelvinsong, licensed under CC BY-SA 3.0 via Commons
66. Old Drawing of Old Cosmological Model (Ptolemy, Aristotle): by Bartolomeu Velho, public domain
68. "Copernicus": public domain
68. "Copernican Heliocentrism Theory Diagram": by Nicolai Copernicus, created in vector format by Scewing, public domain
73. Portrait of Eratosthenes: public domain
73. "Eratosthenes": by Erzbischof, CC BY-SA 3.0
80. "NASA-Apollo8-Dec24-Earthrise": by NASA/Bill Anders, public domain
84. "Solar Internal Structure": by I, Sakurambo, CC BY-SA 3.0
89. Lunar Mission with Moon Rocks: by Wknight94talk, licensed under CC BY-SA 3.0
91. Blood Moon: by Tomruen, licensed under CC BY-SA 3.0
94. Kepler Portrait: by Unknown, licensed under public domain
99. Kepler Retrograde: public domain
99. "Astronomia Nova": by Johannes Kepler, licensed under public domain
100. Elliptical Orbit: Eastern University

103. "Francis Collins Official Portrait": by Bill Branson, NIH, public domain
104. Image of Galileo's Telescope: digital image, n.p., n.d., web. 12 November 2014.
107. "Justus Sustermans—Portrait of Galileo Galilei, 1636": by Justus Sustermans, public domain
109. "Galileo's Sketches of the Moon": by Galileo, public domain
113. "The Atacama Compact Array": by ESO, CC BY 4.0
114. "Giordano Bruno Campo dei Fiori": by Jastrow, public domain
115. Pope Urban VIII: public domain
115. Cardinal Robert Bellarmine: public domain
124. "James Ussher by Sir Peter Lely": by Peter Lely, public domain
129. "Annales Veteris Testamenti page 1": by James Ussher, public domain
130. Ussher in the Bible: public domain
131. "Charles Darwin by Julia Margaret Cameron 2": by Julia Margaret Cameron, reprinted by Davepape, public domain
131. "Lyell 1840": public domain
136. Armstrong on Moon (w/American Flag?): NASA/JPL
139. Apollo 8 Astronauts: NASA/JPL
139. "Madalyn Murray O'Hair": by Alan Light, CC BY 2.0
141. "Aldrin": by NASA, public domain
146. Solar System Scale: NASA/JPL, public domain
149. Planets-Mercury: NASA/JPL
150. Planets-Venus: NASA/JPL
152. Planets-Jupiter: NASA/JPL
153. Planets-Saturn: NASA/JPL
154. Planets-Uranus: NASA/JPL
154. Planets-Neptune: NASA/JPL
155. Planets-Pluto: NASA/JHUAPL/SwRI
158. Image from *Mars Attacks!*: publicity photo
161. Orson Welles: public domain
161. H. G. Wells: public domain
161. Ray Bradbury: cc2.0 photo by Alan Light

161. Gene Roddenberry: public domain

164. "My Favorite Martian Ray Walston 1963": by CBS Television, public domain

167. Water Streaks on Mars: NASA/JPL

170. Mars500: Credit: ESA

172. Meteor Crater: public domain

175. "Daniel Barringer": public domain

177. Comet: by NASA/Dan Burbank, public domain

178. Asteroid Collage: Eastern University

181. Tunguska Event: Leonid Kulik Expedition, public domain

183. "Yucatan Chix Crater": by NASA/JPL-Caltech, modified by David Fuchs, public domain via Commons

184. Bradstreet Asteroid: Eastern University

186. "Very Large Array, 2012": by John Fowler, Flickr: VLA, licensed under CC BY 2.0 via Commons

191. "Leonard Nimoy Spock 1967": by NBC Television-eBayfrontback, public domain

191. Mork: publicity photo

191. ET: publicity photo

191. *Muppets Movie*: publicity photo

193. Kepler: NASA/JPL

194. LL Ori and the Orion Nebula: NASA, ESA, and the Hubble Heritage Team

202. "Jennifer Wiseman": provided by Steve Rabey

206. HH212: image credit: ESO/M, McCaughrean

207. Three different types of stars: Steve Sanders

209. "Crab Nebula": by NASA, ESA, J. Hester, and A. Loll (Arizona State University), public domain

212. Binary Stars: Eastern University

215. "William Herschel01": by Lemuel Francis Abbott, public domain

215. "Herschel Caroline": public domain

219. Binary Stars (plural): Eastern University

219. Binary Star Images: From Binary Maker 3.0, Dr. David Bradstreet

220. Anne Bradstreet: public domain

222. Jeff Bezos: Jeff_Bezos'_iconic_laugh.jpg licensed with CC BY 2.0 by Steve Jurvetson

222. "Richard Branson March 2015 (Cropped)": by Chatham House, CC BY 2.0

222. "Larry Page in the European Parliament, 17.06.2009 (Cropped)": by Stansfield PL, CC BY-SA 3.0

222. "Eric Schmidt at the 37th G8 Summit in Deauville 037": by Guillaume Paumier, CC BY 3.0

222. "Elon Musk 2015": by Steve Jurvetson, CC BY 2.0

222. "JamesCameronHWOFOct2012": by Angela George, CC BY-SA 3.0

224. "Montgolfier Brothers Flight": by Unknown, Bildarchiv Preussuscher Kulturbesitz, Berlin, licensed under public domain via Commons

224. "First flight2": by John T. Daniels, public domain

226. "Blue Origins": by Source. Logo design

227. "Virgin Galactic": by Source. Logo design

228. "Planetary Resources": by Source. Logo design

228. "SpaceX": by Source. Logo design

229. "Xprize": by Source. Logo design

229. Air Force Space Command: image provided by AFSPC/PA

234. "Blackhole": by User:Alain, own work, licensed under CC BY-SA 2.5 via Commons

239. NASA.

242. Earth lights: NASA, by Craig Mayhew and Robert Simmon, NASA GSF, public domain

242. Jeremy Stanley, CC BY 2.0.

244. "Hubble2005–01-barred-spiral-galaxy-NGC1300": by NASA, ESA, and The Hubble Heritage Team STScI/AURA, public domain

247. Edwin Hubble: public domain

247. Hubble Telescope: by Ruffnax (Crew of STS-125), public domain

252. "Heic1323a": public domain

253. Doppler Effect: public domain

255. "HST-SM4": by Ruffnax (Crew of STS-125), public domain

258. Einstein/Lemaitre: publicity photo

261. Lemaitre blackboard: public domain, https://commons.wikimedia.org/w/index.php?curid=577448

264. Lemaitre: public domain

268. "Durer Revelation Four Riders": by Albrecht Dürer, public domain

273. "Ngc2392": by NASA, ESA, Andrew Fruchter (STScI), and the ERO team (STScI + ST-ECF), public domain

274. "Andromeda Galaxy (with H-Alpha)": by Adam Evans; M31, the Andromeda Galaxy (now with h-alpha), uploaded by NotFromUtrecht, CC BY 2.0

278. "Titan 3E with Voyager 1": by NASA, public domain

283. "Voyager 1 Entering Heliosheath Region": by NASA/Walt Feimer, public domain